WHITMAN ILLUMINATED:
SONG *of* MYSELF

Walt Whitman's iconic *Leaves of Grass* has earned a reputation as a sacred American text, so it's fitting that artist and illustrator Allen Crawford has illuminated—like the holy scriptures of medieval monks—the core of Whitman's masterpiece, "Song of Myself." Crawford's handwritten text and illustrations intermingle in a way that's both surprising and wholly in tune with the spirit of the poem—exuberant, rough, and wild. *Whitman Illuminated: Song of Myself* is a sensational reading experience, an artifact in its own right, and a masterful tribute to the Good Gray Poet.

Whitman Illuminated:

Song of Myself

ILLUSTRATED BY
Allen Crawford

TIN HOUSE BOOKS / Portland, Oregon

Published by Tin House Books, Portland, Oregon

Distributed by W. W. Norton & Company

ISBN: 978-1-935639-78-7

First edition 2014
Second edition 2019

www.tinhouse.com

Printed in the USA

for

DAVID C. MUNN

and

BILL HAWTHORNE

FOREWORD

by Allen Crawford

I live outside of Philadelphia, where Walt Whitman spent his last decades. I know the wooded banks of Big Timber Creek, where he rested and slowly recovered from the stroke he suffered after the Civil War. I've kayaked in the cove behind Petty's Island on the Delaware River, where Whitman would picnic on weekends with his friend and amanuensis, Horace Traubel. I've visited his Mickle Street house in Camden many times, and have stood in his bedroom, where his metal washtub is tucked under his heavy wooden bed.

And I know exactly when the mountain laurels outside of his crypt in Harleigh Cemetery are in bloom.

I'm very fortunate to live in Whitman's former backyard: He left a trove of materials and personal effects for local archivists and historians to sift through. It would have been difficult to do a Whitman-based project if I didn't have close access to the Philadelphia institutions that safeguard his legacy. To hold, feel, and study Whitman's books and letters first-hand enriched the endeavor of giving his work a new incarnation.

It's become commonplace, even cliché, to suggest that Whitman's iconic collection of poems, *Leaves of Grass*, is a kind of sacred American text. Whitman himself made such comparisons, going so far as to use biblical verse as a model for his own. So it seems fitting that his work should be transcribed by hand, the way that monks illuminated Holy Scripture in the Middle Ages.

Whitman wanted to create a new form of verse, one that was indigenous to America. He wanted to break free not only in form but also in content: He sought complete candor, not allegory or symbolism. His sensibility was American: exuberant, rough, and wild. He reveled in the vitality and sublimity of the physical. He exalted the nature around and within us. His work is an expression of primal joy: He celebrated our animal senses, and the pleasures of being alive.

What you are now holding in your hands is an illustrated interpretation of Whitman's epic poem, "Song of Myself," which is the centerpiece of *Leaves of Grass*. The version of "Song of Myself" used here is from the original

1855 edition of *Leaves of Grass*. I decided to transcribe and illustrate the 1855 edition because to my unscholarly eye it seems the most energetic, raw, and uncompromising.

With this book, I've tried to make the vigor of "Song of Myself" tangible. I've attempted to liberate the words from their blocks of verse, and allow the lines to flow freely about the page, like a stream or a bustling city crowd. The text and imagery in this book are intended to be in keeping with Whitman's unburnished sensibility. In the process, Whitman's sixty-page poem has been protracted into 234 illustrated pages.

"Protracted" seems a particularly apt word in this case: To complete the book I spent a year in my basement, working well into the wee hours, lapsing into a nocturnal pattern, as I often do with large projects. My setup in the basement is simple: two drafting tables, tracing paper, pens, vellum, and a light box. Each two-page spread started as a thumbnail, and then worked into a full-size pencil layout. It was then inked up, scanned, cleaned up digitally, and edited before being saved as final art. It took about eight to ten hours to complete each two-page spread. By my rough estimate, I devoted about 2,560 hours to this book. During the coldest weeks of winter, I was often wrapped in multiple house robes, socks, boots, and a Russian fur hat. I did my best to make a decent workstation for myself, but at times my shoulders, neck, and wrist were locked up in great pain from holding contorted positions in the cold for hours at a time. Each night before bed, I slathered my hand in sports cream and covered it with a sock, like an aging baseball player.

The book was improvised, not planned. So much effort was put into each spread that I never could work out in advance what I was going to draw on the following day. Each morning I felt as though I was starting all over again. The hardest part was working out what the next image would be. Would it be pictorial? Lyrical? Emblematic? Surreal? Typographical? Playful?

I sometimes think of this project as a visual journal that I kept as I explored the wild expanses of Whitman's poem, surveying and documenting each line as I went. I wanted to make this book an object that is viewed as well as read, and I made every effort to encapsulate a complete thought or mood in each spread before moving on to the next cluster of verse. There are parts where the pages spill into each other, but generally each spread retains its own imagery, personality, and mood—although there is an overall visual theme throughout the book to maintain some measure of cohesion.

I tried to make sure that I wasn't merely reflecting the poem, which would be redundant, predictable, and boring. I'm sure I didn't always succeed, but my goal was to leave an interpretive gap for the reader—or should I say "viewer"—between the poem and my responses (I'm not sure all of the drawings can be properly called "illustrations"). My hope is that you will never quite know what to expect when you turn the page.

To maintain the reader's interest (and my own), I tried to vary the density and complexity from page to page, alternating between pages crammed with text and pages that incorporate imagery. A few pages have little more than imagery.

Deciding what to emphasize was a largely intuitive process as I made my way through the text.

Whitman's verse concerns itself with epic sweeps and grand gestures, which means including nearly everything and everyone. Walt did indeed contain multitudes, and I had to follow his lead if I was going to properly serve his words. At times, this could prove exasperating: Keeping up with Whitman's torrents of people and places sometimes felt like riding a bee-stung bison down the aisle of a bus.

I found that in order to add anything at all to Whitman's panorama of people and places, I had to add a dimension of my own. Events in my daily life affected my approach to each spread, and the Philadelphia of today seeped into the Philadelphia of Whitman's day. Thus, you'll find a variety of contemporary or near-contemporary images in this book. Not doing so would have been a disservice to Whitman's work, which attempts to create a new form of verse for The Here and The Now.

For this project, I wanted to use a drawing style that is slightly awkward and plain, with a minimum of self-consciousness. I spent a couple of weeks testing out certain combinations of pens and paper, until I found a pairing that had the kind of friction that prevents facile, fussy flourishes. I hope this rather plainspoken drawing style will suggest or invoke the sensibilities espoused by Whitman: his rough vigor, his earthy frankness, his dreamy expansiveness, and his reverence for life in all its forms.

I should give thanks and proper credit

to Zak Smith and Matt Kish for inspiring this project. Zak Smith took it upon himself to illustrate every single page of Thomas Pynchon's *Gravity's Rainbow*, and Matt Kish soon followed by illustrating every single page of Herman Melville's *Moby-Dick*. Their steadfast devotion to such ambitious self-appointed projects was an inspiration, and so I decided to join them in their quest to lend new interpretations to American classics. I hope more will follow their lead.

Those of you interested in learning more about Walt Whitman the person should find and read *Specimen Days*, the biography *Walt Whitman: A Life* by Justin Kaplan, and the accounts of Horace Traubel. The bluster of Whitman's poems are swept aside to reveal a flawed but down-to-earth, maternally tender human being. Having read these books, I feel certain that I would have loved the man, if I had known him.

Obviously, to attach one's own name to Walt Whitman's, one of the great names of American letters, is an incredibly presumptuous thing to do. I can only hope that I've atoned for my presumptuousness with my labor, and readers find I've done the words of The Good Gray Poet some justice. In any case, it was a privilege to make such an attempt.

At the close of "Song of Myself," Whitman invites us to look for him under our boot-soles. It's my hope that readers of this book might also find a little of him under my pen.

Song of Myself

by Walt Whitman

1855

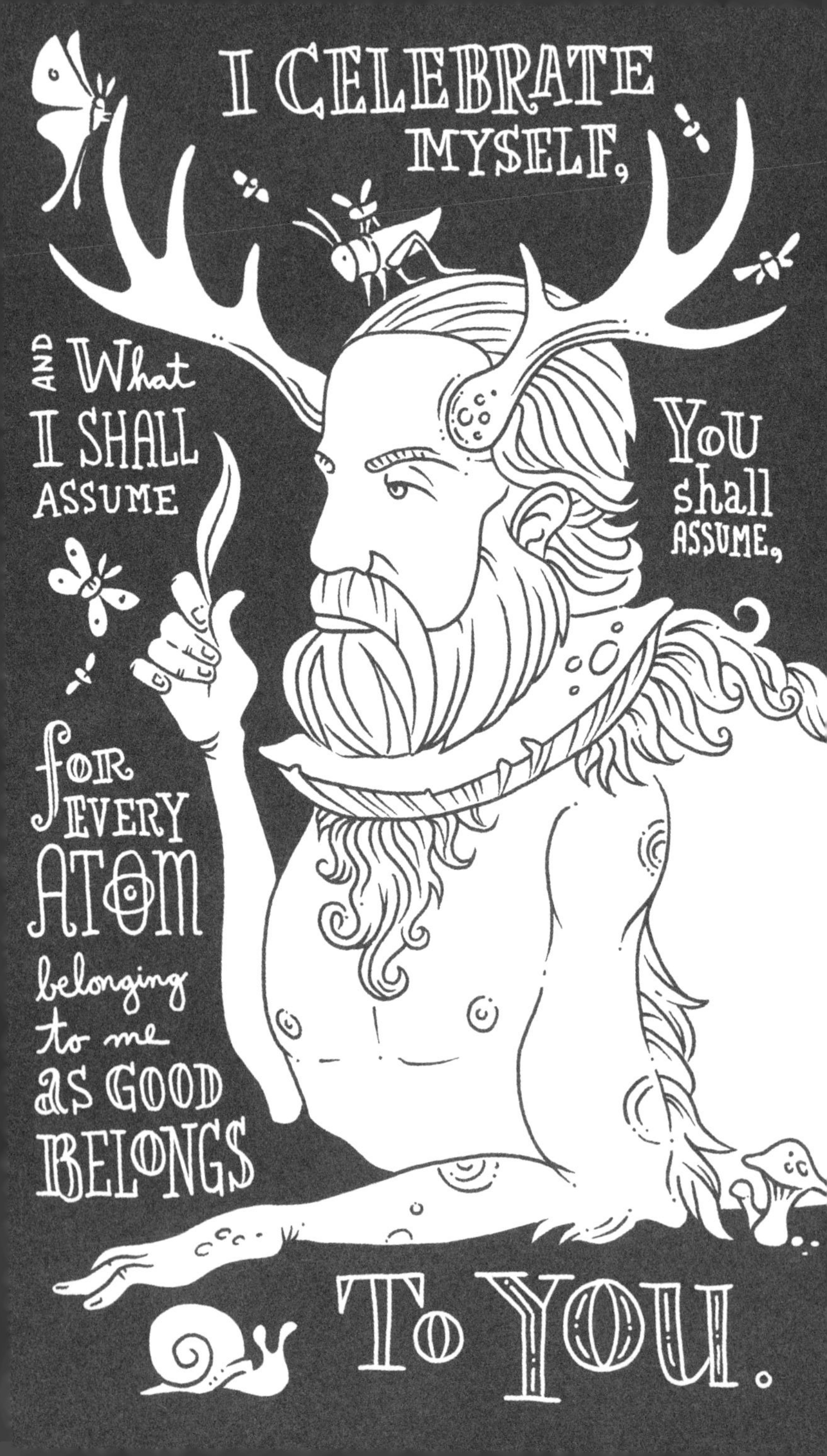
I CELEBRATE
MYSELF,
AND What
I SHALL
ASSUME
YOU
shall
ASSUME,
FOR
EVERY
ATOM
belonging
to me
as GOOD
BELONGS
TO YOU.

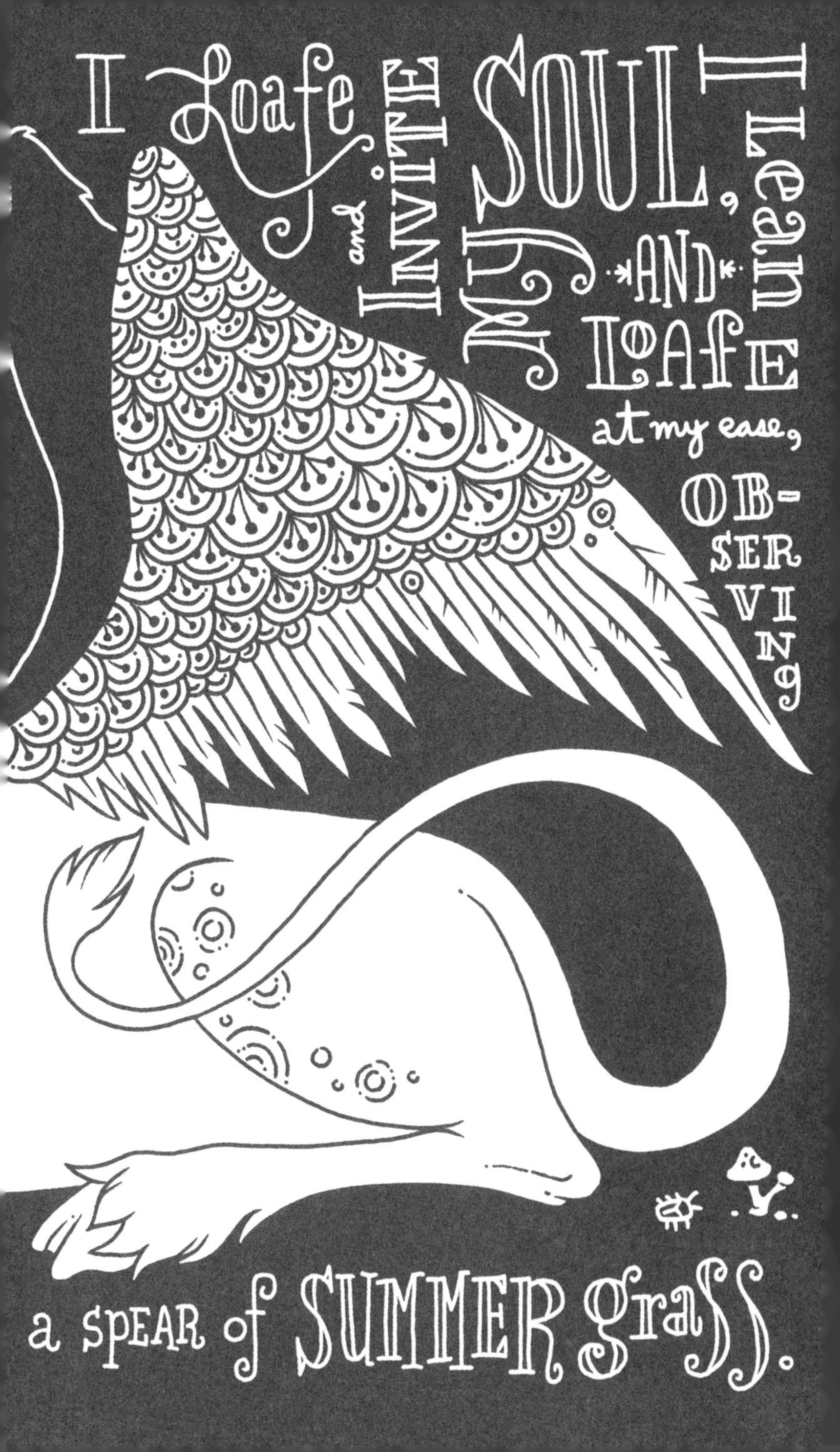
I Loafe and INVITE MY SOUL,
I lean AND LOAFE
at my ease,
OB-SER-VI-NG
a SPEAR of SUMMER grass.

HOUSES AND ROOMS ARE full of PERFUMES..

The shelves are crowded with PERFUMES,

I BREATHE the fragrance myself, AND KNOW IT AND LIKE IT,

the DISTILLATION would intoxicate me also, BUT I SHALL NOT LET it.

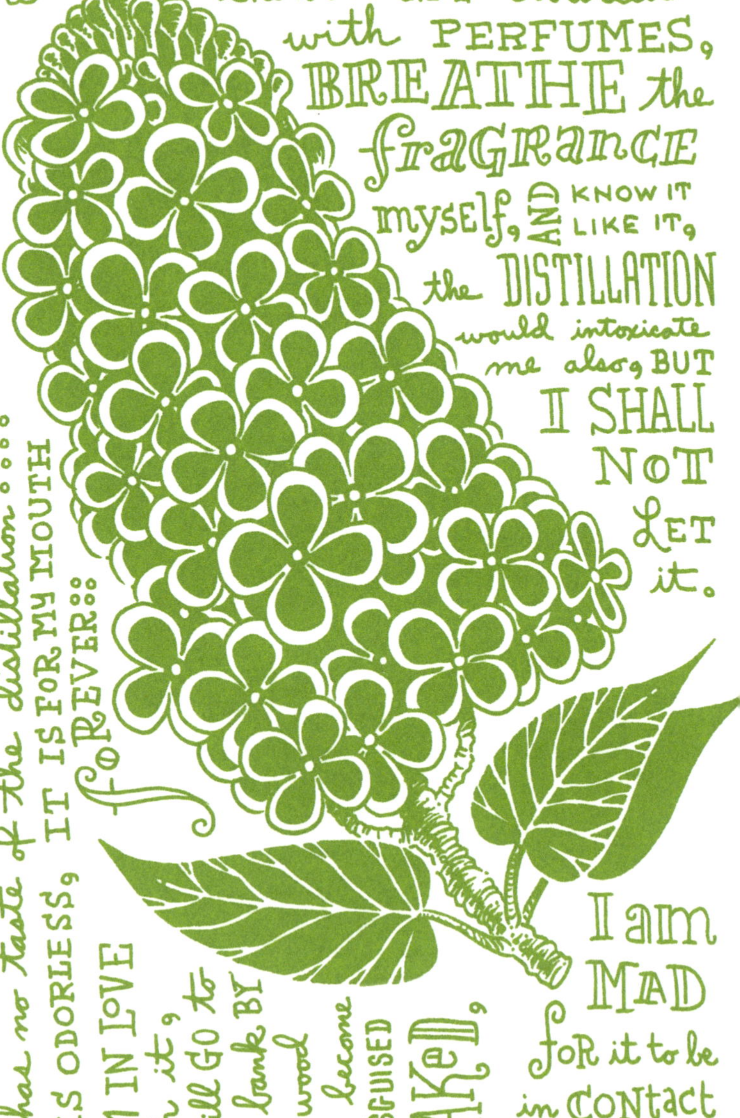

THE ATMOSPHERE is not a PERFUME...

it has no taste of the distillation...

IT IS ODORLESS, IT IS FOR MY MOUTH FOREVER..

I AM IN LOVE with it,

I will GO to the bank BY the wood and become UNDISGUISED AND NAKED,

I am MAD for it to be in CONTACT With ME.

THE SMOKE of MY OWN BREATH,

ECHOES, RIPPLES, AND BUZZED whispers .... LOVE-ROOT, SILKTHREAD CROTCH AND VINE,

MY RESPIRATION AND INSPIRATION, ... the BEATING of MY HEART .... the PASSING of BLOOD and AIR THROUGH MY LUNGS

the SNIFF of GREEN LEAVES AND DRY LEAVES,

AND of the SHORE and DARKCOLORED SEA-ROCKS, and OF THE HAY IN THE BARN,

THE SOUND OF THE BELCHED WORDS OF MY VOICE .... WORDS loosed TO THE EDDIES OF THE Wind,

A few light kisses, a few embraces, a reaching around of arms, the play of shine and shade on the trees as the supple boughs wag, the delight alone or in the rush of the streets, or along the fields and hillsides, the feeling of health, the full noon trill, the song of me rising from bed and meeting the sun. Have you reckoned a thousand acres much? Have you reckoned the earth much? Have you practiced so long to read? Have you felt so proud to get at the meaning of poems?

STOP THIS DAY AND NIGHT WITH ME AND YOU SHALL POSSESS the ORIGIN OF ALL POEMS,

YOU SHALL POSSESS THE GOOD of the EARTH AND SUN .... (THERE are MILLIONS of SUNS left)

YOU SHALL NO LONGER take things at second or THIRD HAND .... nor LOOK THROUGH the EYES of the DEAD, ... nor FEED ON THE SPECTRES in BOOKS,

YOU SHALL NOT LOOK THROUGH my EYES EITHER, nor TAKE things FROM me,

YOU shall LISTEN to ALL SIDES and FILTER them FROM YOURSELF.

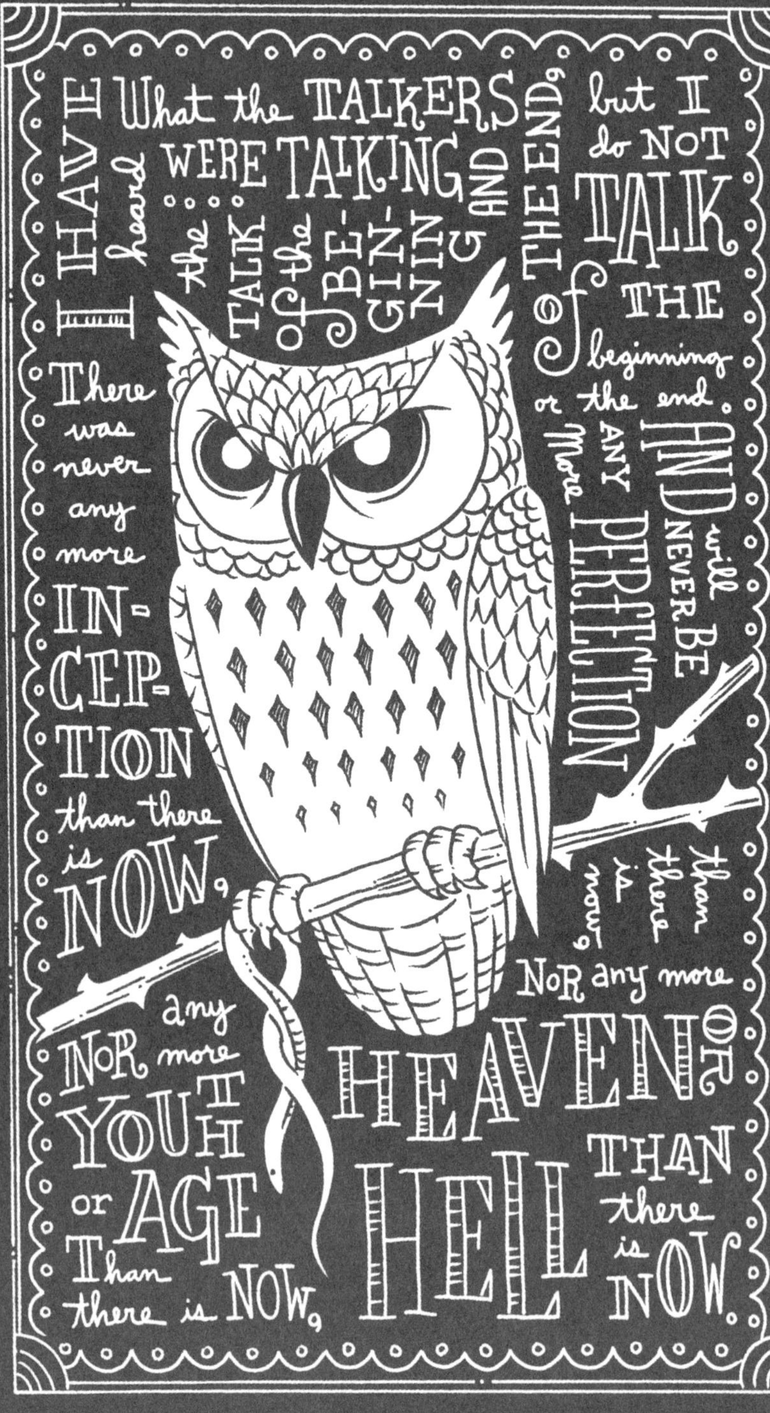

I HAVE heard
What the TALKERS
WERE TALKING,
the TALK of the BE-GIN-NING AND THE END,
but I do NOT TALK
of THE beginning
or the end.
There was never any more IN-CEP-TION
than there is NOW,
AND will NEVER BE ANY More PERFECTION
than there is now,
NOR any more YOUTH or AGE
Than there is NOW,
NoR any more
HEAVEN OR HELL
THAN there is NOW.

Urge and urge and urge,
Always the procreant urge of the world.

Out of the dimness opposite equals advance, always substance and increase,

always identity, always distinction, always a breed of life.

Always a knit of identity, always distinction, always a breed of life.

To elaborate is no avail, learned and unlearned feel that it is so.

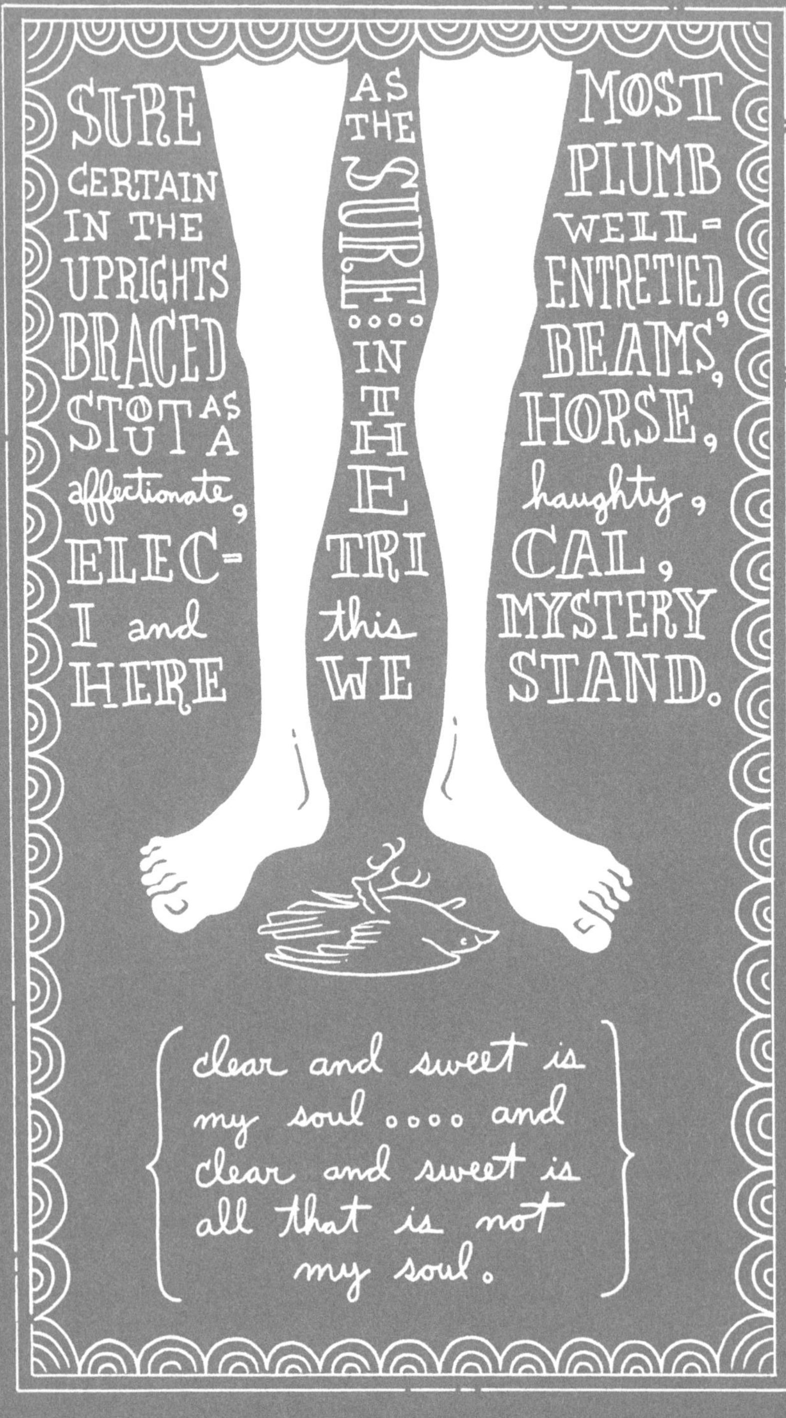
SURE AS THE MOST
CERTAIN SURE PLUMB
IN THE UPRIGHTS WELL-ENTRETIED
BRACED IN THE BEAMS,
STOUT AS A HORSE,
affectionate, haughty,
ELEC-TRI-CAL,
I and this MYSTERY
HERE WE STAND.
clear and sweet is my soul .... and clear and sweet is all that is not my soul.

Lack one lacks both, and the unseen is proved by the seen,
Till that becomes unseen and receives proof in its turn.

Showing the best and dividing it from the worst, age vexes age,
Knowing the perfect fitness and equanimity of things, while they discuss I am silent, and go bathe and admire myself.

Welcome is every organ and attribute of me, and of any man hearty and clean,
Not an inch nor a particle of an inch is vile, and none shall be less familiar than the rest.

I AM SATISFIED: I SEE, DANCE, Laugh, SING;

as GOD COMES A loving bedfellow AND SLEEPS at My side all NIGHT and CLOSE ON THE PEEP of DAY,

And leaves for me BASKETS covered with white TOWELS bulging the HOUSE with their PLENTY, SHALL I POST-PONE my accept-ation and real-ization AND SCREAM at my EYES,

THAT THEY TURN FROM GAZING AFTER AND DOWN the ROAD,

AND forTHWiTH CipHER AND SHOW ME TO A CENT, EXACTly the CONTENTS OF ONE, and EXACTLY the CONTENTS of TWO, and WHICH is AHEAD?

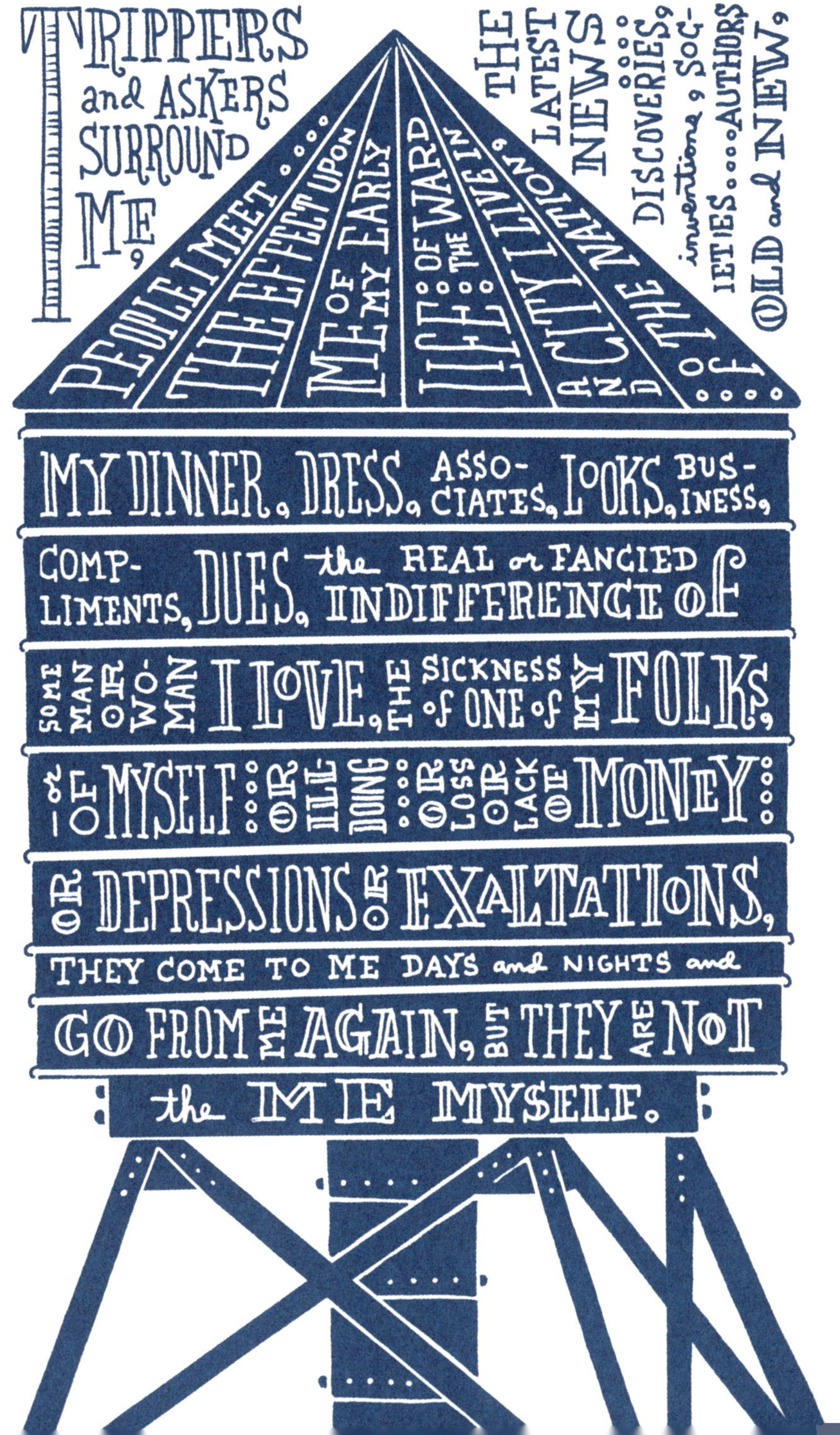
TRIPPERS and ASKERS SURROUND ME,
PEOPLE I MEET....
THE EFFECT UPON
ME OF MY EARLY
LIFE.. OF THE WARD
AND CITY I LIVE IN,
OF THE NATION....
THE LATEST NEWS....
DISCOVERIES, inventions, SOCIETIES....AUTHORS, OLD and NEW,
MY DINNER, DRESS, ASSOCIATES, LOOKS, BUSINESS,
COMPLIMENTS, DUES, the REAL or FANCIED INDIFFERENCE OF
SOME MAN OR WOMAN I LOVE, THE SICKNESS OF ONE OF MY FOLKS,
-or OF MYSELF.... OR ILL-DOING.... OR LOSS OR LACK OF MONEY....
OR DEPRESSIONS OR EXALTATIONS,
THEY COME TO ME DAYS and NIGHTS and
GO FROM ME AGAIN, BUT THEY ARE NOT
the ME MYSELF.

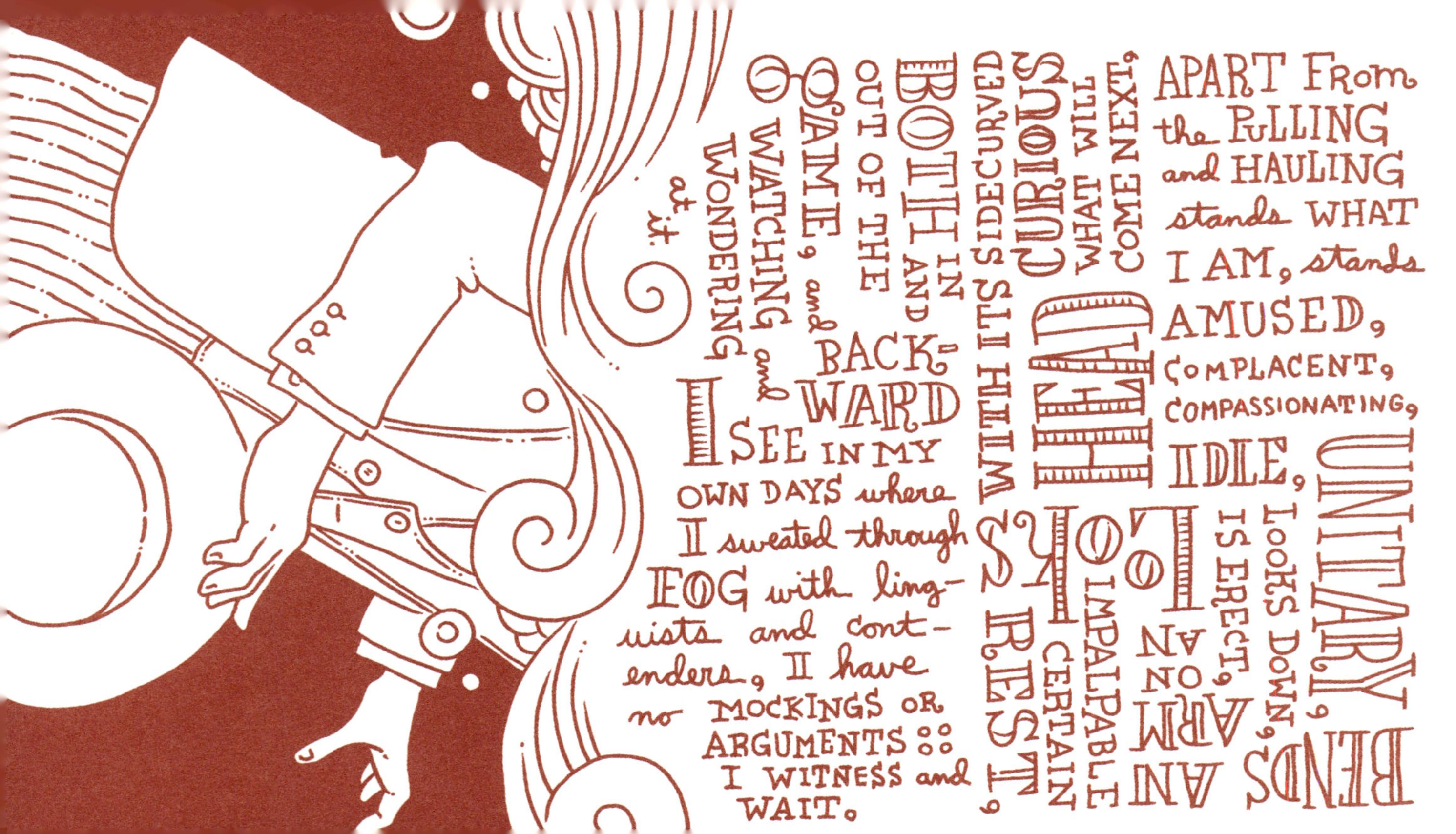
APART FROM the PULLING and HAULING stands WHAT I AM, stands AMUSED, COMPLACENT, COMPASSIONATING, IDLE, UNITARY,
LOOKS DOWN, IS ERECT, OR BENDS AN ARM ON AN IMPALPABLE CERTAIN REST,
LOOKS WITH ITS SIDECURVED HEAD CURIOUS WHAT WILL COME NEXT,
BOTH IN AND OUT OF THE GAME, and WATCHING and WONDERING at it.
BACKWARD I SEE IN MY OWN DAYS where I sweated through FOG with linguists and contenders, I have no MOCKINGS OR ARGUMENTS :: I WITNESS and WAIT.

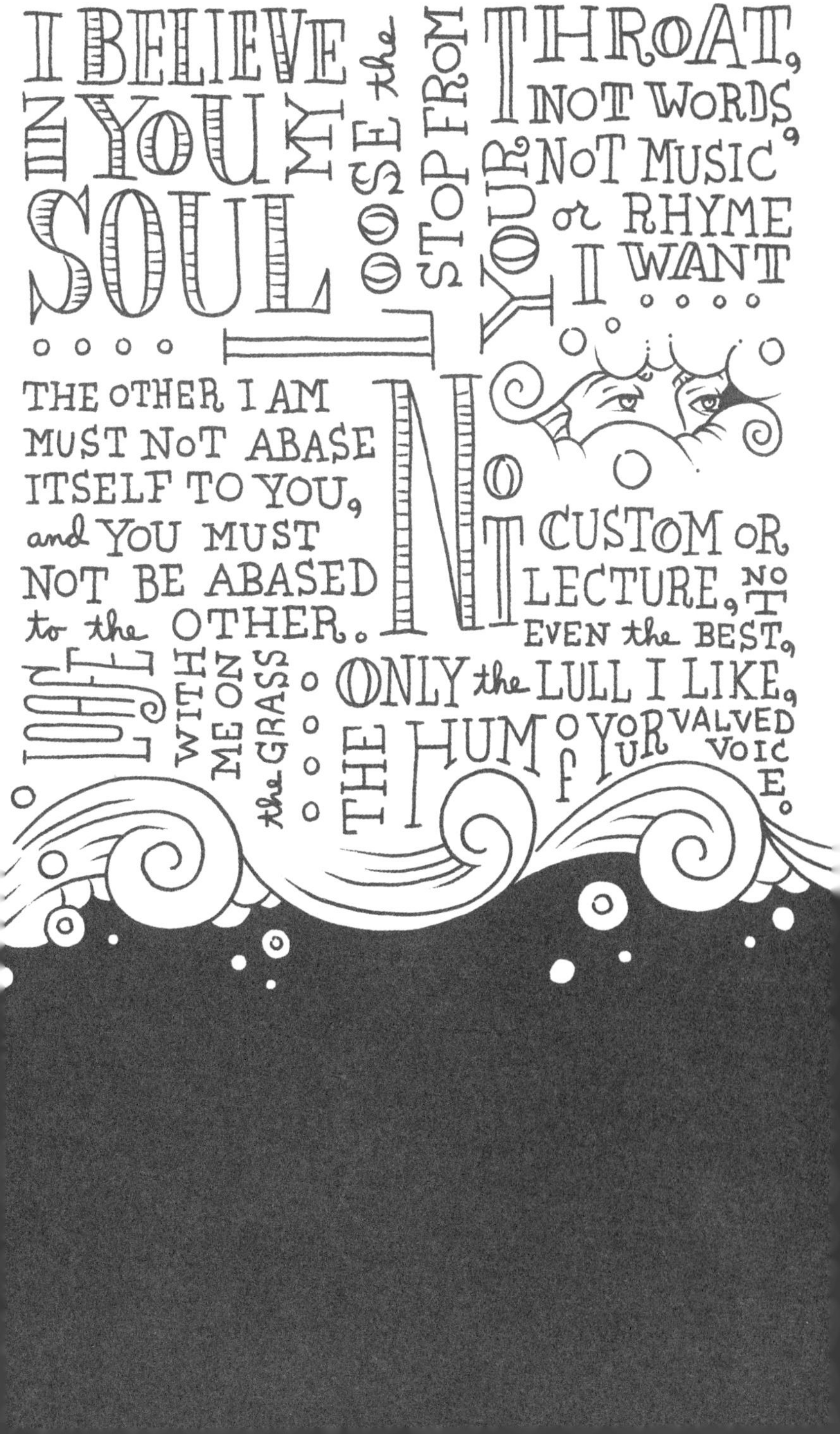

I BELIEVE IN YOU MY SOUL
THE OTHER I AM MUST NOT ABASE ITSELF TO YOU,
and YOU MUST NOT BE ABASED to the OTHER.
LOAFE WITH ME ON the GRASS
LOOSE the STOP FROM YOUR THROAT,
NOT WORDS, NOT MUSIC or RHYME I WANT
NOT CUSTOM OR LECTURE, NOT EVEN the BEST,
ONLY the LULL I LIKE,
THE HUM of YOUR VALVED VOICE.

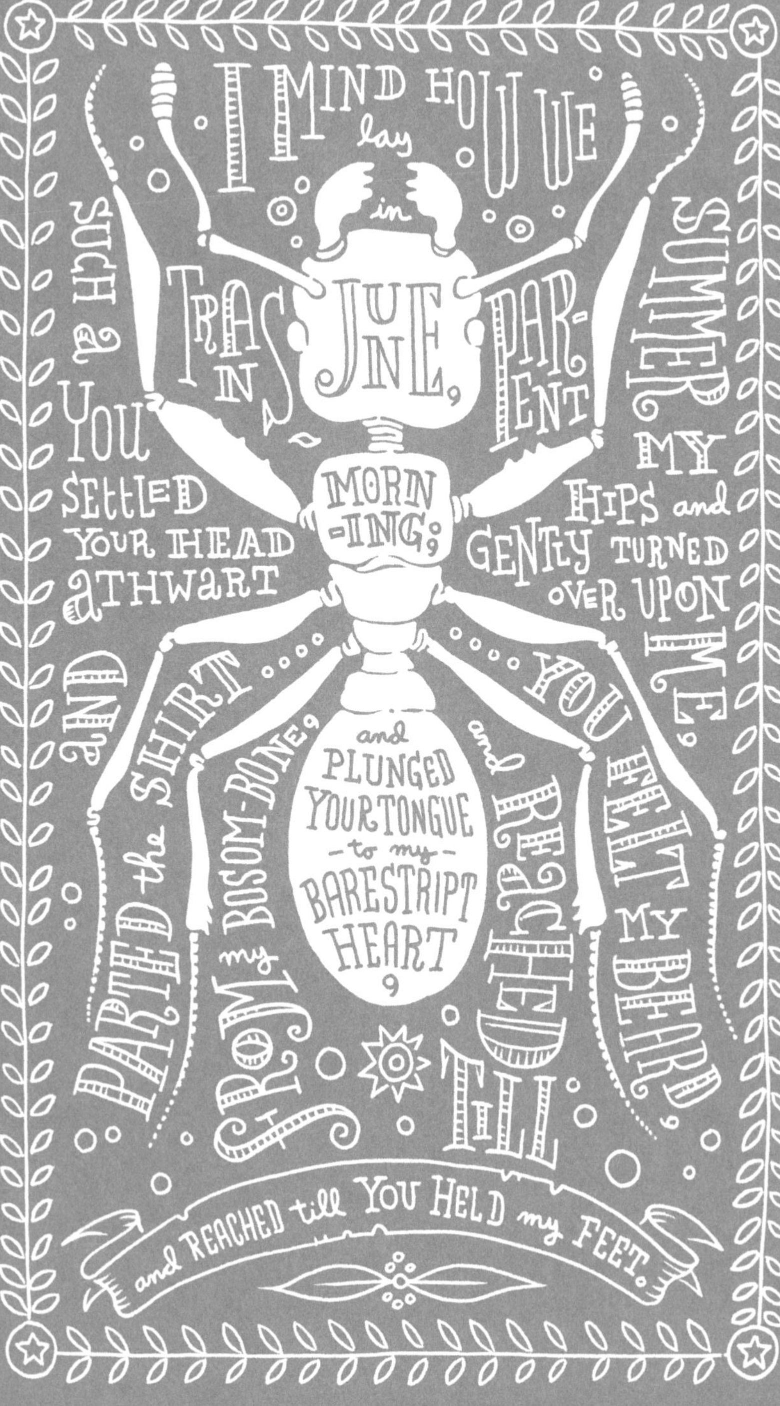

I MIND HOW WE lay in JUNE,
SUCH a TRANSPARENT SUMMER MORNING;
YOU SETTLED YOUR HEAD ATHWART MY HIPS and GENTLY TURNED OVER UPON ME,
AND PARTED the SHIRT FROM my BOSOM-BONE,
and PLUNGED YOUR TONGUE to my BARESTRIPT HEART,
and REACHED TILL YOU FELT MY BEARD,
and REACHED till YOU HELD my FEET.

SWIFTLY AROSE and SPREAD AND AROUND ME THE PEACE AND JOY AND KNOWLEDGE THAT PASS all the ARGUMENT of the EARTH;

and I KNOW that the HAND of GOD is the ELDERHAND of my OWN,

AND I KNOW that THE SPIRIT of GOD is the ELDEST brother of MY OWN,

AND THAT ALL THE MEN EVER BORN ARE ALSO MY BROTHERS .... and the WOMEN MY SISTERS AND LOVERS,

and that A KELSON OF THE CREATION IS LOVE;

and LIMITLESS are LEAVES STIFF OR DROOPING IN the FIELDS,

AND BROWN ANTS IN THE LITTLE WELLS BENEATH THEM,

and MOSSY SCABS OF THE WORMFENCE, and HEAPED STONES, and ELDER and MULLEN and POKEWEED.

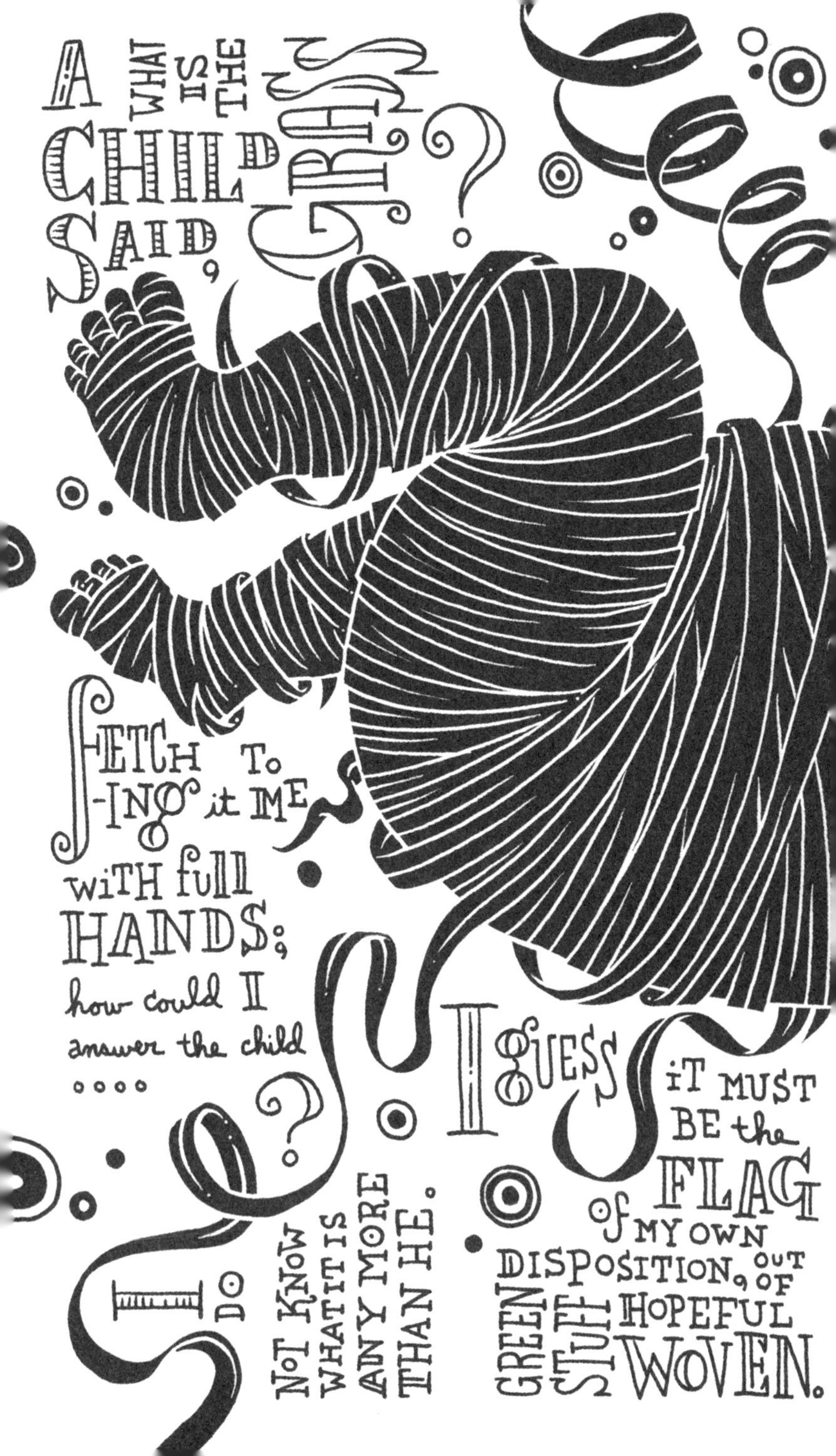
A CHILD SAID, WHAT IS THE GRASS?
FETCH-ING IT TO ME
WITH FULL HANDS;
how could I answer the child ....
I DO NOT KNOW WHAT IT IS ANY MORE THAN HE.
I GUESS IT MUST BE THE FLAG OF MY OWN DISPOSITION, OUT OF HOPEFUL GREEN STUFF WOVEN.

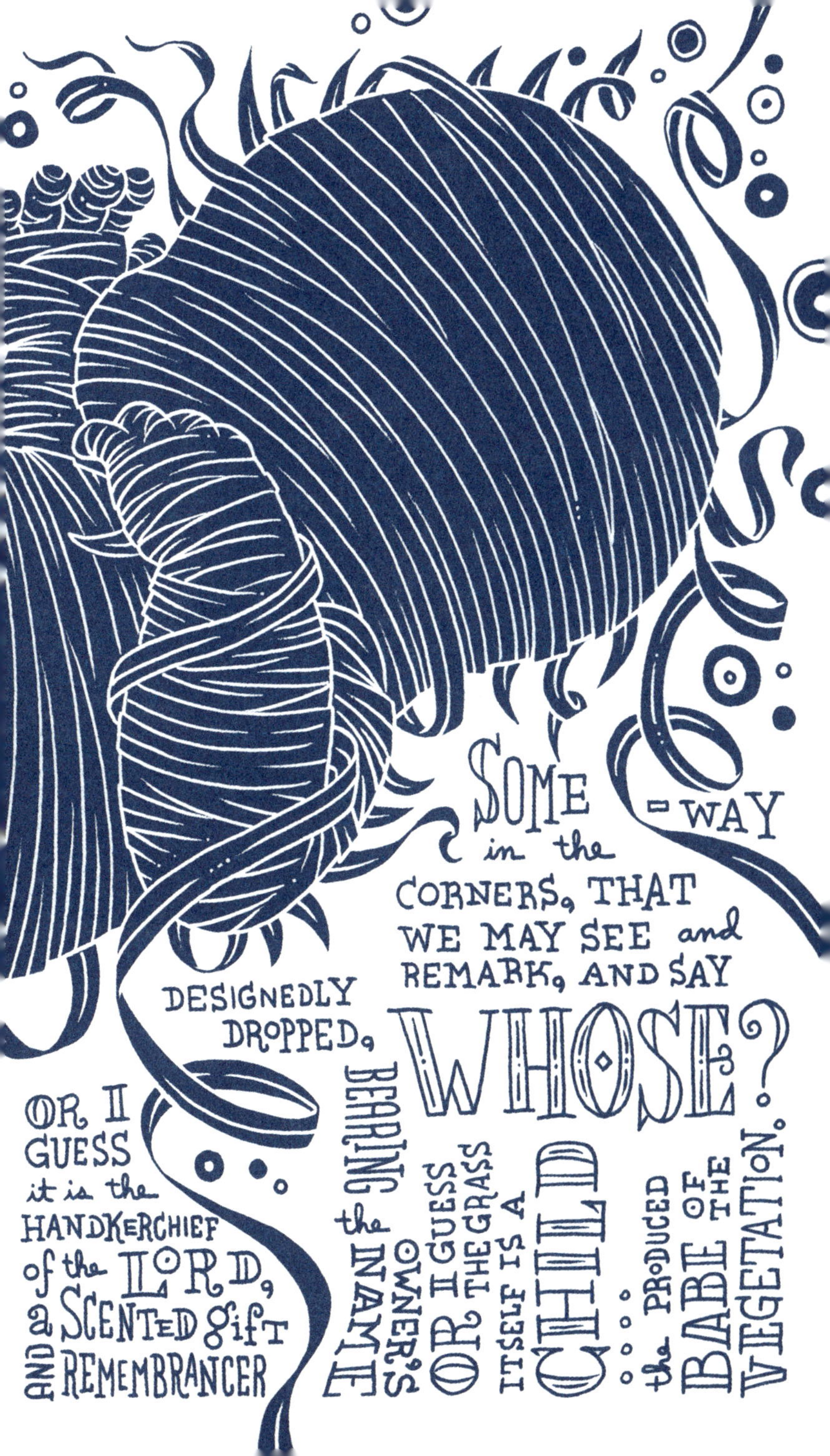
OR I GUESS it is the HANDKERCHIEF of the LORD,
a SCENTED gift AND REMEMBRANCER
DESIGNEDLY DROPPED,
BEARING the NAME OWNER'S
SOME-WAY in the CORNERS, THAT WE MAY SEE and REMARK, AND SAY
WHOSE?
OR I GUESS THE GRASS ITSELF IS A CHILD...
the PRODUCED BABE OF THE VEGETATION.

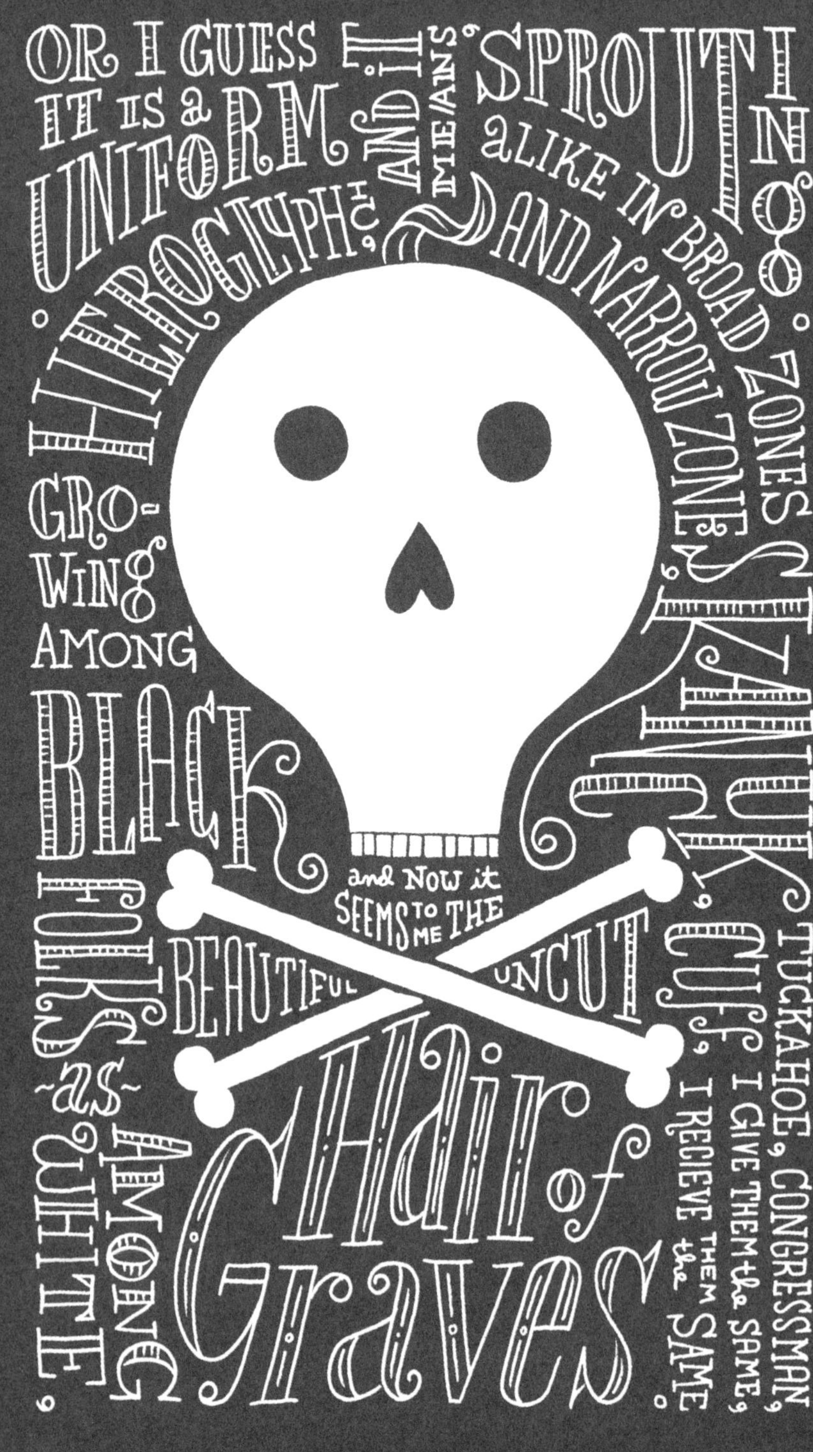
OR I GUESS IT IS a UNIFORM HIEROGLYPHIC,
AND IT MEANS, SPROUTING alike IN BROAD ZONES AND NARROW ZONES,
GROWING AMONG BLACK FOLKS ~as~ AMONG WHITE,
KANUCK, TUCKAHOE, CONGRESSMAN, CUFF,
I GIVE THEM the SAME,
I RECIEVE THEM the SAME.
and NOW it SEEMS TO ME THE BEAUTIFUL UNCUT Hair of Graves.

Tenderly will I use you curling grass,
It may be you transpire from the breasts of young men,
It may be if I had known them I would have loved them;
It may be you are from old people and from women, and from offspring taken soon out of their mothers' laps,
And here you are the mothers' laps.

This grass is very dark to be from the white heads of old mothers,
Darker than the colorless beards of old men,
Dark to come from under the faint red roofs of mouths.

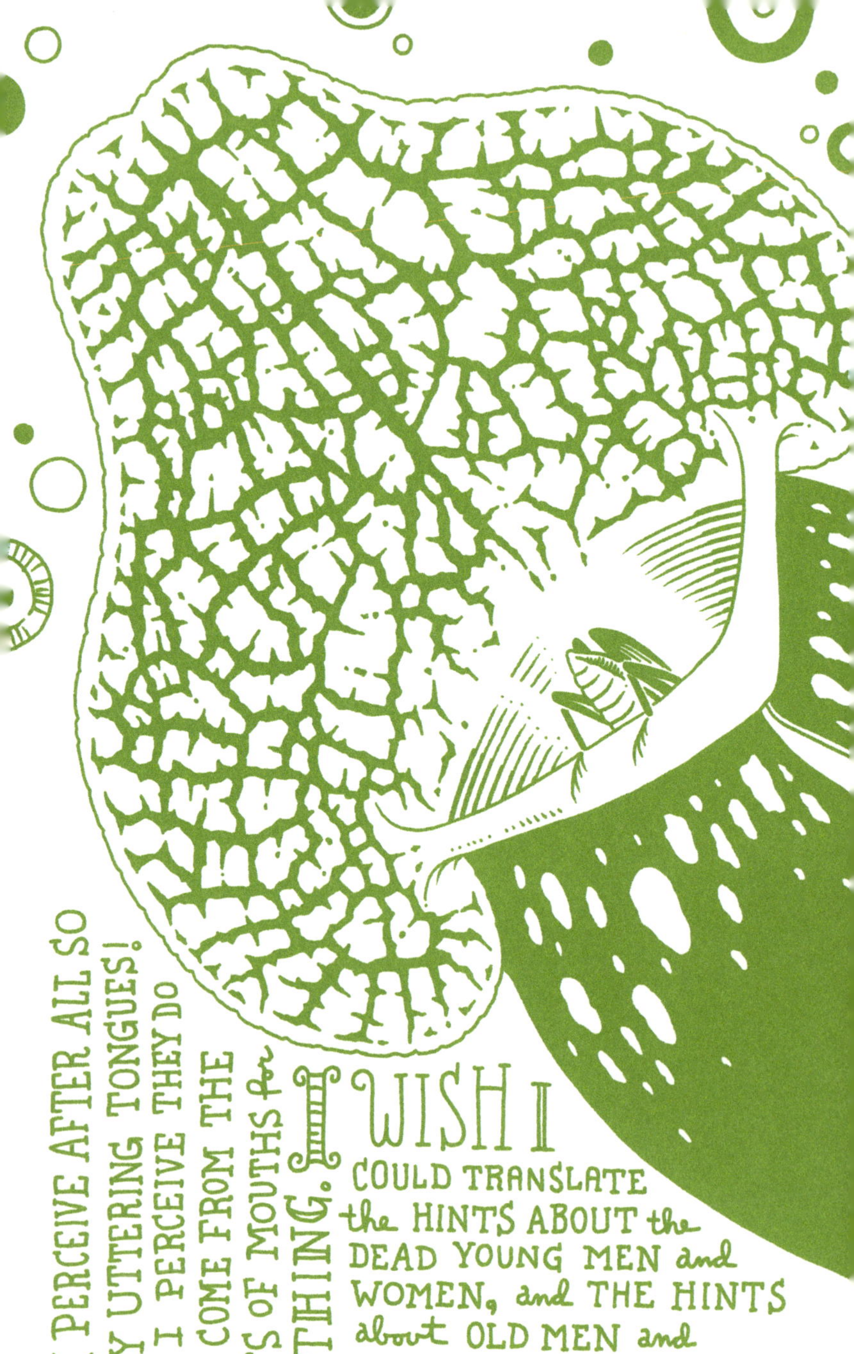

O I PERCEIVE AFTER ALL SO MANY UTTERING TONGUES! and I PERCEIVE THEY DO NOT COME FROM THE ROOFS OF MOUTHS for NOTHING. I WISH I COULD TRANSLATE the HINTS ABOUT the DEAD YOUNG MEN and WOMEN, and THE HINTS about OLD MEN and MOTHERS, and the OFFSPRING TAKEN SOON out of THEIR LAPS.

WHAT DO YOU THINK HAS BECOME OF THE YOUNG and OLD MEN?

AND WHAT DO YOU THINK HAS BECOME of the WOMEN and CHILDREN?

THEY ARE ALIVE and WELL SOME-WHERE; THE SMALLEST SPROUT SHOWS THERE IS REALLY NO DEATH,

AND if EVER THERE WAS IT LED FORWARD LIFE, and DOES NOT WAIT at the END to ARREST IT, and CEASED the MOMENT LIFE APP-EARED.

ALL GOES ON-WARD AND OUTWARD... and NOTHING COLLAPSES, AND TO DIE IS DIFFERENT from WHAT ANY ONE SUPPOSED and LUCKIER.

HAS ANY-ONE SUPPOSED IT LUCKY TO BE BORN? I HASTEN TO INFORM HIM OR HER, IT IS JUST AS LUCKY TO DIE, AND I KNOW IT.

I PASS DEATH WITH the DYING, and BIRTH WITH THE NEW-WASHED BABE.... and AM not CONTAINED BETWEEN MY HAT and BOOTS .... AND PERUSE MANIFOLD OBJECTS, NO TWO ALIKE, AND EVERY ONE GOOD, THE EARTH GOOD, and THE STARS GOOD, and THEIR AD-JUNCTS ALL GO OD.

I AM NOT AN EARTH NOR AN ADJUNCT OF AN EARTH, I AM THE MATE and COM-PANION OF PEOPLE, ALL JUST as IMMORT-AL and FATHOMLESS AS MYSELF.

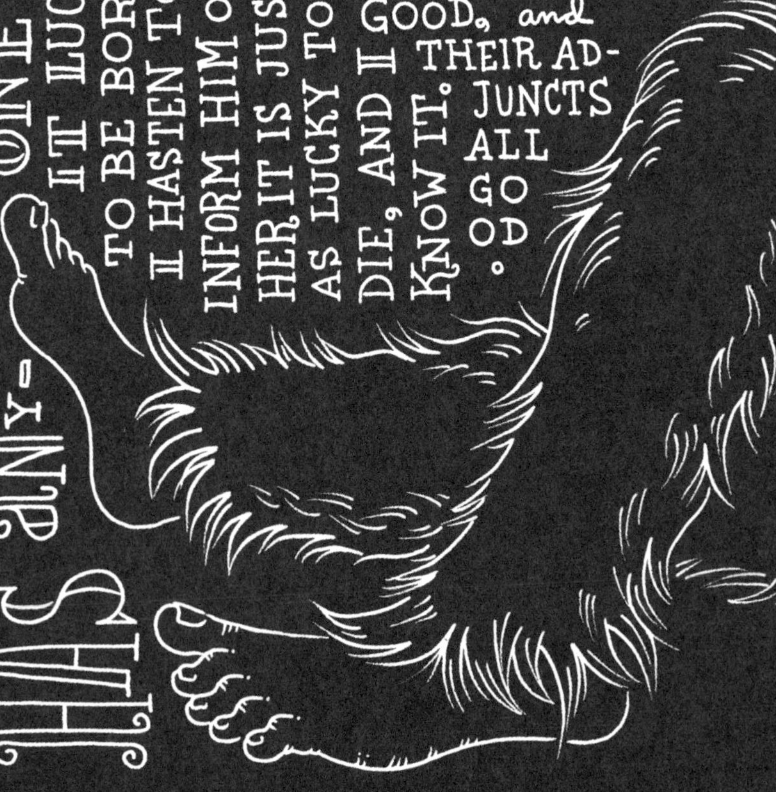

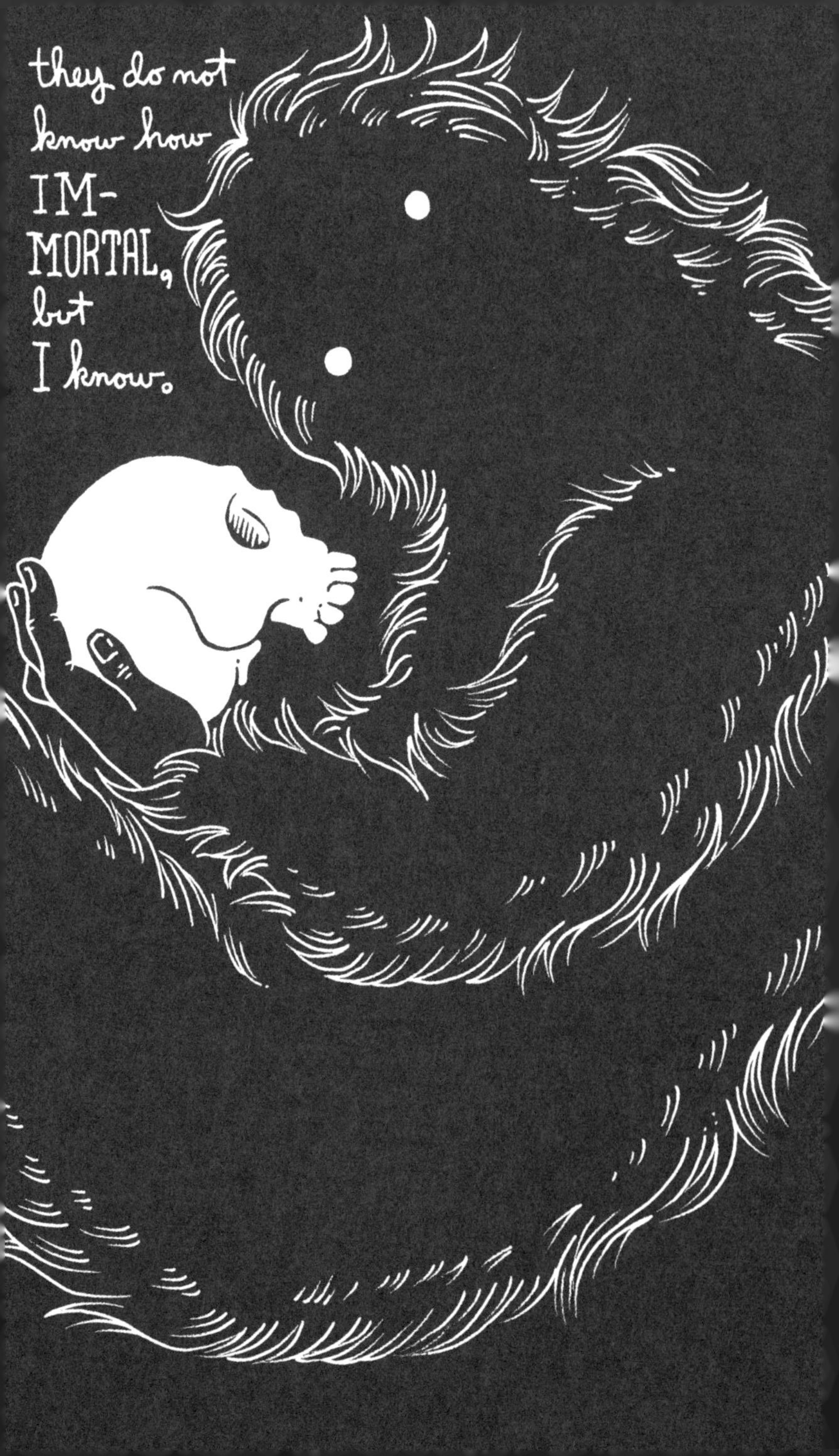
they do not know how IM-MORTAL, but I know.

EVERY KIND FOR ITSELF AND ITS OWN: FOR ME MINE MALE AND FEMALE,
FOR ME ALL THAT HAVE BEEN BOYS AND THAT LOVE WOMEN,

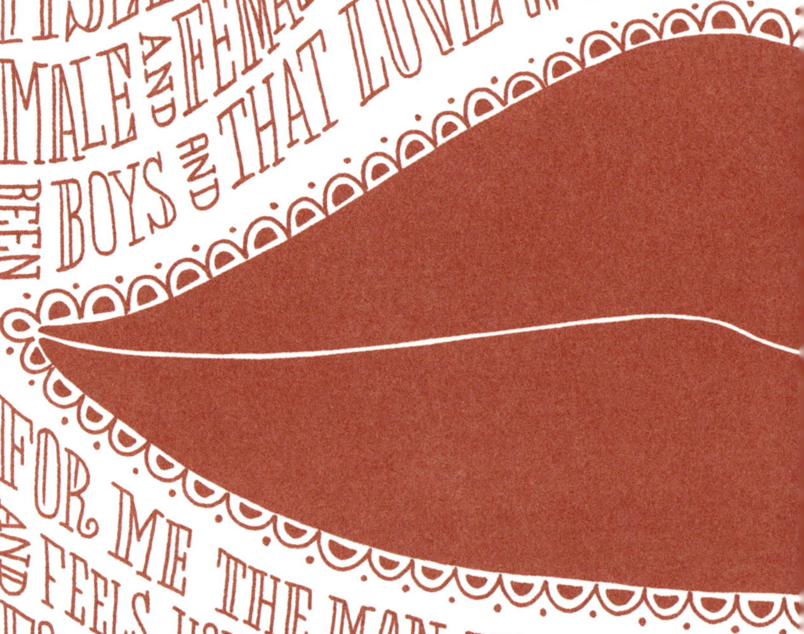

FOR ME THE MAN THAT IS PROUD AND FEELS HOW IT STINGS TO BE SLIGHTED;
FOR ME THE SWEETHEART AND THE OLD MAID:
FOR ME MOTHERS AND THE MOTHERS OF MOTHERS,
FOR ME LIPS THAT HAVE SMILED, EYES THAT HAVE SHED TEARS,

FOR ME CHILDREN AND THE BEGETTERS OF CHILDREN.

WHO NEED BE AFRAID OF THE MERGE?

UNDRAPE . . . YOU ARE NOT GUILTY TO ME, NOR STALE NOR DISCARDED, I SEE THROUGH THE

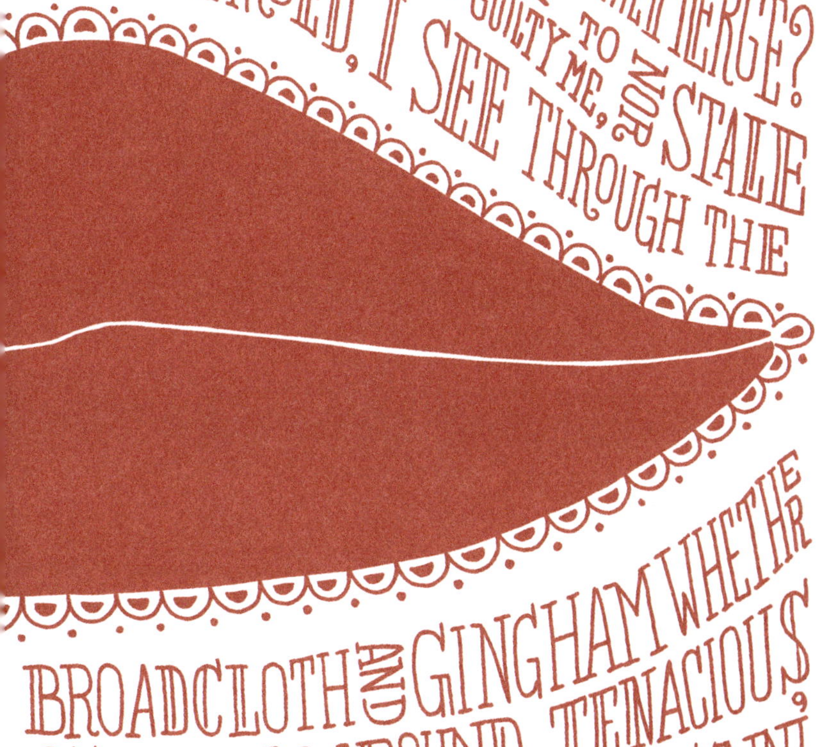

BROADCLOTH AND GINGHAM WHETHER OR NO, AND AM AROUND, TENACIOUS, ACQUISITIVE, TIRELESS . . . AND CAN NEVER BE SHAKEN AWAY.

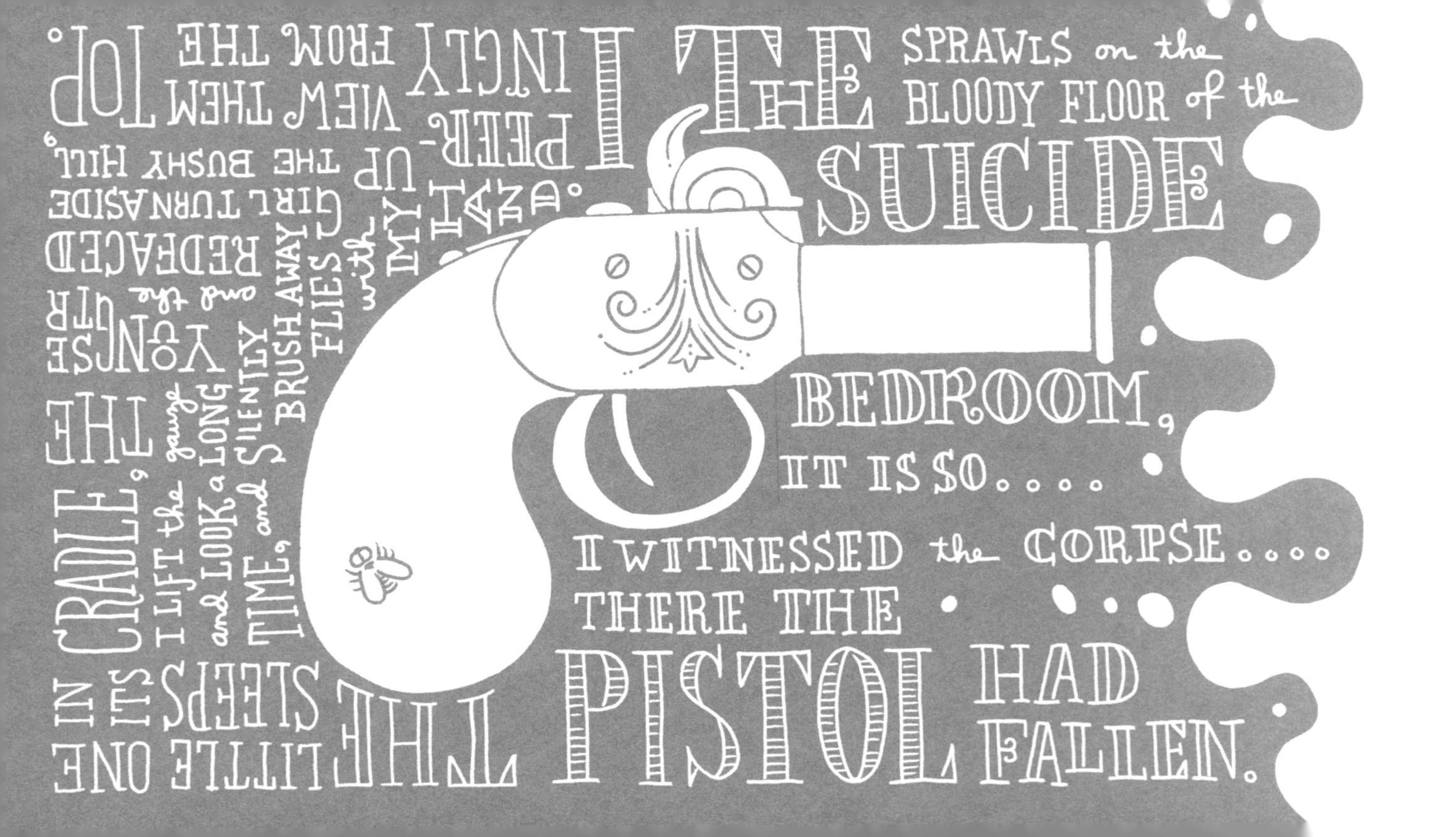
THE LITTLE ONE SLEEPS IN ITS CRADLE,
I LIFT the gauze and LOOK a LONG TIME, and SILENTLY BRUSH AWAY FLIES with MY HAND.
THE YOUNGSTER and the REDFACED GIRL TURN ASIDE UP THE BUSHY HILL,
I PEER-INGLY VIEW THEM FROM THE TOP.
THE SUICIDE SPRAWLS on the BLOODY FLOOR of the BEDROOM,
IT IS SO.....
I WITNESSED the CORPSE.....
THERE THE PISTOL HAD FALLEN.

THE BLAB OF THE PAVE, THE TIRES OF CARTS AND SLUFF OF BOOT-SOLES AND TALK OF THE PROMENADERS, THE HEAVY OMNIBUS, THE DRIVER WITH HIS INTER-ROGATING THUMB, THE CLANK OF THE SHOD HORSES ON THE GRANITE FLOOR, THE CARNIVAL OF SLEIGHS, THE CLINKING AND SHOUTED JOKES AND PELTS OF SNOWBALLS; THE HURRAHS FOR POPULAR FAVORITES: THE FURY OF ROUSED MOBS; THE FLAP OF THE CURTAINED LITTER — THE SICK MAN INSIDE BORNE TO THE HOSP-ITAL;

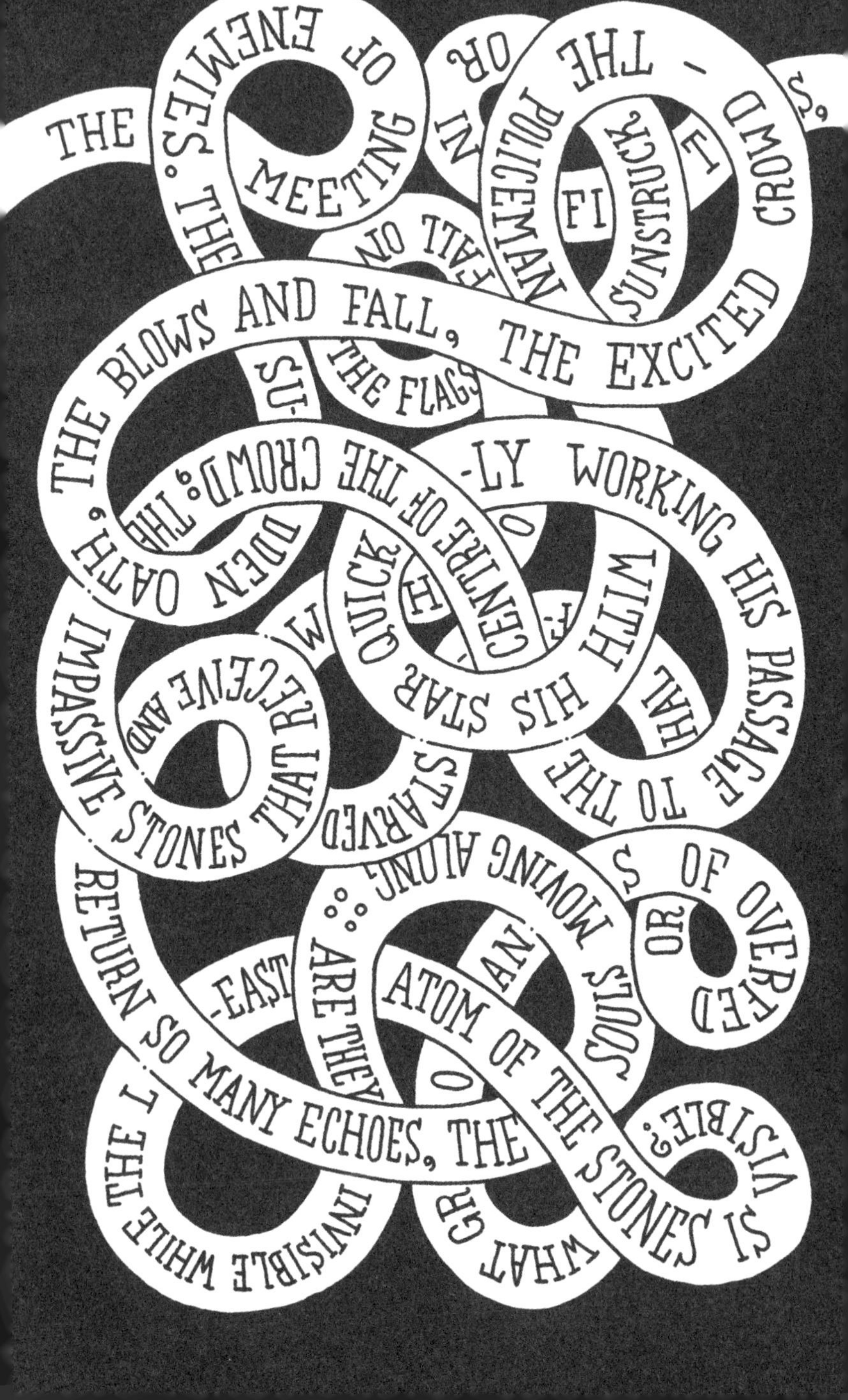
THE
MEETING
OF ENEMIES. THE
THE
SU-
DDEN OATH, THE
BLOWS AND FALL, THE EXCITED
CROWD - THE POLICEMAN
IN OR
FALL ON
THE FLAGS
SUNSTRUCK
FI
CROWD'S
THE CROWD: THE
QUICK
-LY WORKING HIS PASSAGE
WITH HIS STAR
CENTRE OF THE
TO THE HALL
IMPASSIVE STONES THAT RECEIVE AND
STARVED
MOVING ALONG
S OF OVERFED
OR
SOULS
ARE THEY
ATOM OF THE STONES IS
AN
-EAST
RETURN SO MANY ECHOES, THE
INVISIBLE WHILE THE
WHAT GR
VISIBLE?

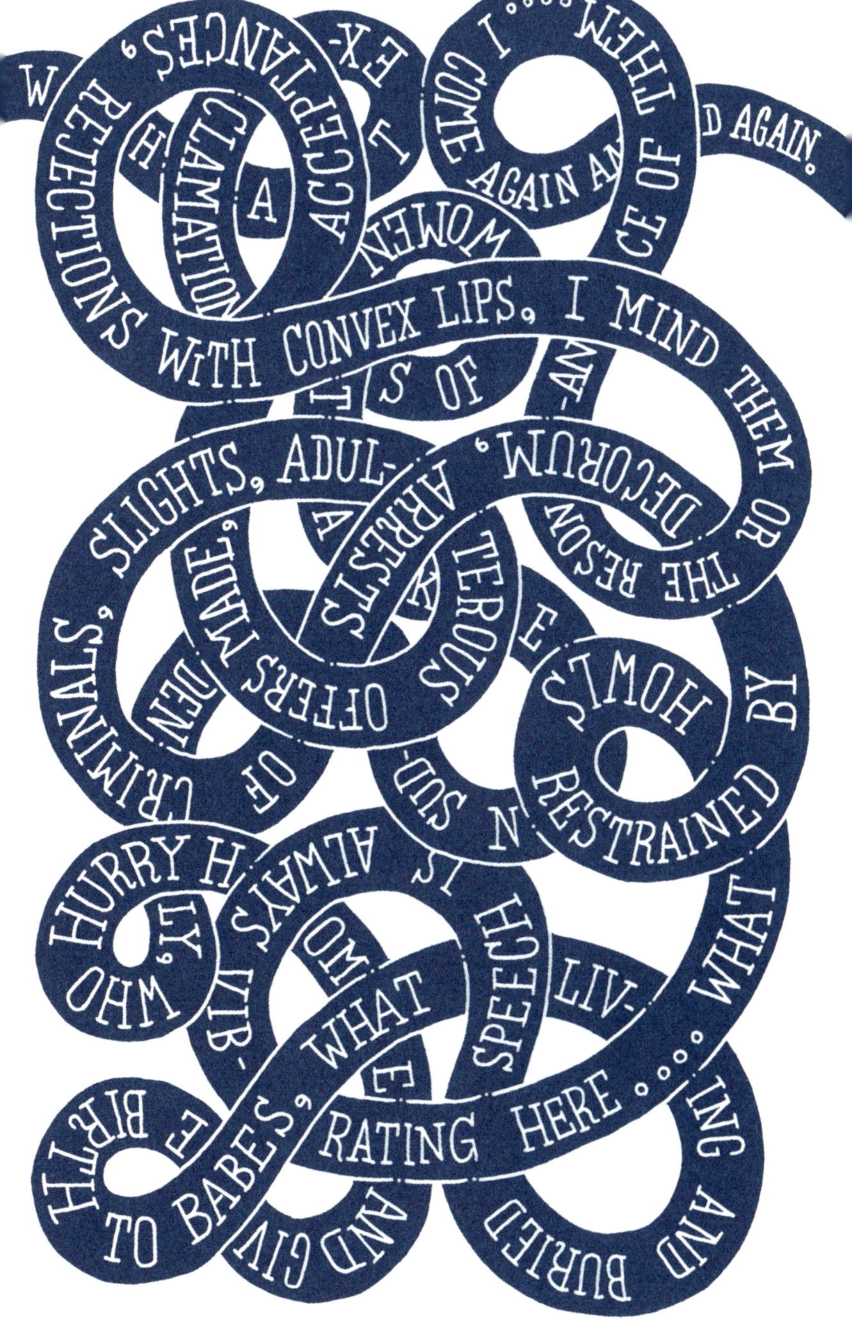

WHAT EX-CLAMATIONS OF WOMEN
TAKEN SUDDEN
WHO HURRY HOME AND GIVE BIRTH TO BABES,
WHAT LIV-ING AND BURIED SPEECH IS ALWAYS VIB-RATING HERE.... WHAT HOWLS RESTRAINED BY DECORUM,
ARRESTS OF CRIMINALS, SLIGHTS, ADUL-TEROUS OFFERS MADE, ACCEPTANCES, REJECTIONS WITH CONVEX LIPS, I MIND THEM OR THE RESON-ANCE OF THEM.... I COME AGAIN AND AGAIN.

the big doors of the country-barn
stand open and ready, the dried
grass of the harvest-time loads the
slow-drawn wagon, the clear light
plays on the brown gray and green
intertinged, the armfuls are packed
to the sagging mow:
I am there .... I help ....
I came stretched atop of the
load, I felt its soft jolts ....
one leg reclined on the other,
I jump from the crossbeams,
and seize the clover and timothy,
and roll head over heels, and tangle
my hair full of wisps.

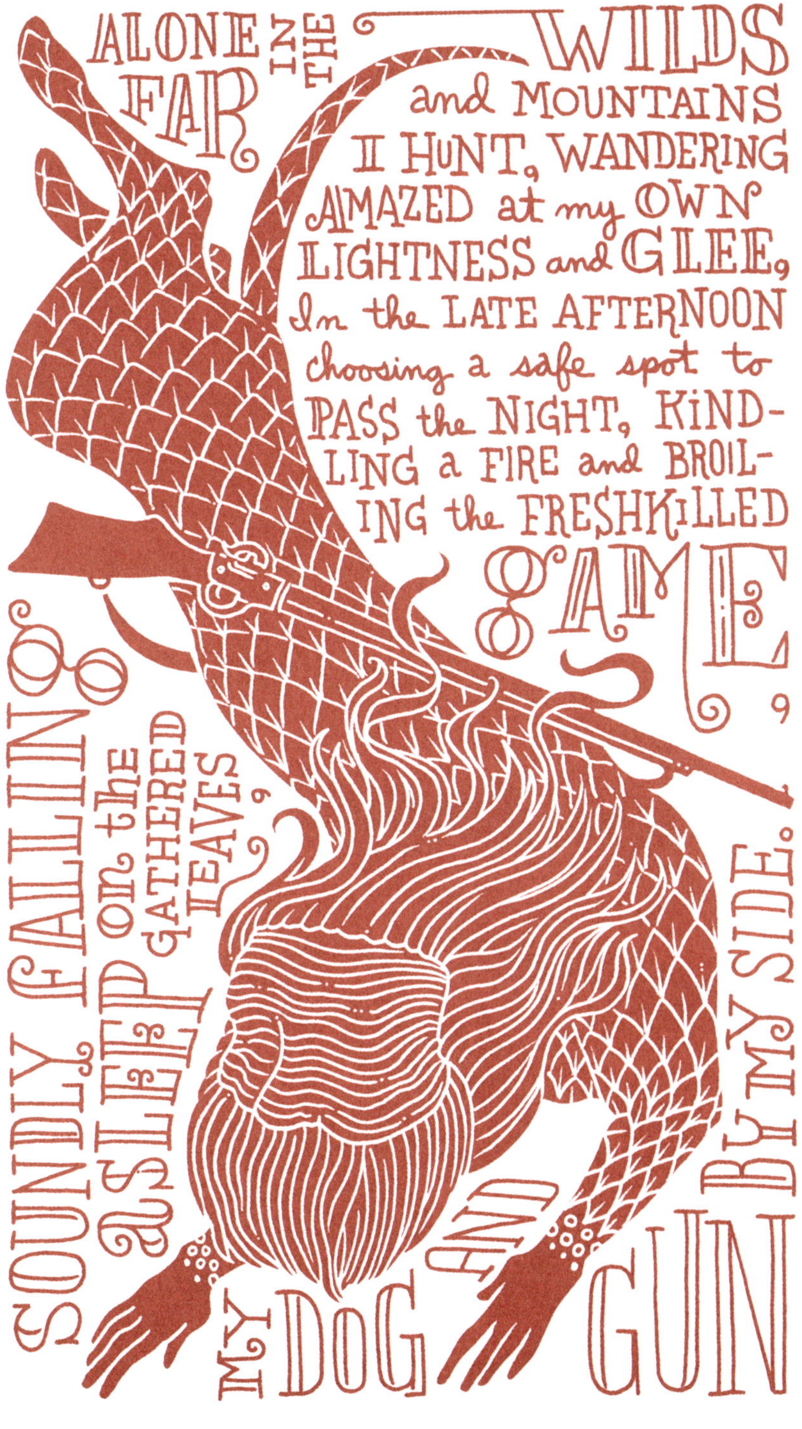

ALONE FAR IN THE WILDS
and MOUNTAINS
I HUNT, WANDERING
AMAZED at my OWN
LIGHTNESS and GLEE,
In the LATE AFTERNOON
choosing a safe spot to
PASS the NIGHT, KIND-
LING a FIRE and BROIL-
ING the FRESHKILLED
GAME,
SOUNDLY FALLING ASLEEP on the GATHERED LEAVES,
MY DOG AND GUN BY MY SIDE.

THE YANKEE CLIPPER IS UNDER HER THREE SKYSAILS,
SHE CUTS the SPARKLE AND SCUD,
MY EYES SETTLE the LAND,
I BEND AT HER PROW, OR SHOUT JOYOUSLY FROM the DECK.

THE BOAT-
MEN
and
CLAM-
DIGGERS
AROSE
EARLY
AND
STOP-
PED
for ME,

I TUCKED MY
TROUSER-ENDS IN MY
BOOTS AND
WENT

AND
HAD A
GOOD
TIME,

YOU SHOULD HAVE
BEEN WITH US
THAT DAY
ROUND
the
CHOWDER-
KETTLE.

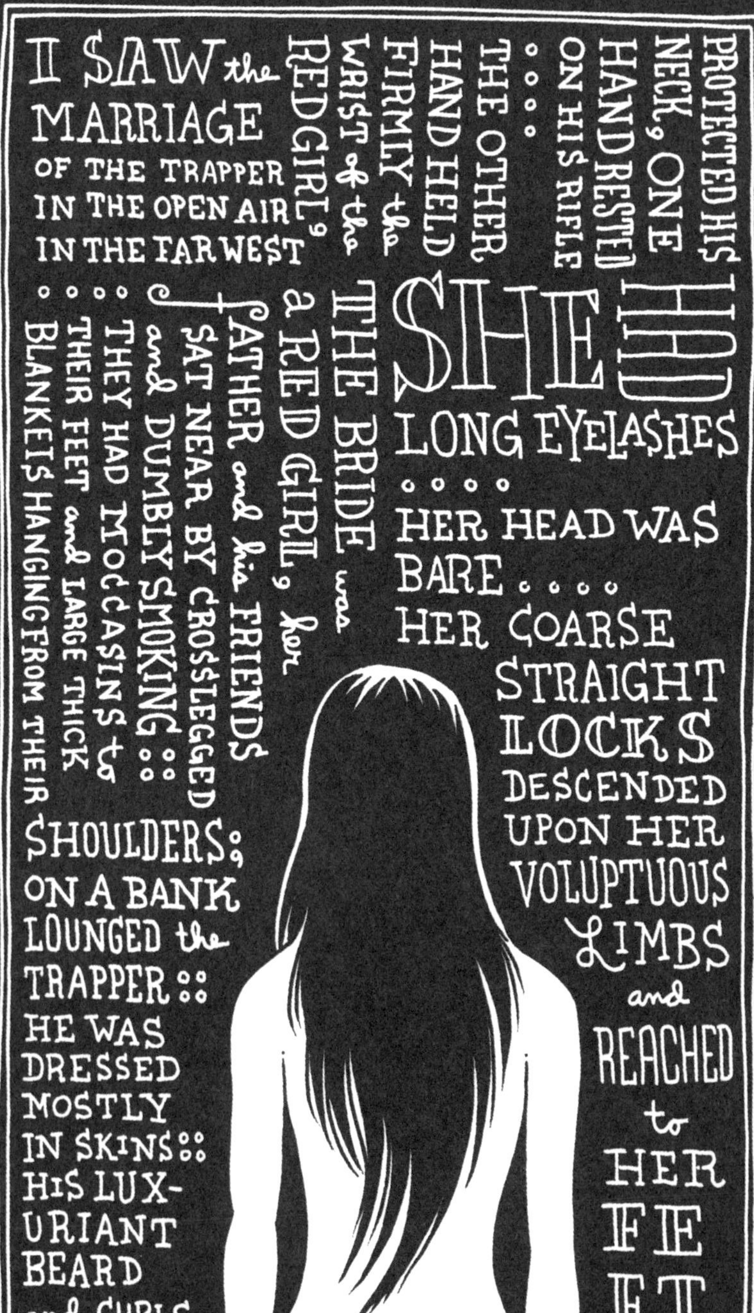
I SAW the MARRIAGE OF THE TRAPPER IN THE OPEN AIR IN THE FAR WEST
.... THE BRIDE was a RED GIRL, her FATHER and his FRIENDS SAT NEAR BY CROSSLEGGED and DUMBLY SMOKING:: THEY HAD MOCCASINS to THEIR FEET and LARGE THICK BLANKETS HANGING FROM THEIR SHOULDERS;
ON A BANK LOUNGED the TRAPPER:: HE WAS DRESSED MOSTLY IN SKINS:: HIS LUX-URIANT BEARD and CURLS
PROTECTED HIS NECK, ONE HAND RESTED ON HIS RIFLE .... THE OTHER HAND HELD FIRMLY the WRIST of the REDGIRL,
SHE HAD LONG EYELASHES .... HER HEAD WAS BARE .... HER COARSE STRAIGHT LOCKS DESCENDED UPON HER VOLUPTUOUS LIMBS and REACHED to HER FEET.

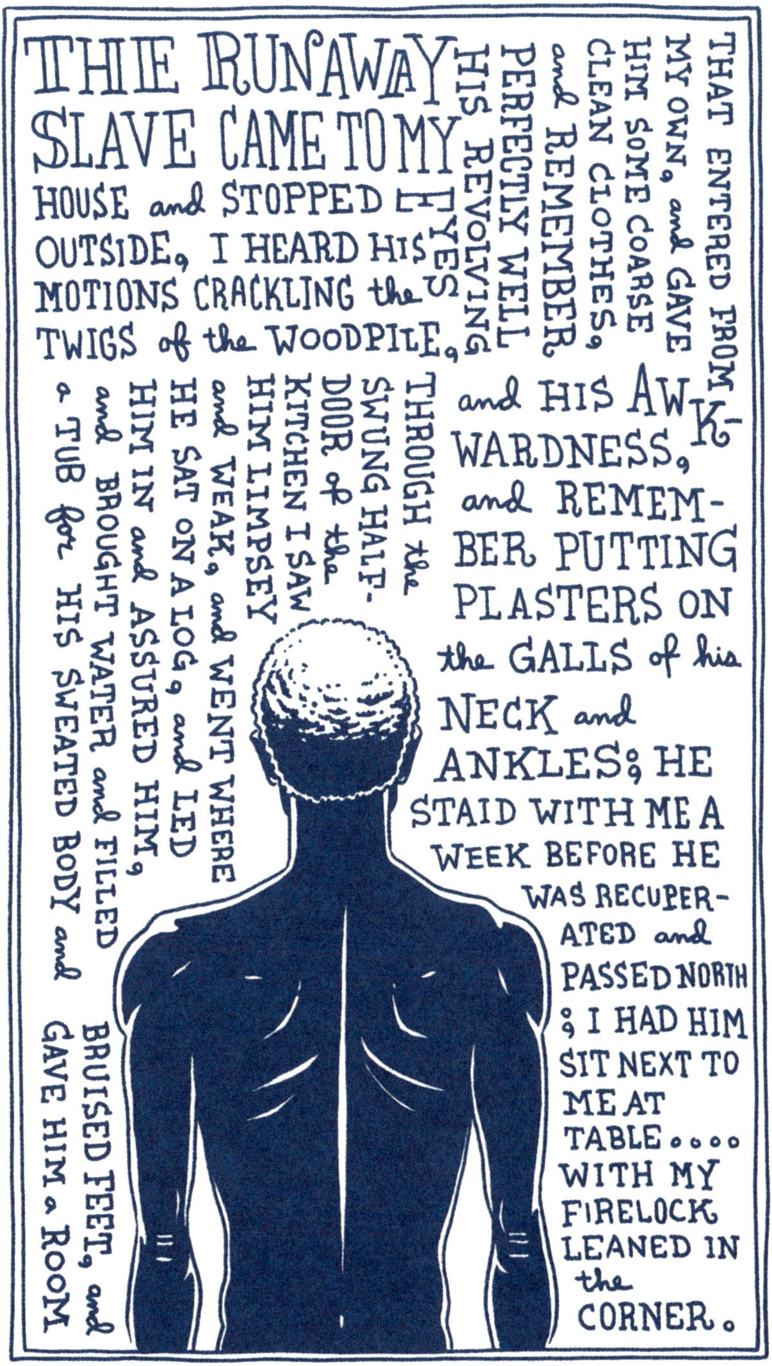
THE RUNAWAY SLAVE CAME TO MY HOUSE and STOPPED OUTSIDE, I HEARD HIS MOTIONS CRACKLING the TWIGS of the WOODPILE,
THROUGH the SWUNG HALF-DOOR of the KITCHEN I SAW HIM LIMPSEY and WEAK, and WENT WHERE HE SAT ON A LOG, and LED HIM IN and ASSURED HIM, and BROUGHT WATER and FILLED a TUB for HIS SWEATED BODY and BRUISED FEET, and GAVE HIM a ROOM
THAT ENTERED FROM MY OWN, and GAVE HIM SOME COARSE CLEAN CLOTHES, and REMEMBER PERFECTLY WELL HIS REVOLVING EYES
and HIS AWKWARDNESS, and REMEMBER PUTTING PLASTERS ON the GALLS of his NECK and ANKLES; HE STAID WITH ME A WEEK BEFORE HE WAS RECUPERATED and PASSED NORTH; I HAD HIM SIT NEXT TO ME AT TABLE.... WITH MY FIRELOCK LEANED IN the CORNER.

TWENTY-EIGHT
young men bathe
by the shore,
TWENTY-EIGHT
young men,
and all so
friendly,

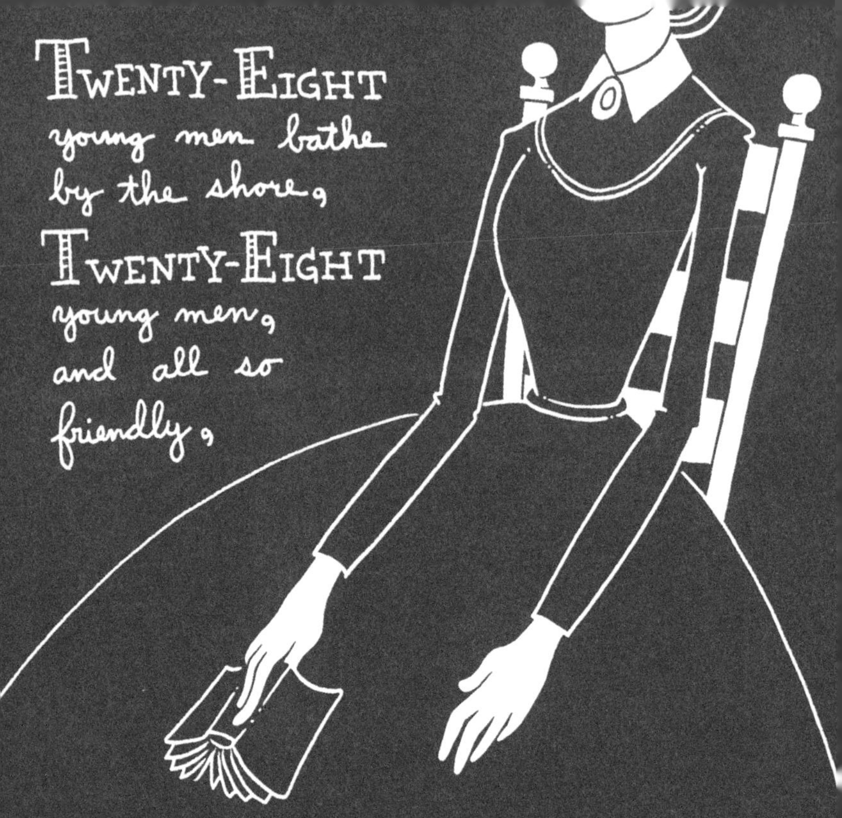

TWENTY-EIGHT
years of womanly life,
and all so lonesome.

She owns the fine house
by the rise of the bank,
She hides handsome and
richly drest aft the
blinds of the
window,

WHICH OF THE YOUNG MEN DOES SHE LIKE THE BEST?
AH THE HOMELIEST OF THEM IS BEAUTIFUL TO HER.

WHERE ARE YOU OFF TO, LADY? FOR I SEE YOU,
YOU SPLASH IN THE WATER THERE, YET STAY STOCK STILL IN YOUR ROOM.

DANCING and LAUGHING ALONG the BEACH CAME the TWENTY-NINTH BATHER,
THE REST DID NOT SEE HER, BUT SHE SAW THEM and LOVED THEM.

THE BEARDS OF the YOUNG MEN GLISTENED WITH WET, IT RAN FROM THEIR LONG HAIR, LITTLE STREAMS PASSED OVER THEIR BODIES.

AN UN-SEEN HAND ALSO PASSED OVER THEIR BODIES, IT DESCENDED TREM-BLINGLY FROM THEIR TEMPLES and RIBS.

THE YOUNG MEN FLOAT ON THEIR BACKS, THEIR WHITE BELLIES SWELL to the SUN.... THEY DO NOT ASK WHO SIEZES FAST TO THEM, THEY DO NOT KNOW WHO PUFFS and DECLINES WITH PEN-DANT and BENDING ARCH, THEY DO NOT THINK WHOM THEY SOUSE with SPRAY.

THE BUTCHER BOY PUTS OFF HIS KILLING-CLOTHES, OR SHARPENS HIS KNIFE at the STALL in the MARKETS I LOITER ENJOYING HIS REPARTEE and HIS SHUFFLE and BREAKDOWN.

BLACKSMITHS WITH GRIMED AND HAIRY CHESTS ENVIRON THE ANVIL, EACH HAS HIS MAIN-SLEDGE.... THEY ARE ALL OUT .... THERE IS A GREAT HEAT in the FIRE.

FROM the CINDER-STREWED THRESHOLD I FOLLOW THEIR MOVEMENTS, the LITHE SHEER OF THEIR WAISTS PLAYS EVEN WITH THEIR MASSIVE ARMS, OVERHAND the HAMMERS ROLL- OVERHAND SO SLOW - OVERHAND SO SURE, THEY DO NOT HASTEN, EACH MAN HITS IN HIS PLACE.

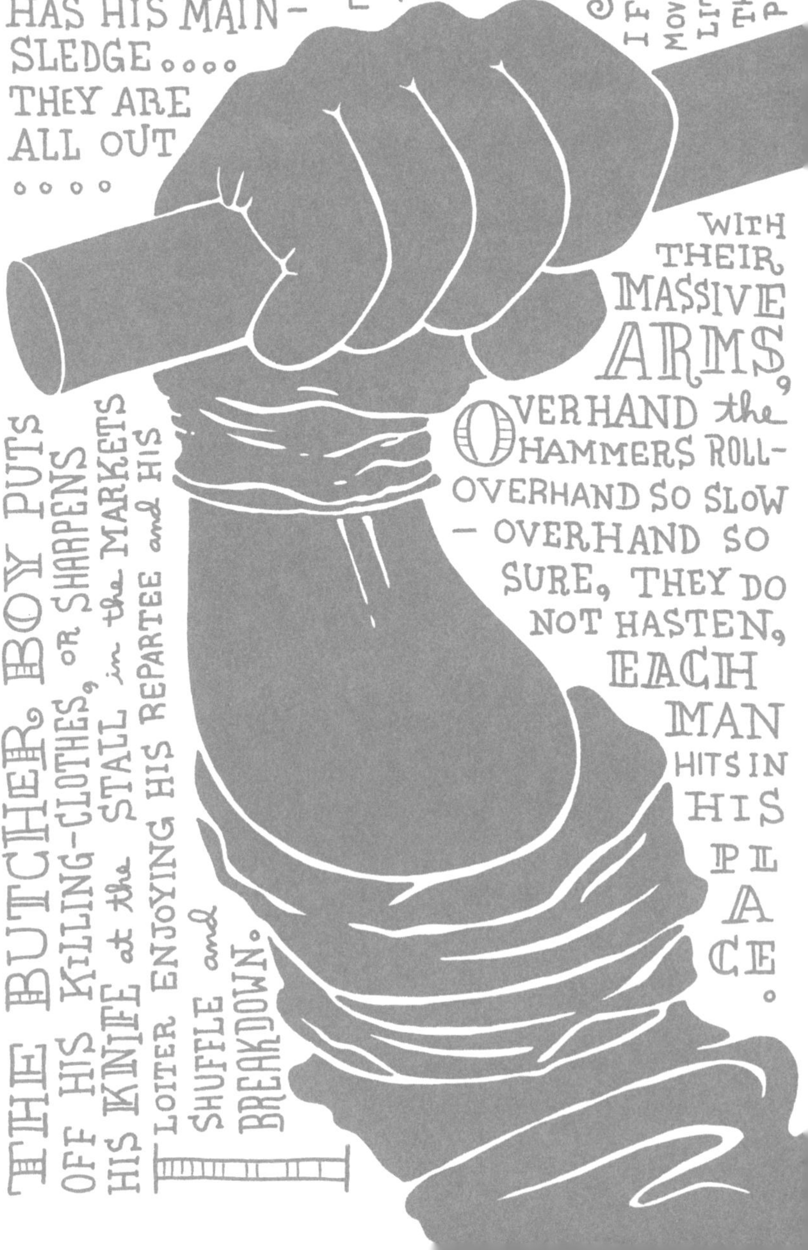

THE NEGRO HOLDS FIRMLY THE REINS of HIS FOUR HORSES

THE BLOCK SWAGS UNDER-NEATH on its TIED-OVER CHAIN, ...

The NEGRO THAT DRIVES the HUGE DRAY of the STONEYARD ... STEADY and TALL HE STANDS POISED on ONE LEG on the STRINGPIECE, HIS BLUE SHIRT EXPOSES HIS AMPLE NECK and BREAST AND LOOSENS OVER HIS HIPBAND,

HIS GLANCE IS CALM and COMMANDING:: HE TOSSES the SLOUCH of HIS HAT AWAY from HIS FOREHEAD,

THE SUN FALLS ON HIS CRISPY HAIR and MOUSTACHE ... FALLS ON the BLACK OF HIS POLISH'D AND PERFECT LIMBS.

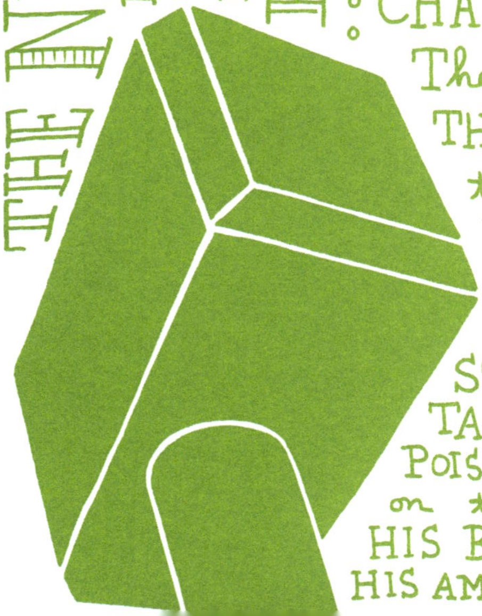

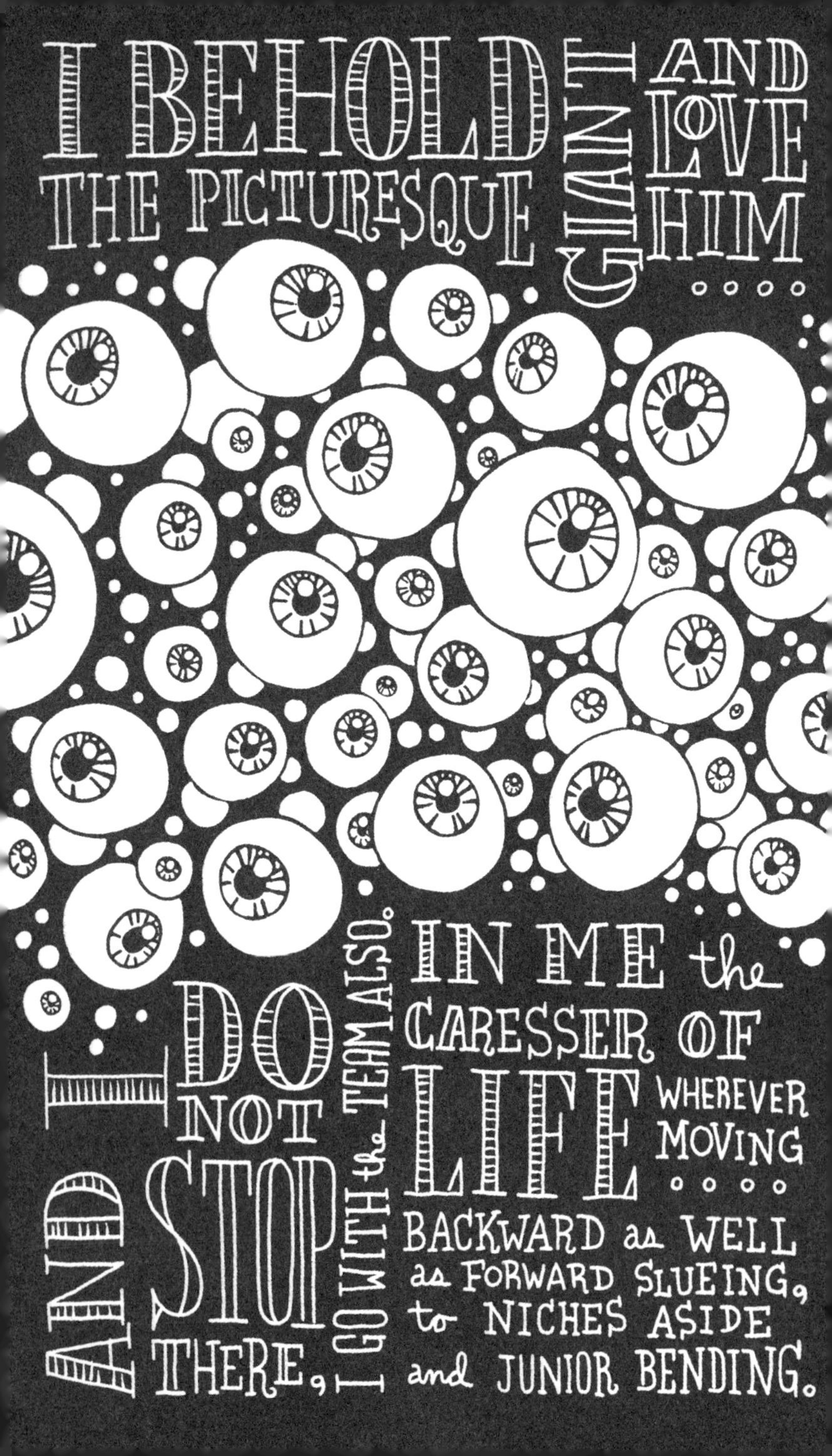
I BEHOLD THE PICTURESQUE GIANT AND LOVE HIM ....
AND I DO NOT STOP THERE, I GO WITH the TEAM ALSO.
IN ME the CARESSER OF LIFE WHEREVER MOVING ....
BACKWARD as WELL as FORWARD SLUEING, to NICHES ASIDE and JUNIOR BENDING.

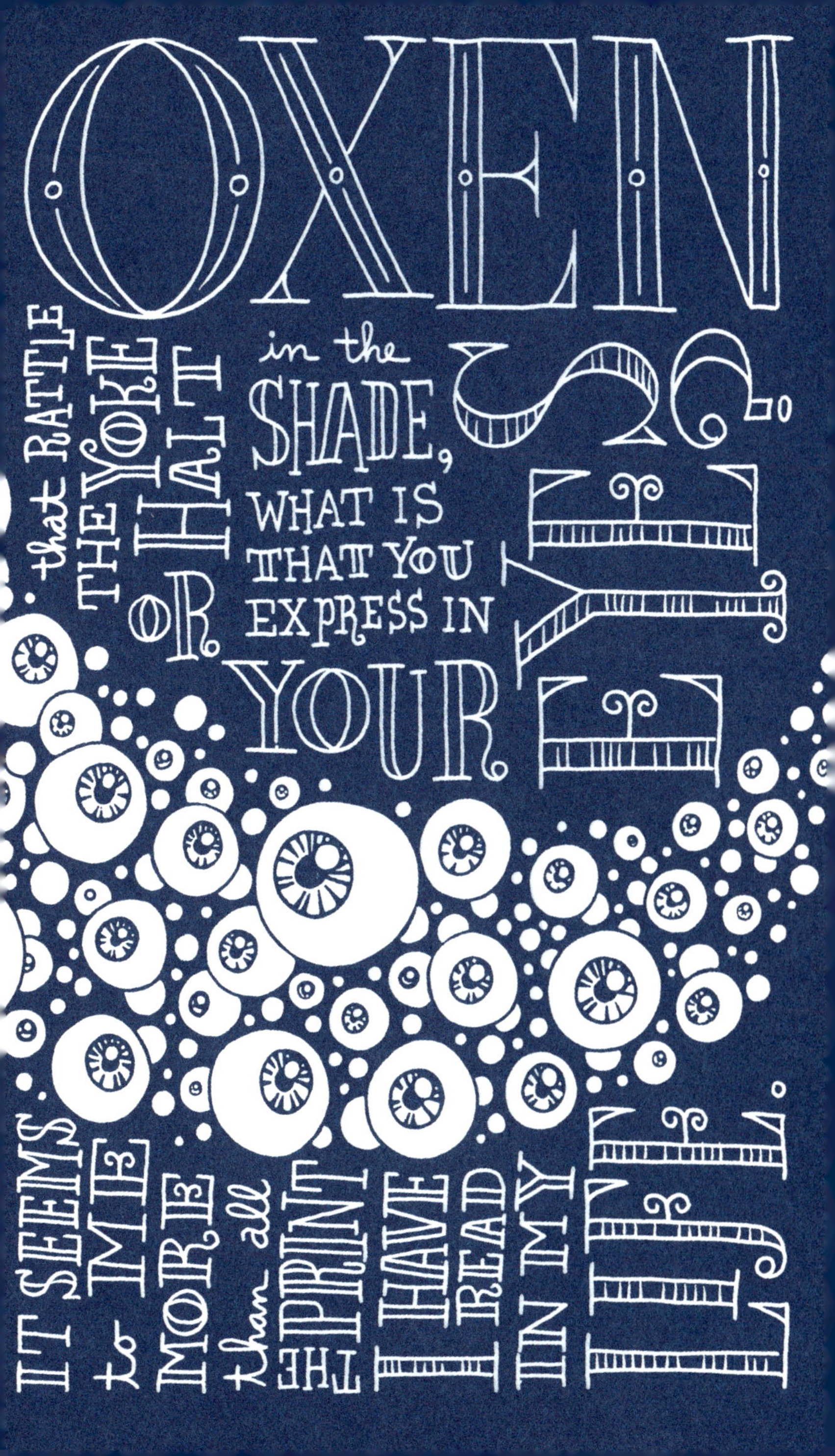
OXEN
that RATTLE
THE YOKE
OR HALT
in the
SHADE,
WHAT IS
THAT YOU
EXPRESS IN
YOUR
EYES?
IT SEEMS
to ME
MORE
than all
THE PRINT
I HAVE
READ
IN MY
LIFE.

MY TREAD SCARES the WOOD-DRAKE and WOOD-DUCK
ON MY DISTANT AND DAYLONG RAMBLE,
THEY RISE TOGETHER, they SLOWLY CIRCLE AROUND.
I BELIEVE IN THOSE WINGED PURPOSES,
AND ACKNOWLEDGE the RED YELLOW and WHITE PLAYING WITHIN ME,
AND CONSIDER THE GREEN and VIOLET and THE TUFTED CROWN INTENTIONAL; and
DO NOT CALL THE TORTOISE UNWORTHY BECAUSE SHE IS NOT SOMETHING ELSE,
AND THE MOCKING BIRD IN the SWAMP NEVER STUDIED the GAMUT,
YET TRILLS PRETTY WELL to ME,
AND THE LOOK OF the BAY MARE SHAMES SILLINESS OUT OF ME.

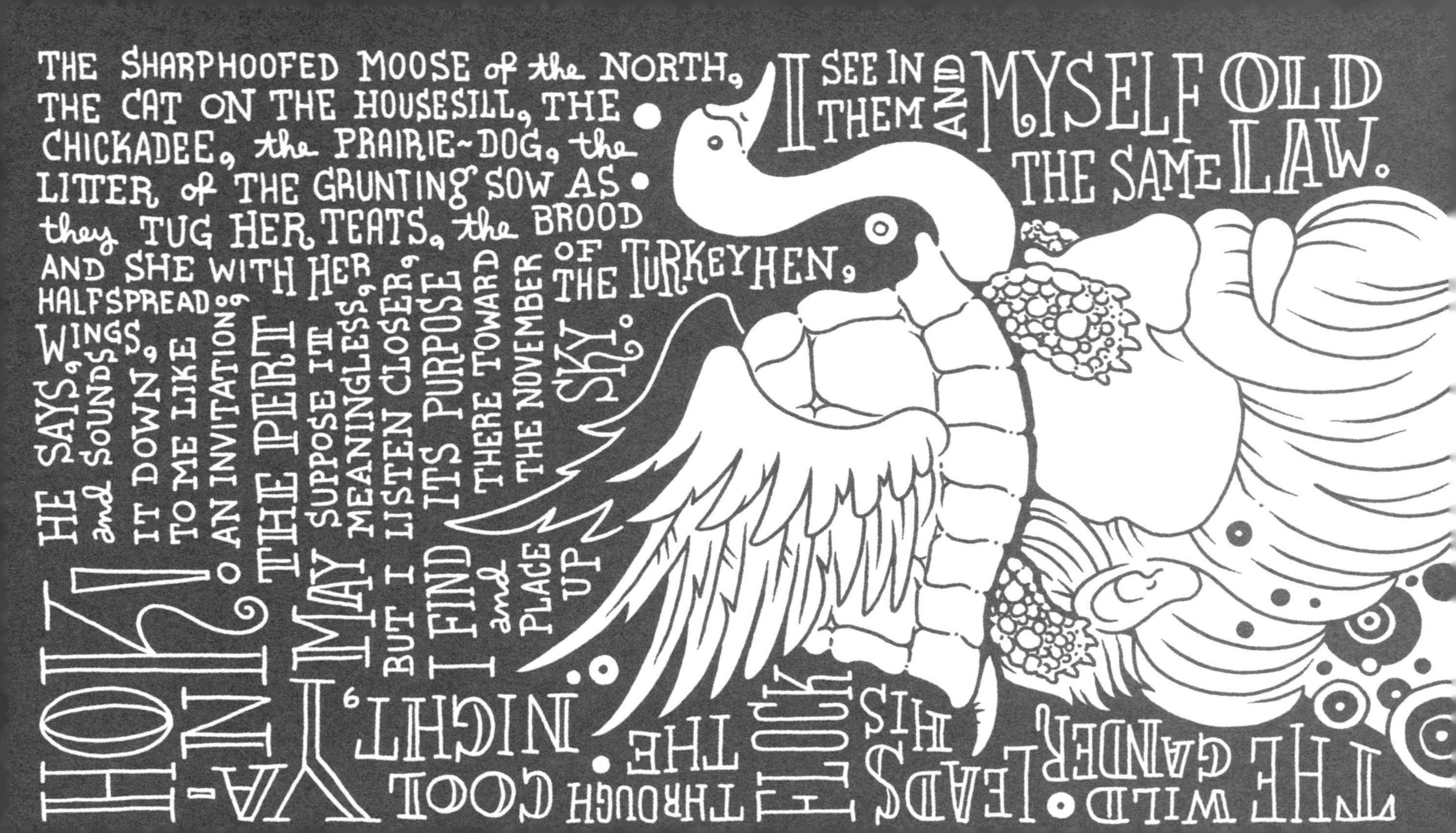
THE WILD GANDER LEADS HIS FLOCK THROUGH THE COOL NIGHT,
YA-HONK! HE SAYS, and SOUNDS IT DOWN TO ME LIKE AN INVITATION;
THE PERT MAY SUPPOSE IT MEANINGLESS, BUT I LISTEN CLOSER,
I FIND ITS PURPOSE and PLACE UP THERE TOWARD THE NOVEMBER SKY.
THE SHARPHOOFED MOOSE of the NORTH, THE CAT ON THE HOUSESILL, THE CHICKADEE, the PRAIRIE-DOG, the LITTER of THE GRUNTING SOW AS they TUG HER TEATS, the BROOD OF THE TURKEYHEN, AND SHE WITH HER HALFSPREAD WINGS,
I SEE IN THEM AND MYSELF THE SAME OLD LAW.

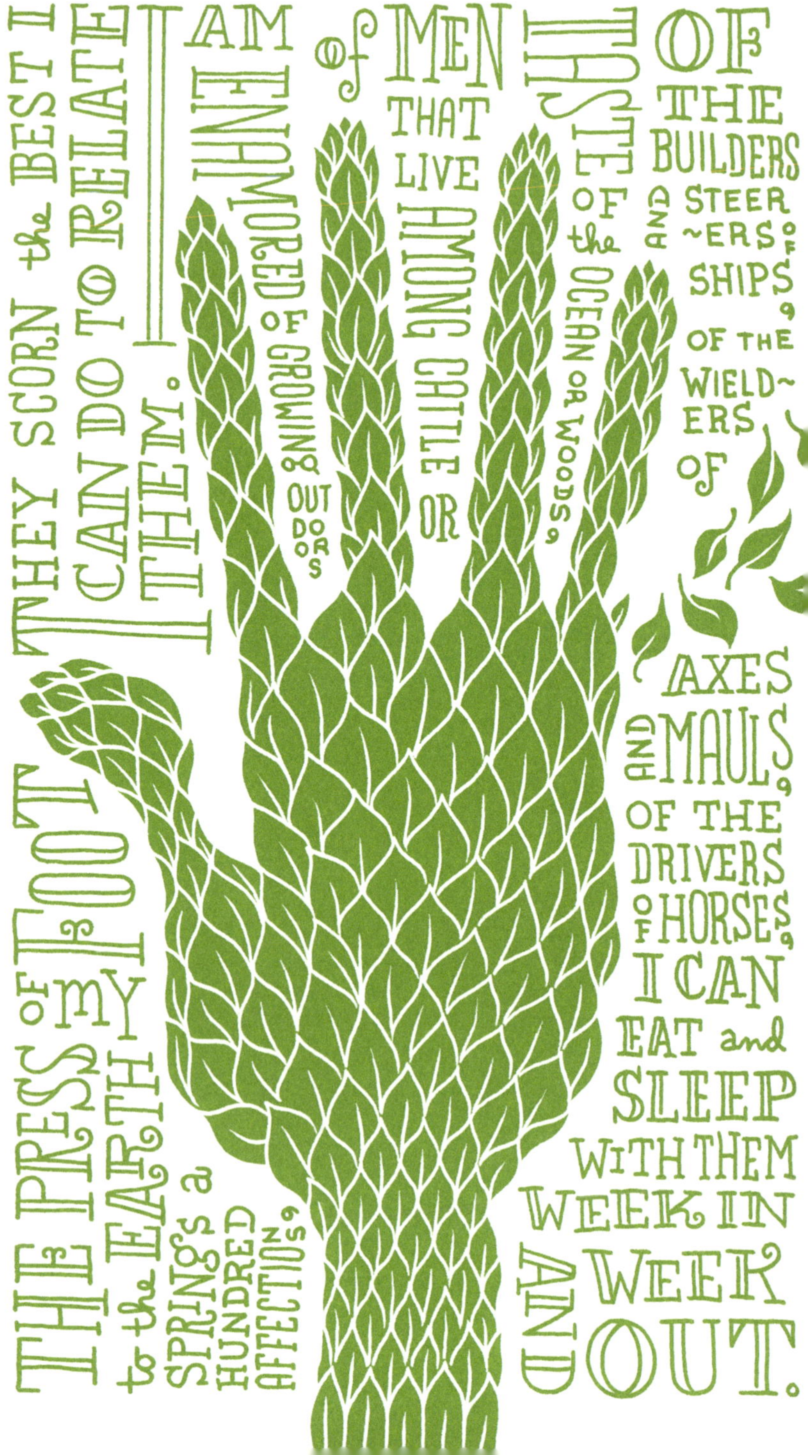
THE PRESS OF MY FOOT to the EARTH SPRINGS a HUNDRED AFFECTIONS,
THEY SCORN the BEST I CAN DO TO RELATE THEM.
I AM ENAMORED OF GROWING OUTDOORS
of MEN THAT LIVE AMONG CATTLE OR TASTE OF the OCEAN OR WOODS,
OF THE BUILDERS AND STEER~ERS OF SHIPS, OF THE WIELD~ERS OF AXES AND MAULS, OF THE DRIVERS OF HORSES,
I CAN EAT and SLEEP WITH THEM WEEK IN AND WEEK OUT.

WHAT IS COMMONEST and NEAREST and EASIEST is ME, ME GOING IN for MY CHANCES, SPENDING for VAST RETURNS, ADORNING MYSELF to BESTOW MYSELF ON THE FIRST THAT WILL TAKE ME, NOT ASKING the SKY to COME DOWN to MY GOODWILL, SCATTERING it FREELY FOR~EV~ER.

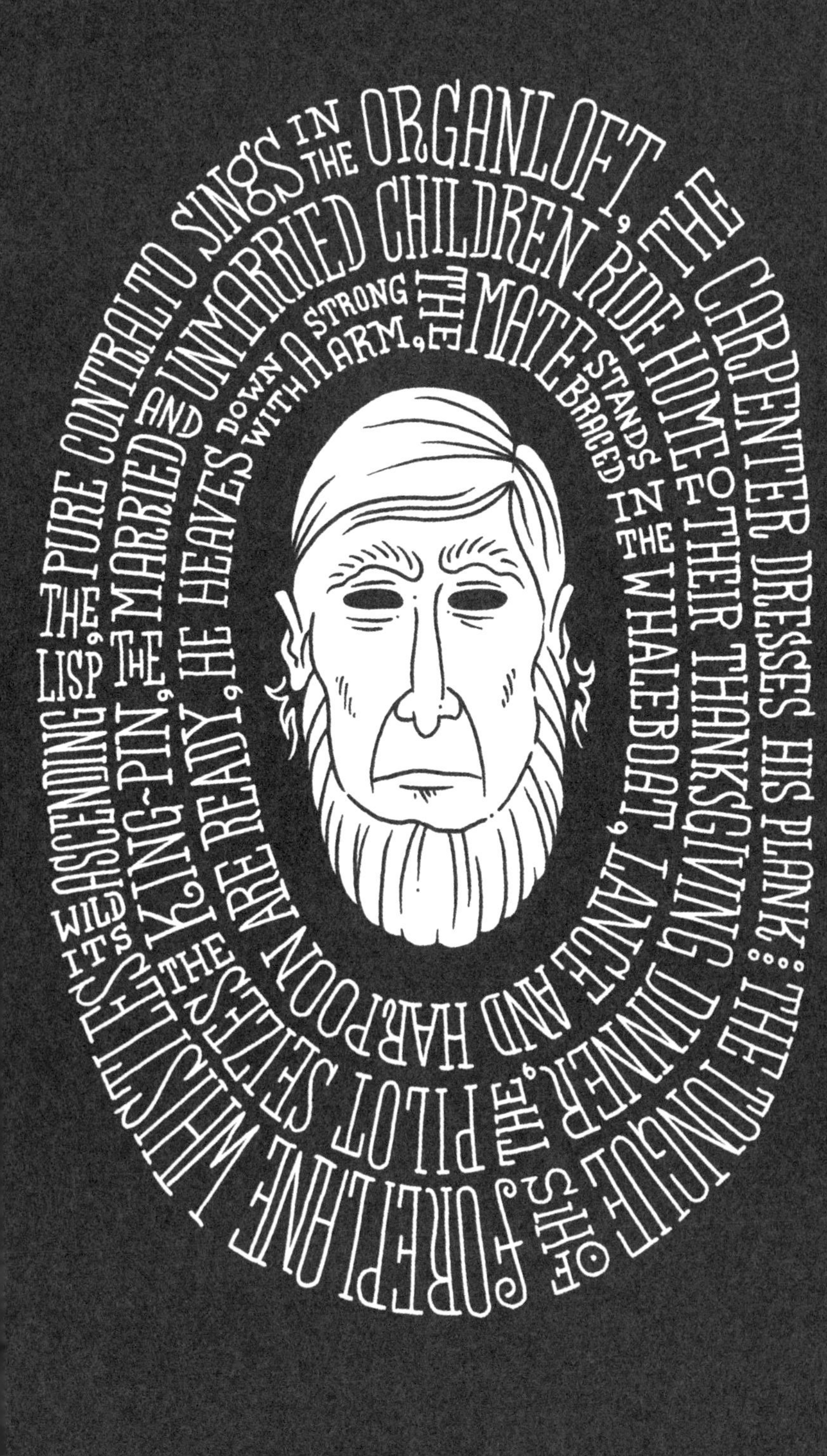
THE PURE CONTRALTO SINGS IN THE ORGANLOFT, THE CARPENTER DRESSES HIS PLANK... THE TONGUE OF HIS FOREPLANE WHISTLES ITS WILD ASCENDING LISP, THE MARRIED AND UNMARRIED CHILDREN RIDE HOME TO THEIR THANKSGIVING DINNER, THE PILOT SEIZES THE KING-PIN, HE HEAVES DOWN WITH A STRONG ARM, THE MATE STANDS BRACED IN THE WHALEBOAT, LANCE AND HARPOON ARE READY,

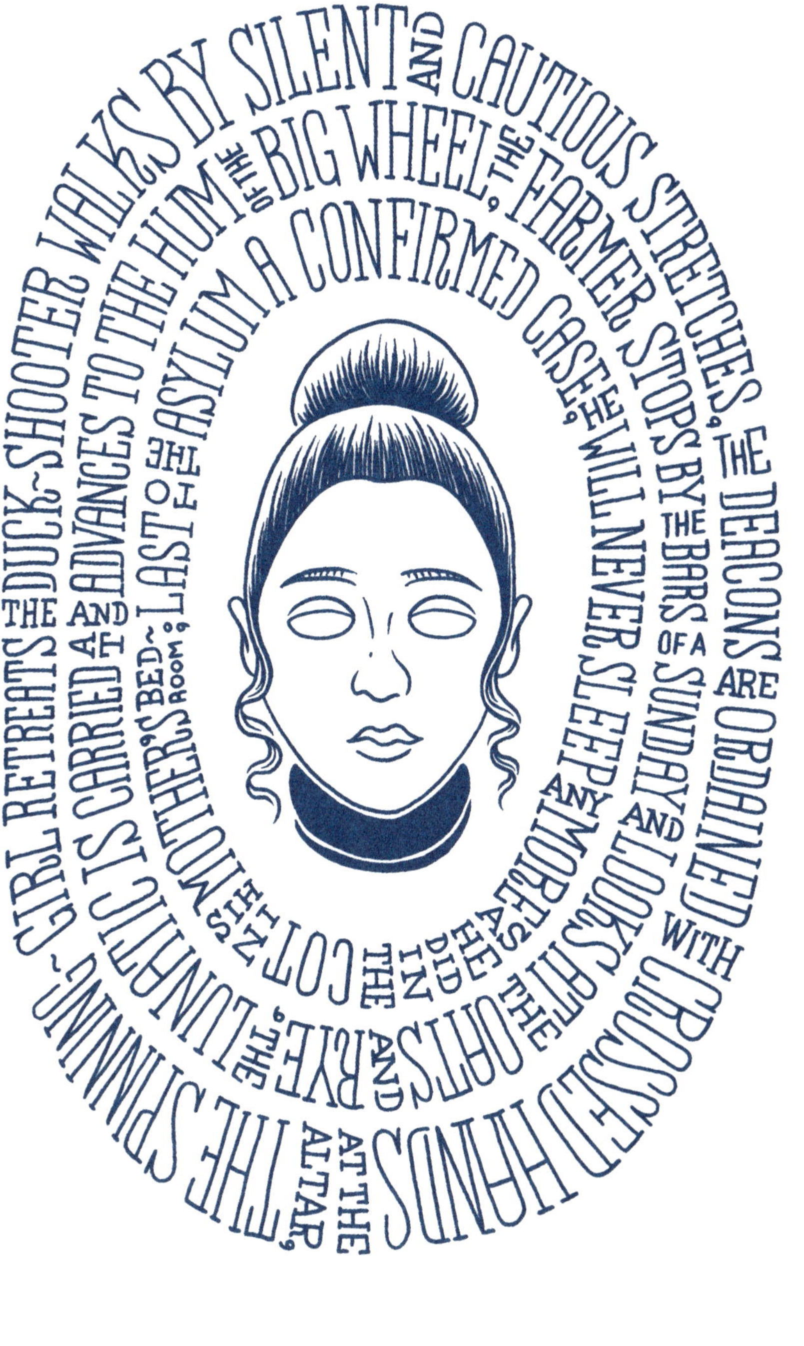
THE SPINNING~GIRL RETREATS AND ADVANCES TO THE HUM OF THE BIG WHEEL, THE FARMER STOPS BY THE BARS OF A SUNDAY AND LOOKS AT THE OATS AND RYE, THE LUNATIC IS CARRIED AT LAST TO THE ASYLUM A CONFIRMED CASE, HE WILL NEVER SLEEP ANY MORE AS HE DID IN THE COT IN HIS MOTHER'S BED~ROOM;
THE DUCK~SHOOTER WALKS BY SILENT AND CAUTIOUS STRETCHES, THE DEACONS ARE ORDAINED WITH CROSSED HANDS AT THE ALTAR,

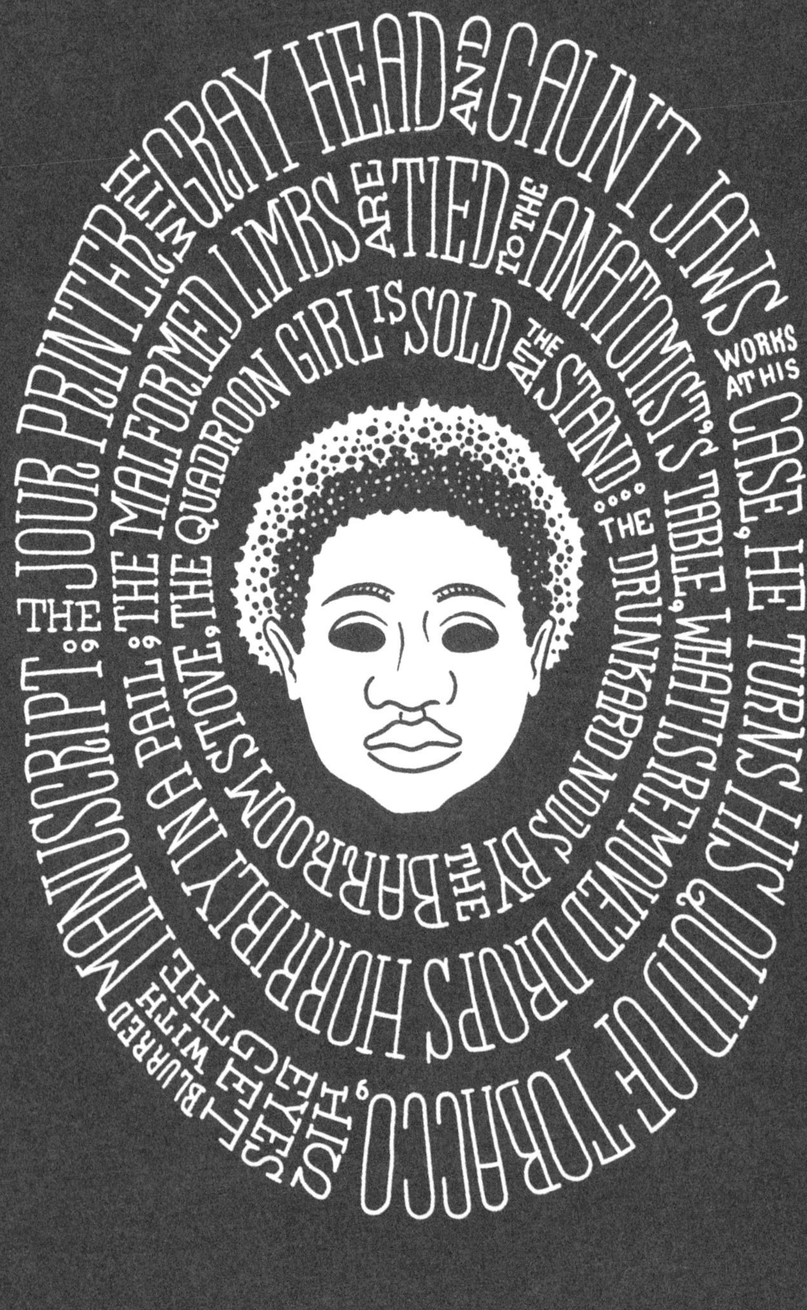
THE JOUR PRINTER WITH GRAY HEAD AND GAUNT JAWS WORKS AT HIS CASE, HE TURNS HIS QUID OF TOBACCO, HIS EYES BLURRED WITH THE MANUSCRIPT;
THE MALFORMED LIMBS ARE TIED TO THE ANATOMIST'S TABLE, WHAT IS REMOVED DROPS HORRIBLY IN A PAIL;
THE QUADROON GIRL IS SOLD AT THE STAND.... THE DRUNKARD NODS BY THE BARROOM STOVE,

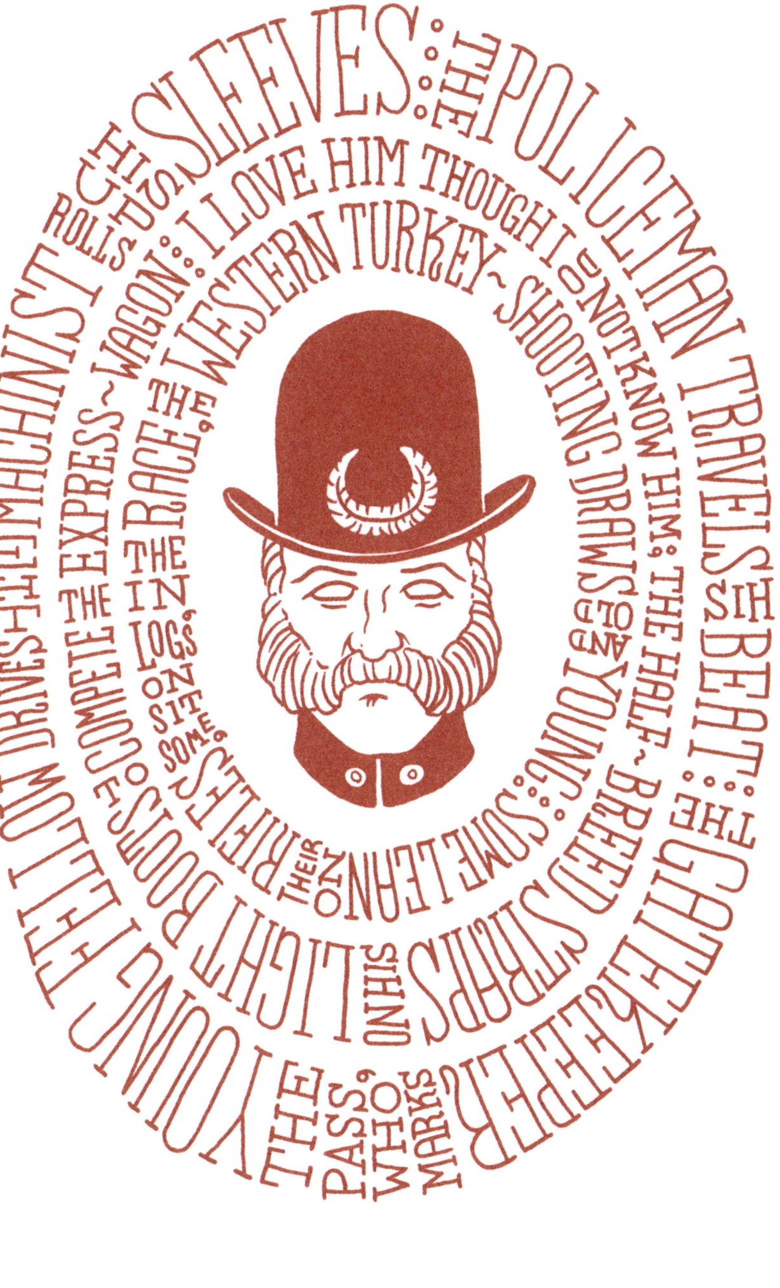
THE MACHINIST ROLLS UP HIS SLEEVES: THE POLICEMAN TRAVELS HIS BEAT: THE GATEKEEPER MARKS WHO PASS, THE YOUNG FELLOW DRIVES THE EXPRESS~WAGON: I LOVE HIM THOUGH I DO NOT KNOW HIM; THE HALF~BREED STRAPS ON HIS LIGHT BOOTS TO COMPETE IN THE RACE, THE WESTERN TURKEY~SHOOTING DRAWS OLD AND YOUNG: SOME LEAN ON THEIR RIFLES, SOME SIT ON LOGS,

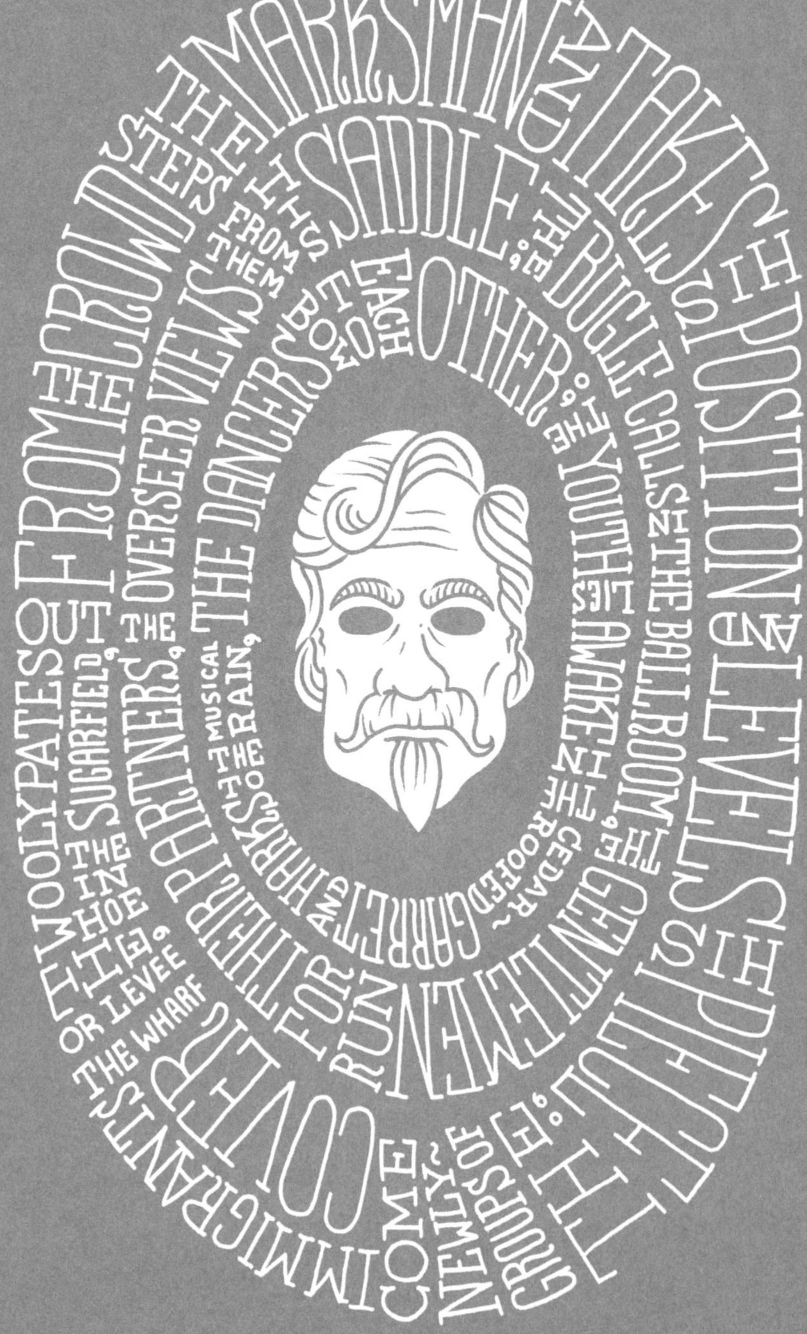

OUT FROM THE CROWD STEPS THE MARKSMAN AND TAKES HIS POSITION AND LEVELS HIS PIECE;
THE GROUPS OF NEWLY-COME IMMIGRANTS COVER THE WHARF OR LEVEE,
THE WOOLYPATES HOE IN THE SUGARFIELD, THE OVERSEER VIEWS THEM FROM HIS SADDLE;
THE BUGLE CALLS IN THE BALLROOM, THE GENTLEMEN RUN FOR THEIR PARTNERS, THE DANCERS BOW TO EACH OTHER;
THE YOUTH LIES AWAKE IN THE CEDAR-ROOFED GARRET AND HARKS TO THE MUSICAL RAIN,

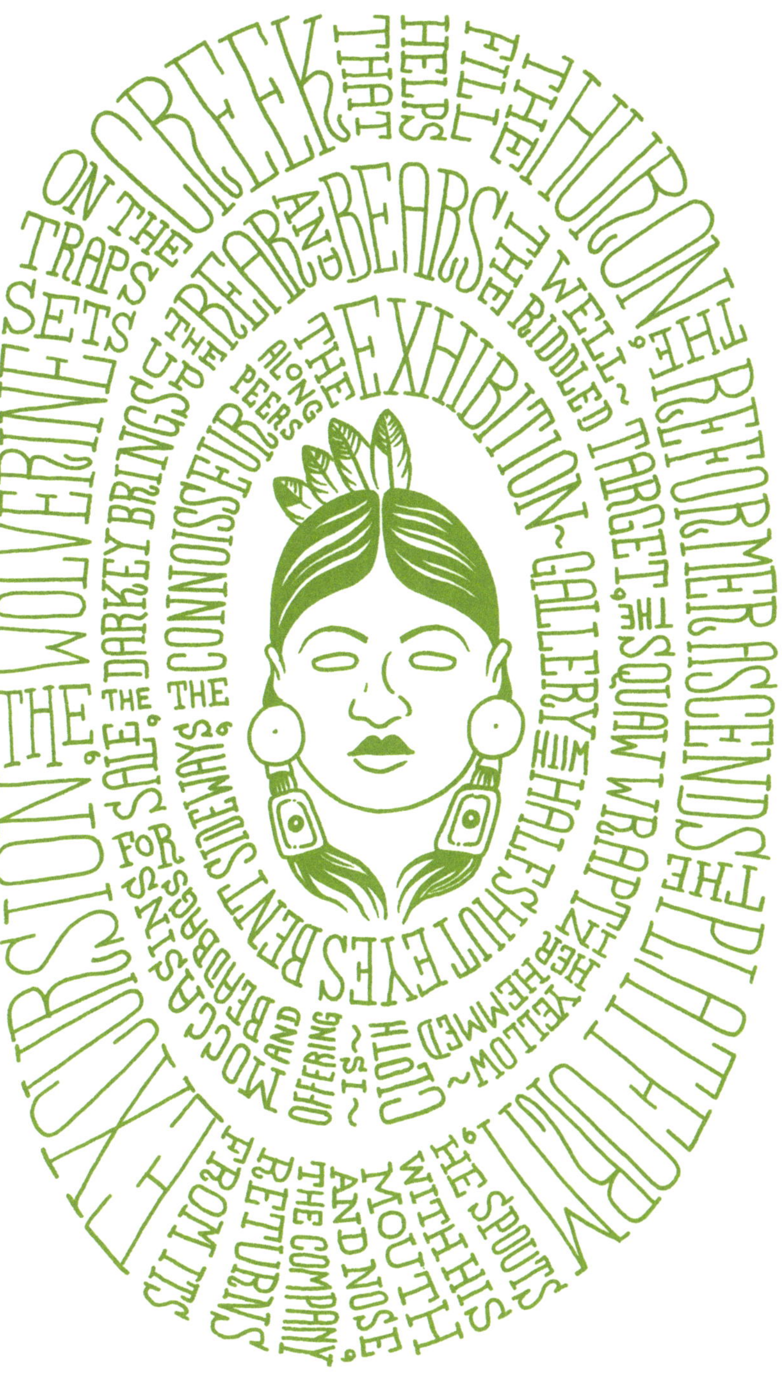
THE WOLVERINE SETS TRAPS ON THE CREEK THAT HELPS FILL THE HURON,
THE FORMER ASCENDS THE PLATFORM, HE SPOUTS WITH HIS MOUTH AND NOSE,
THE COMPANY RETURNS FROM ITS EXCURSION, THE DARKEY BRINGS UP THE REAR AND BEARS THE WELL~RIDDLED TARGET,
THE SQUAW WRAPT IN HER YELLOW~HEMMED CLOTH ~ IS ~ OFFERING MOCCASINS AND BEAD~BAGS FOR SALE,
THE CONNOISSEUR PEERS ALONG THE EXHIBITION~GALLERY WITH HALF~SHUT EYES BENT SIDEWAYS,

THE DECKHANDS make Fast THE steamboat, the plank is thrown for the SHOREGOING PASSENGERS, The young sister holds out the skein, the elder sister winds it off in a ball and STOPS now and then for the knots, THE one-year wife is RECOVERING and happy, a week ago she bore her FIRST CHILD, The cleanhaired YANKEE GIRL works with her sewing~machine, or in the factory or mill,

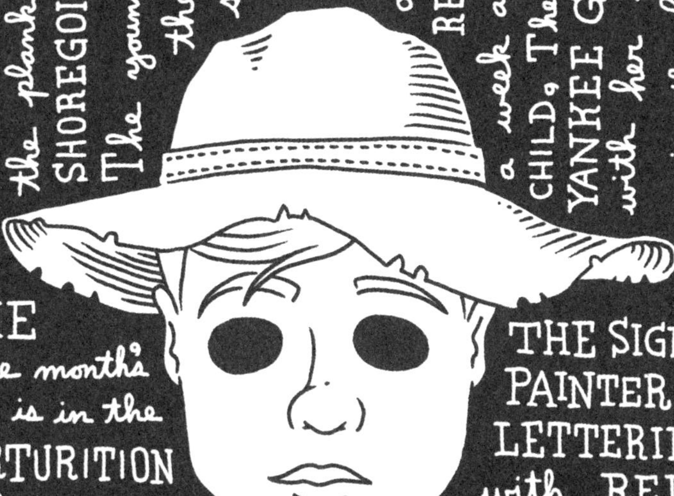

THE nine months' gone is in the PARTURITION CHAMBER, her FAINTNESS and PAINS are advancing; The PAVINGMAN leans on his two-handed rammer ~ the reporter's lead flies swiftly over the notebook ~

THE SIGN-PAINTER is LETTERING with RED and GOLD, THE CANAL~BOY TROTS on the TOWPATH~ the BOOKKEEPER counts at his desk ~ the SHOEMAKER WAXES his THREAD,

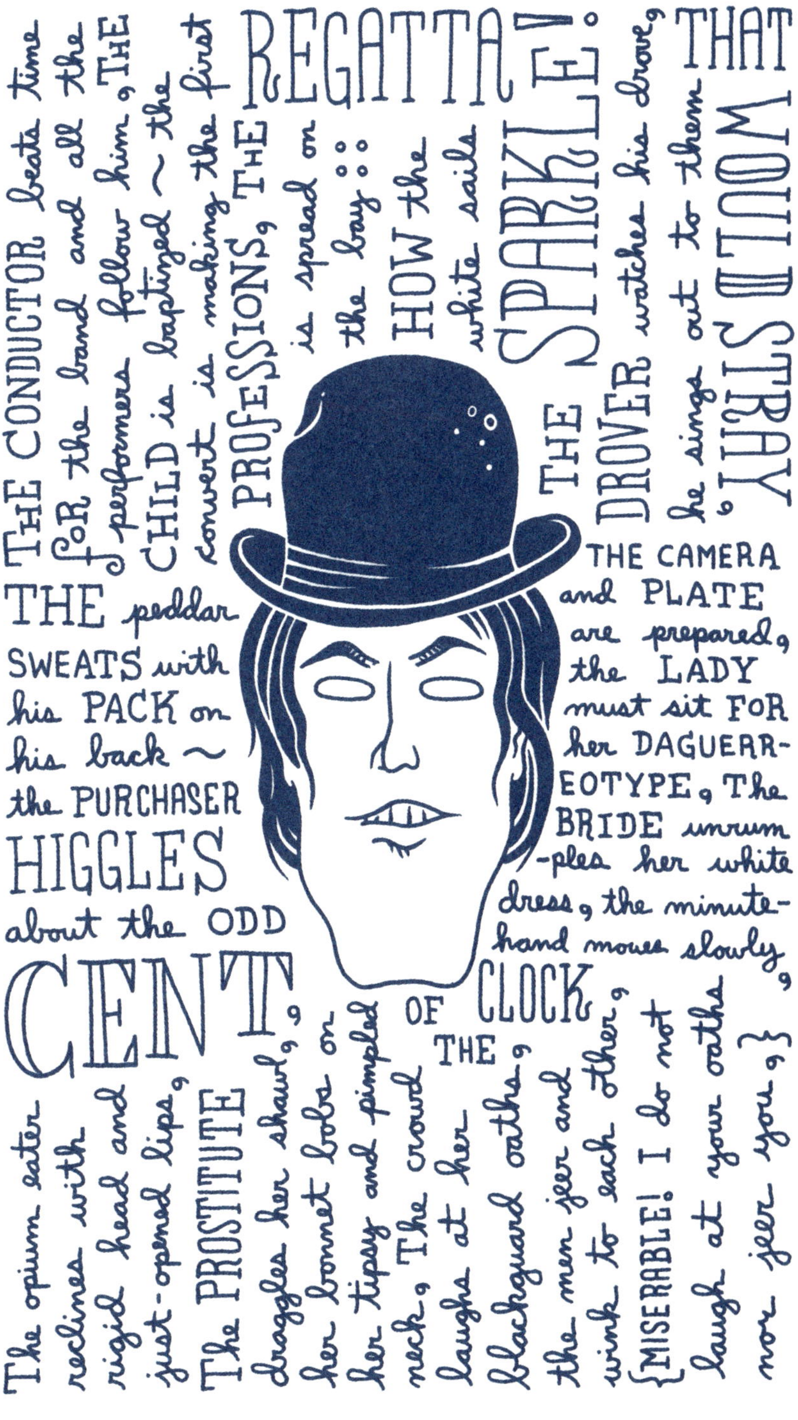

THE CONDUCTOR beats time for the band and all the performers follow him, THE CHILD is baptized ~ the convert is making the first PROFESSIONS, THE REGATTA is spread on the bay:: HOW the white sails SPARKLE!
THE DROVER watches his drove, he sings out to them THAT WOULD STRAY,
THE peddar SWEATS with his PACK on his back ~ the PURCHASER HIGGLES about the ODD CENT,
THE CAMERA and PLATE are prepared, the LADY must sit FOR her DAGUERR-EOTYPE, The BRIDE unrumples her white dress, the minute-hand moves slowly, OF THE CLOCK,
The opium eater reclines with rigid head and just-opened lips, The PROSTITUTE draggles her shawl, her bonnet bobs on her tipsy and pimpled neck, The crowd laughs at her blackguard oaths, the men jeer and wink to each other, {MISERABLE! I do not laugh at your oaths nor jeer you,}

THE PRESIDENT holds a CABINET COUNCIL, he is surrounded by the great SECRETARIES, On the PIAZZA walk five friendly matrons with twined arms; The crew of the FISH~SMACK pack repeated layers of HALIBUT in the hold, THE MISSOURIAN crosses the plains toting his wares and his cattle, the FARE~COLLECTOR goes through the TRAIN ~ he GIVES notice BY the JINGLING of loose change,

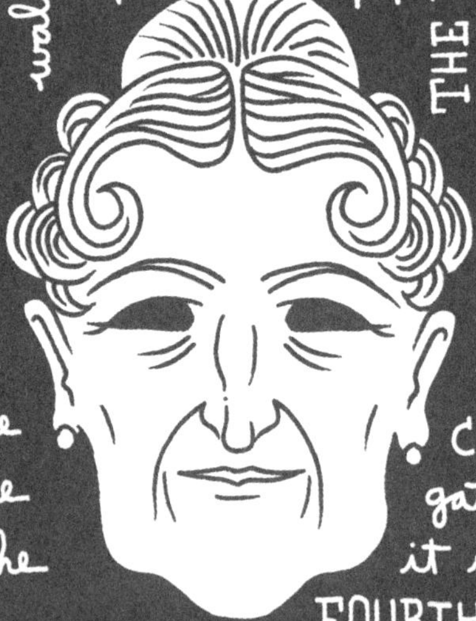

The FLOOR-MEN are laying the floor ~ the tinners are tinning the roof ~ the masons are calling for mortar, IN single file each shouldering his hod pass onward the laborers; SEASONS pursuing each other

The INDESCRIBABLE CROWD is gathered :: it is the FOURTH of JULY ... what SALUTES of CANNON and SMALL ARMS! Seasons pursuing each other the PLOUGHER PLOUGHS and the MOWER MOWS and the wintergrain falls in the GROUND;

OFF ON THE LAKES the PIKEFISHER watches and waits by the HOLE in the frozen surface, The stumps stand thick round the clearing, the SQUATTER strikes DEEP with his AXE, The FLAT~BOATMEN make fast toward dusk near the cottonwood or pekantrees, THE COON~SEEKERS go now through the regions of the RED river, or through those drained by the TENNESSEE, or through those of the ARKANSAS, The TORCHES shine in the dark that hangs on the CHATTAHOOCHEE or ALTAMAHAW;

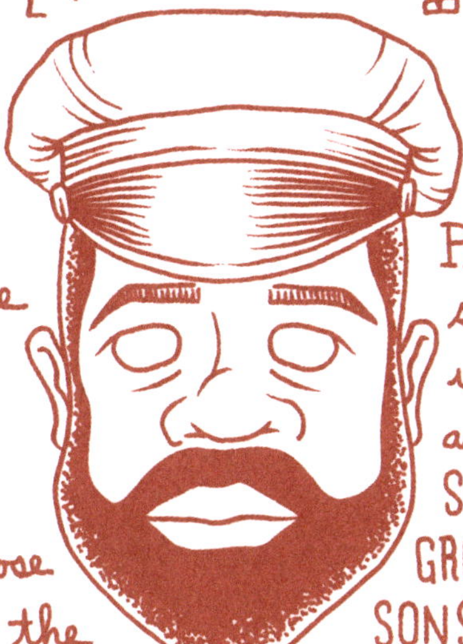

PATRIARCHS sit at supper with SONS and GRAND~SONS and GREAT~GRAND~SONS around them, IN WALLS OF ADOBIE, IN CANVAS TENTS, rest HUNTERS and TRAPPERS after their DAY'S SPORT.

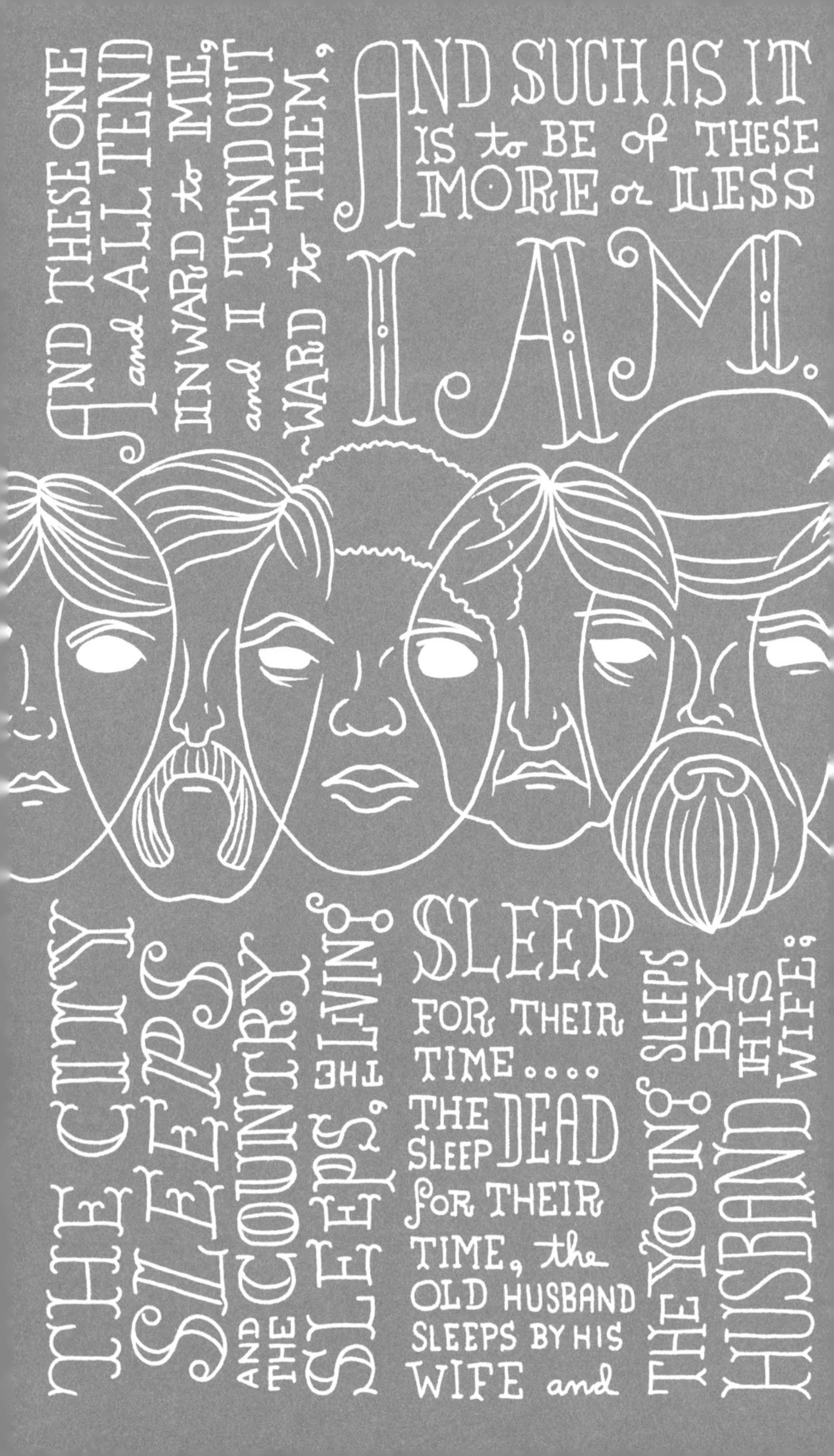
And these one and all tend inward to me, and I tend outward to them,
And such as it is to be of these more or less I am.
The city sleeps and the country sleeps,
the living sleep for their time....
the dead sleep for their time,
the old husband sleeps by his wife and
the young husband sleeps by his wife;

I AM of OLD and YOUNG,
of THE FOOLISH as
MUCH AS the WISE,
REGARDLESS OF
OTHERS, EVER REGARDFUL
of OTHERS, MATERNAL
as WELL as PATERNAL,
A CHILD AS WELL AS A
MAN, STUFFED WITH
THE STUFF THAT IS COARSE,
AND STUFFED WITH THE STUFF
THAT IS FINE,

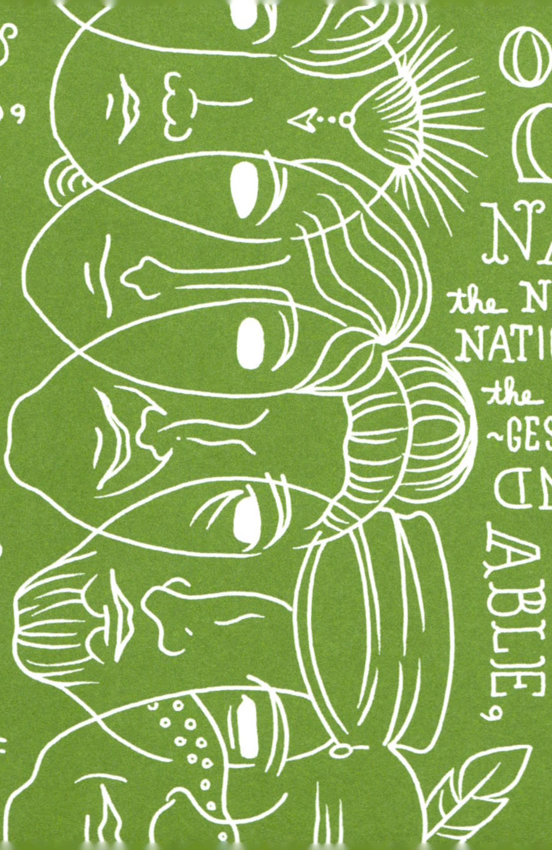

ONE of THE
GREAT
NATIONS,
the NATION of MANY
NATIONS ~ the SMALLEST
the SAME and the LAR
~GEST the SAME,

A SOUTHERNER as
SOON as a NORTHERNER,
A PLANTER
NONCHALANT
AND HOSPIT~
ABLE,

A YANKEE BOUND MY OWN WAY.... READY FOR TRADE.... MY JOINTS the LIMBEREST JOINTS ON EARTH, A KENTUCKIAN WALKING THE VALE OF THE ELKHORN in my DEERSKIN LEGGINGS, A BOATMAN OVER the LAKES or BAYS or ALONG COASTS.... A HOOSIER, A BADGER, A BUCKEYE, A LOUISIANIAN or GEORGIAN, a POKE-EASY FROM SANDHILLS and PINES, AT HOME on CANADIAN SNOWSHOES or UP in the BUSH, or with FISHERMEN OFF NEWFOUNDLAND, AT HOME in the FLEET OF ICEBOATS, SAILING with the REST and TACKING, AT HOME on the HILLS OF VERMONT or in the WOODS OF MAINE or the TEXAN RANCH, COMRADE OF CALIFORNIANS:: COMRADE OF FREE NORTHWESTERNERS, LOVING THEIR BIG PROPORTIONS, COMRADE OF RAFTS-MEN and COALMEN ~ COMRADE OF all who SHAKE HANDS and WELCOME to DRINK and MEAT;

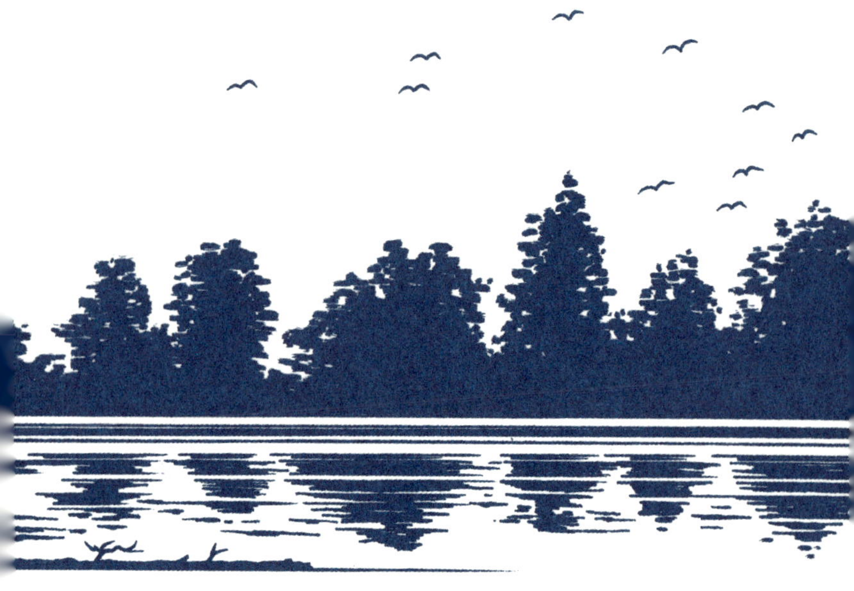

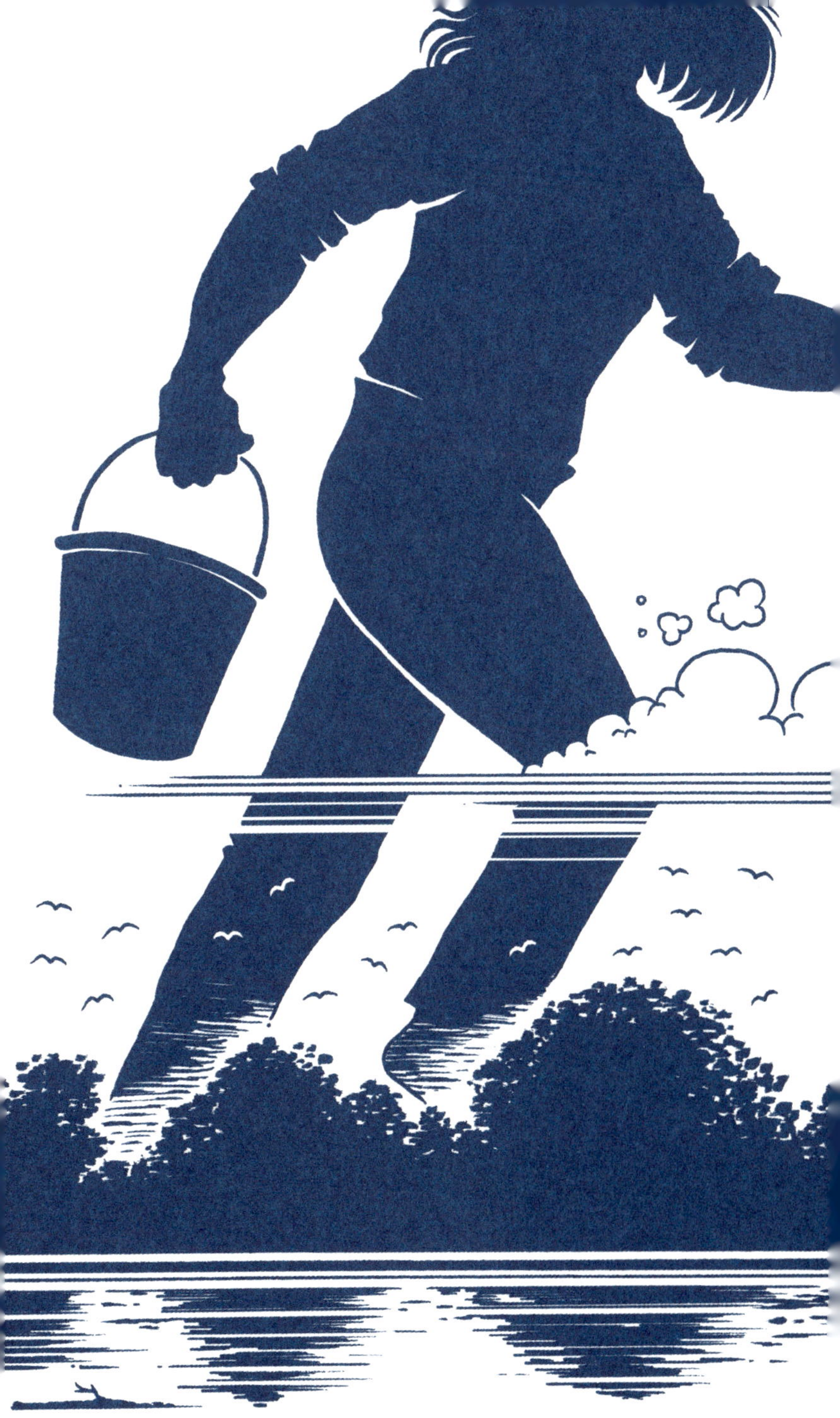

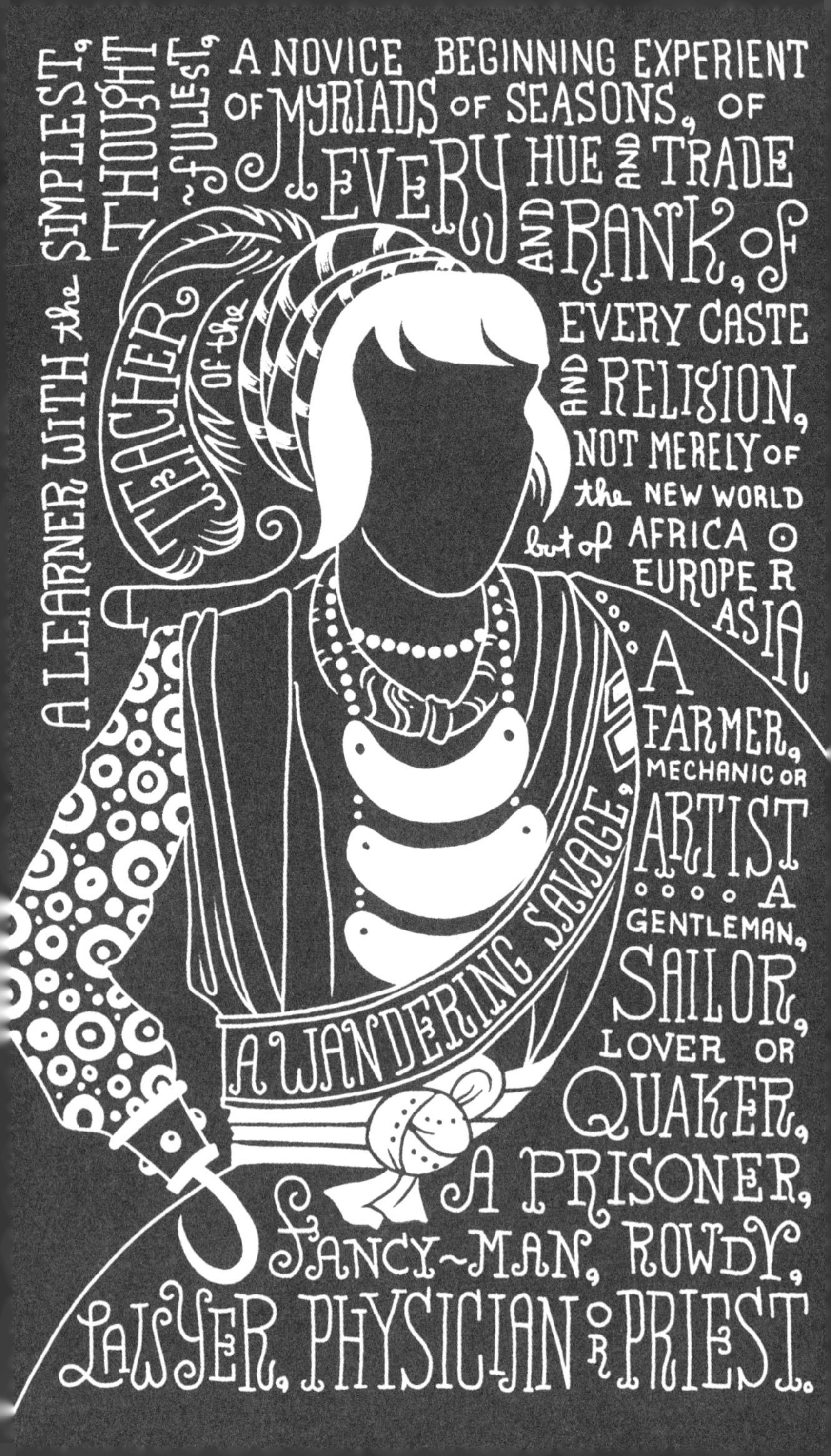
A LEARNER WITH the SIMPLEST,
A TEACHER OF the THOUGHTFULLEST,
A NOVICE BEGINNING EXPERIENT
OF MYRIADS OF SEASONS, OF
EVERY HUE AND TRADE
AND RANK, OF
EVERY CASTE
AND RELIGION,
NOT MERELY OF
the NEW WORLD
but of AFRICA
EUROPE R
ASIA
A WANDERING SAVAGE,
A
FARMER,
MECHANIC OR
ARTIST
A
GENTLEMAN,
SAILOR,
LOVER OR
QUAKER,
A PRISONER,
FANCY~MAN, ROWDY,
LAWYER, PHYSICIAN OR PRIEST.

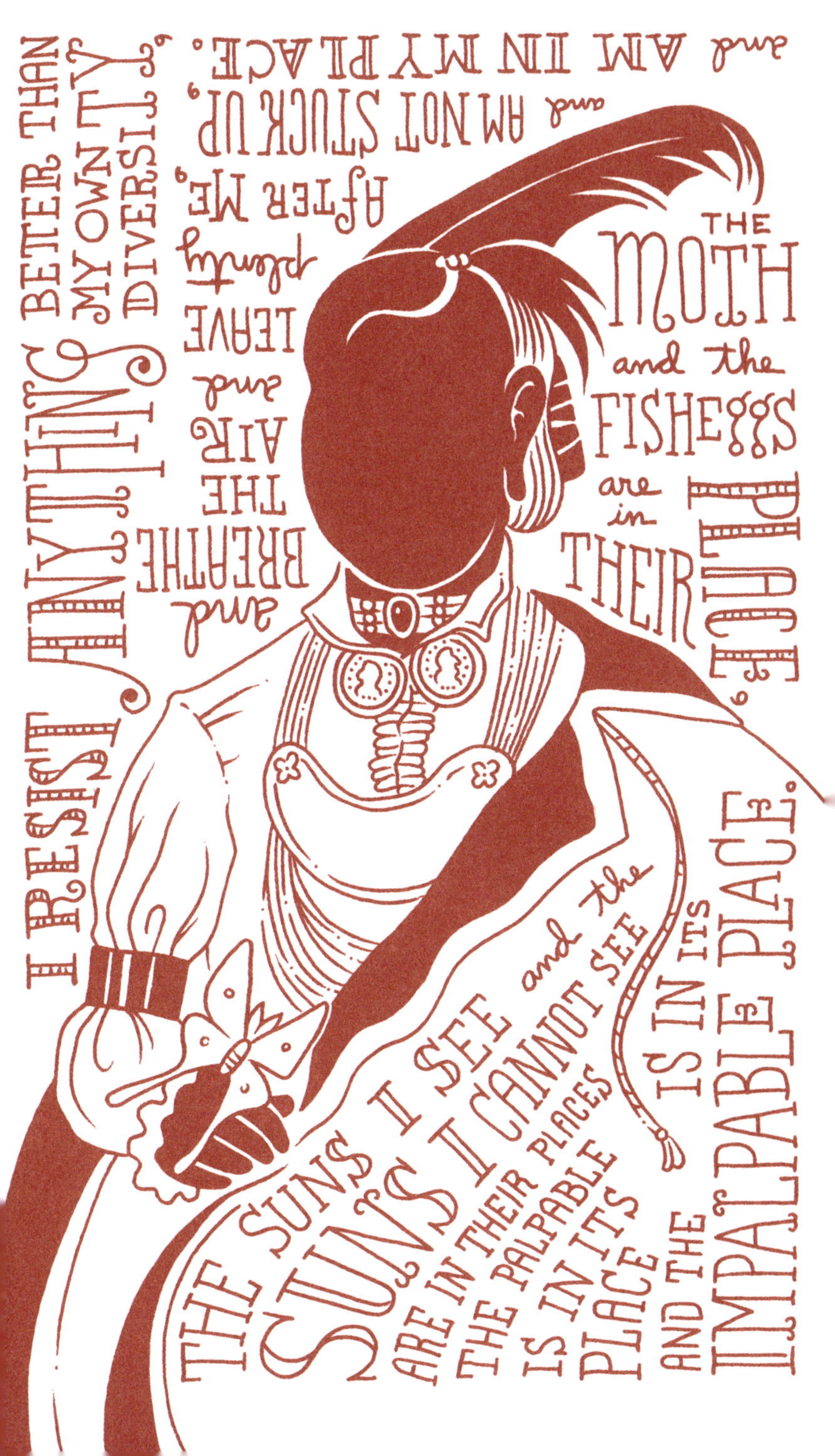
I RESIST ANYTHING BETTER THAN MY OWN DIVERSITY,
and BREATHE THE AIR and LEAVE plenty AFTER ME,
and AM NOT STUCK UP,
and AM IN MY PLACE.
THE MOTH and the FISHeggs are in THEIR PLACE,
THE SUNS I SEE and the SUNS I CANNOT SEE ARE IN THEIR PLACES
THE PALPABLE IS IN ITS PLACE
AND THE IMPALPABLE IS IN ITS PLACE.

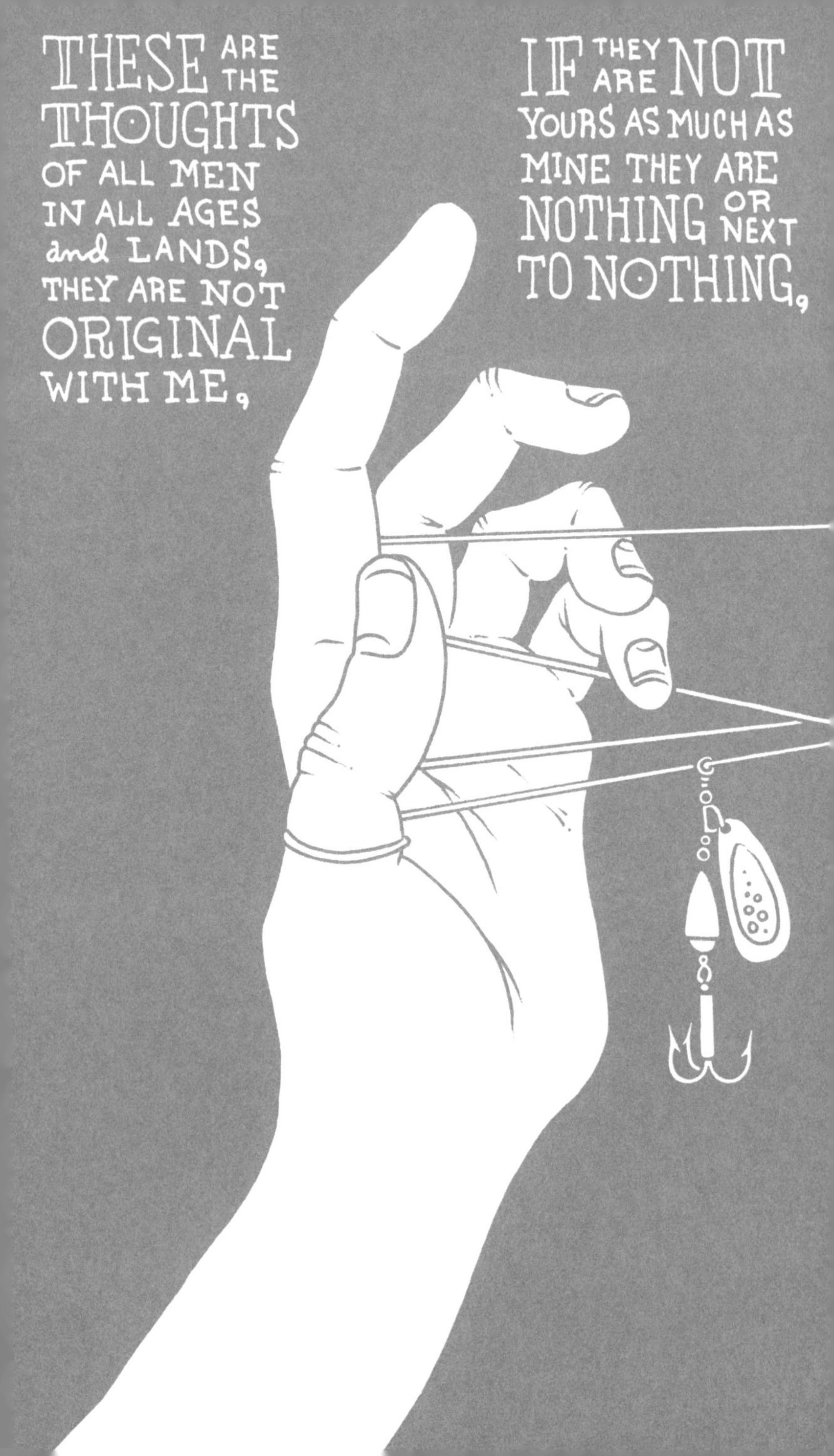
THESE ARE THE THOUGHTS OF ALL MEN IN ALL AGES and LANDS, THEY ARE NOT ORIGINAL WITH ME,
IF THEY ARE NOT YOURS AS MUCH AS MINE THEY ARE NOTHING OR NEXT TO NOTHING,

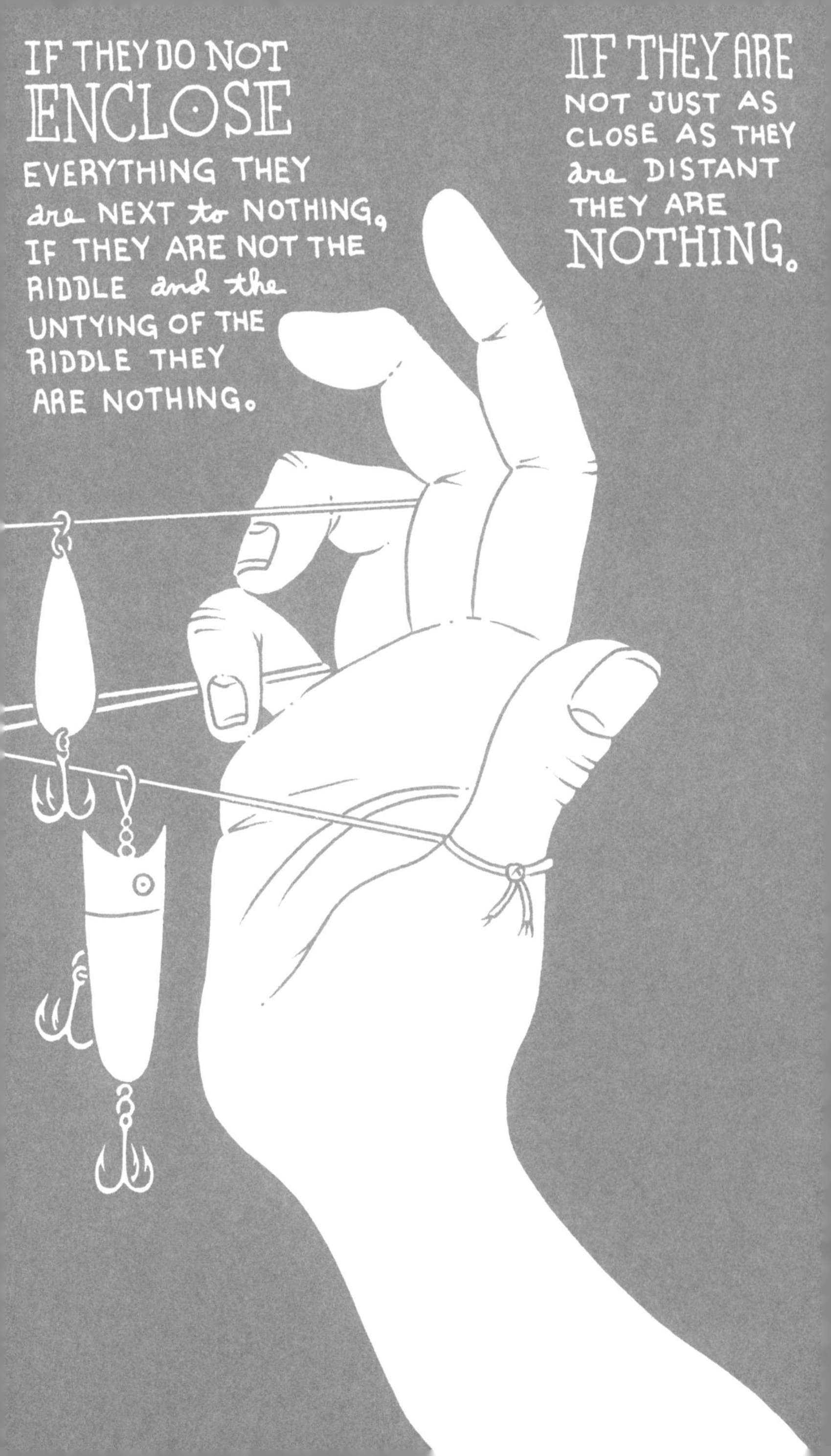
IF THEY DO NOT ENCLOSE EVERYTHING THEY are NEXT to NOTHING,
IF THEY ARE NOT THE RIDDLE and the UNTYING OF THE RIDDLE THEY ARE NOTHING.
IF THEY ARE NOT JUST AS CLOSE AS THEY are DISTANT THEY ARE NOTHING.

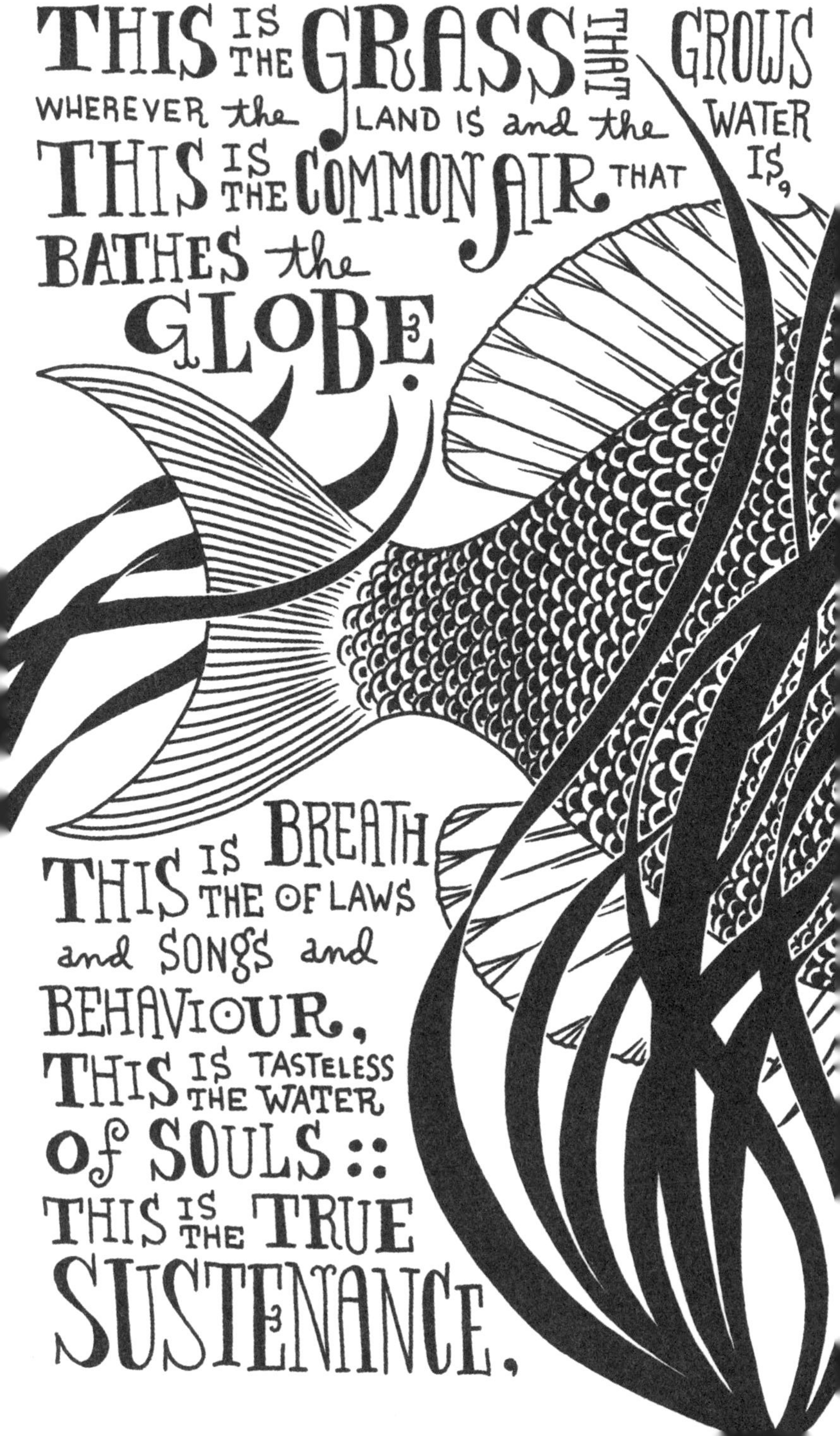

THIS IS THE GRASS THAT GROWS
WHEREVER the LAND IS and the WATER IS,
THIS IS THE COMMON AIR THAT BATHES the GLOBE.
THIS IS THE BREATH OF LAWS and SONGS and BEHAVIOUR,
THIS IS THE TASTELESS WATER OF SOULS ::
THIS IS THE TRUE SUSTENANCE,

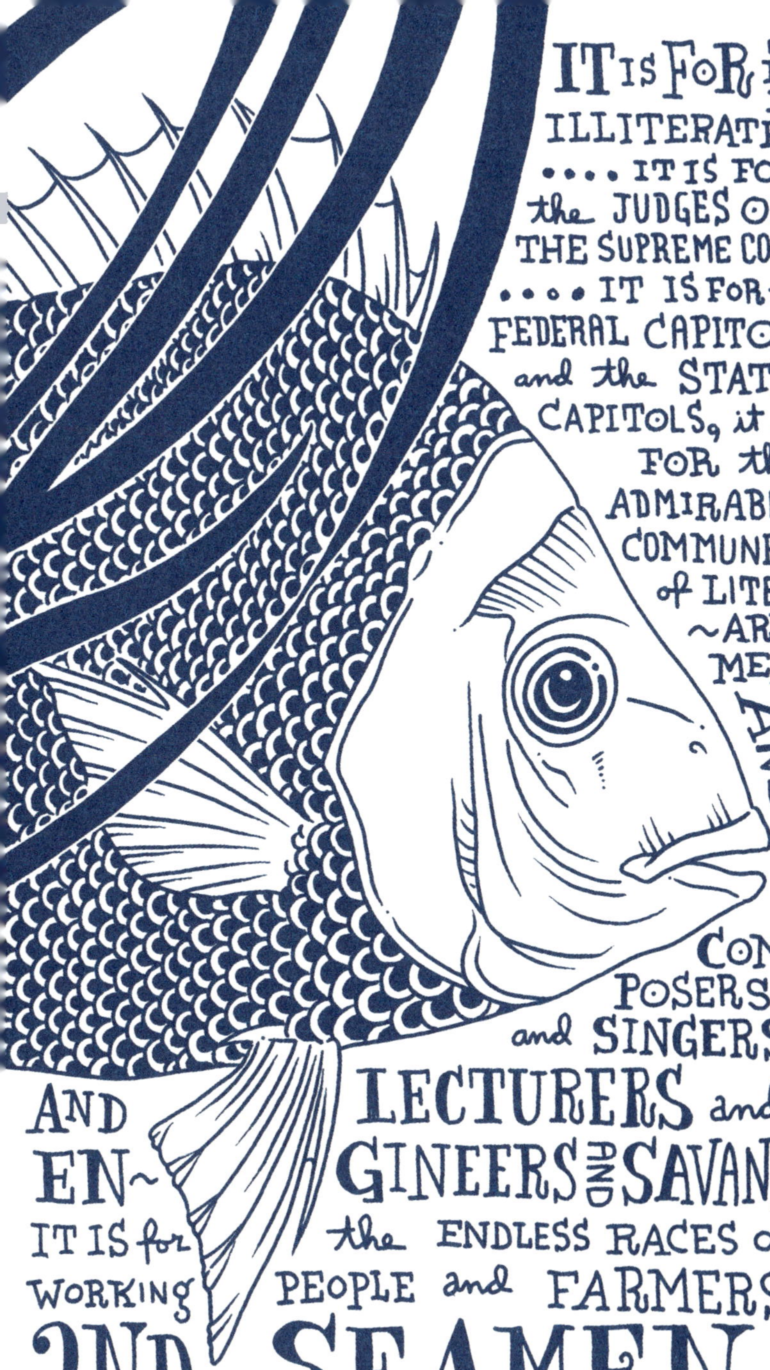

IT IS FOR THE ILLITERATE .... IT IS FOR the JUDGES OF THE SUPREME COURT .... IT IS FOR the FEDERAL CAPITOL and the STATE CAPITOLS, it is FOR the ADMIRABLE COMMUNES of LITERARY MEN AND COMPOSERS and SINGERS AND LECTURERS and ENGINEERS AND SAVANS, IT IS for the ENDLESS RACES OF WORKING PEOPLE and FARMERS AND SEAMEN.

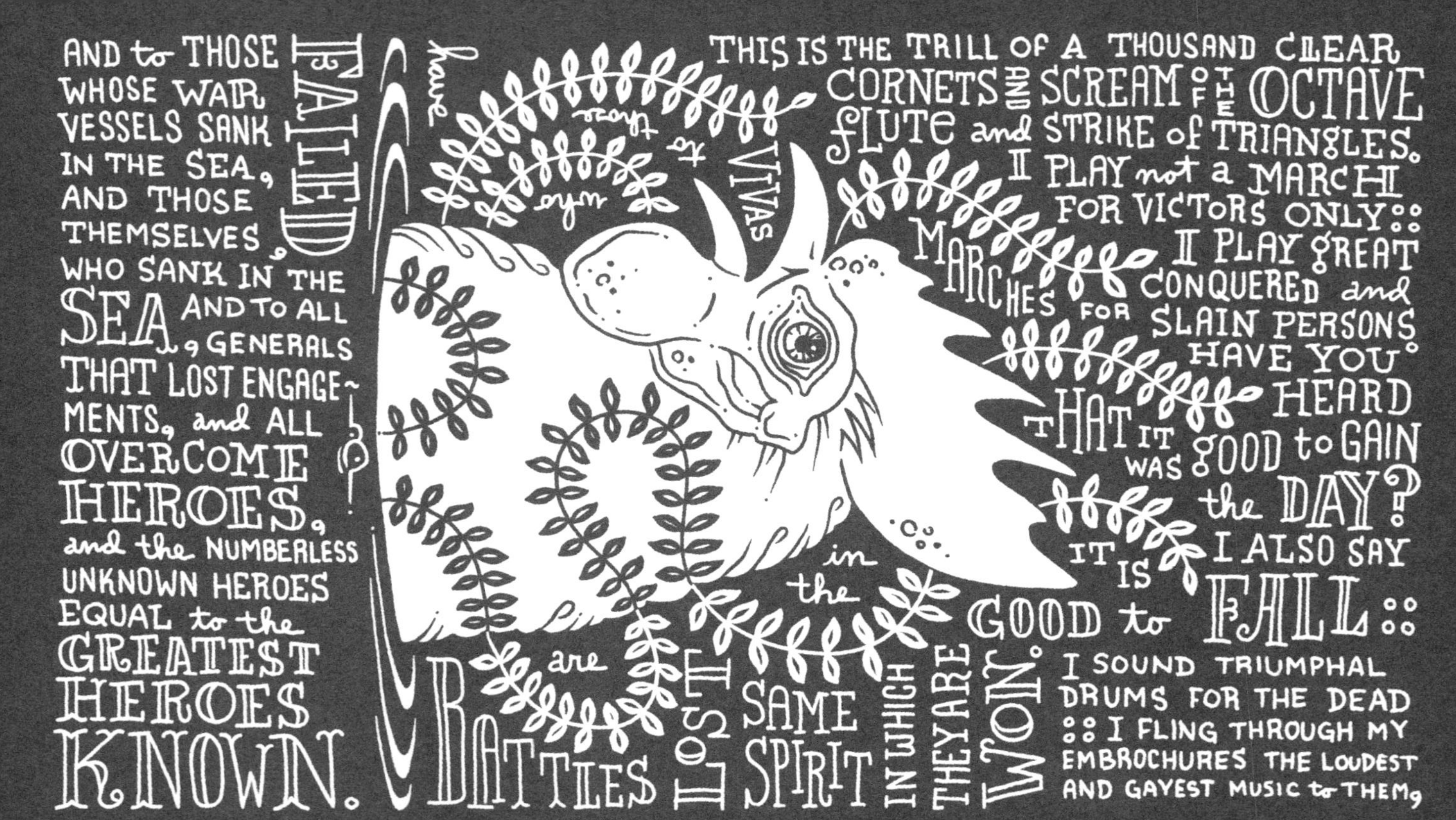
THIS IS THE TRILL OF A THOUSAND CLEAR CORNETS AND SCREAM OF THE OCTAVE FLUTE and STRIKE of TRIANGLES.
I PLAY not a MARCH FOR VICTORS ONLY:
I PLAY GREAT MARCHES FOR CONQUERED and SLAIN PERSONS
HAVE YOU HEARD THAT IT WAS GOOD to GAIN the DAY?
I ALSO SAY IT IS GOOD to FALL:
BATTLES are LOST in the SAME SPIRIT IN WHICH THEY ARE WON.
I SOUND TRIUMPHAL DRUMS FOR THE DEAD
: I FLING THROUGH MY EMBROCHURES THE LOUDEST AND GAYEST MUSIC to THEM,
VIVAS to those who have FAILED!
AND to THOSE WHOSE WAR VESSELS SANK IN THE SEA,
AND THOSE THEMSELVES, WHO SANK IN THE SEA,
AND TO ALL GENERALS THAT LOST ENGAGEMENTS, and ALL OVERCOME HEROES,
and the NUMBERLESS UNKNOWN HEROES EQUAL to the GREATEST HEROES KNOWN.

THIS is the MEAL PLEASANTLY SET, ... THIS is the MEAT and DRINK FOR NATURAL HUNGER,

IT IS for the WICKED JUST the SAME as the RIGHTEOUS .... I MAKE APPOINTMENTS with all, I WILL NOT HAVE A SINGLE PERSON SLIGHTED OR LEFT AWAY, the KEPTWOMAN and SPONGER and THIEF are HEREBY INVITED .... the HEAVY~LIPPED SLAVE IS INVITED .... THE VENER~EALEE is IN~VITED,

THERE SHALL be NO DIFFERENCE BETWEEN them and the REST.

THIS is the PRESS of a BASHFUL HAND .... this is the FLOAT and ODOR of HAIR .... THIS IS the TOUCH of MY LIPS to YOURS .... THIS is the MURMUR of YEARNING,

THIS is the FAR~off DEPTH and HEIGHT REFLECTING MY OWN FACE, THIS is the THOUGHTFUL MERGE of MYSELF and the OUTLET AGAIN.

DO YOU GUESS I HAVE SOME INTRICATE PURPOSE? WELL I HAVE .... FOR THE APRIL RAIN HAS, and the MICA ON the SIDE OF A ROCK HAS.

DO YOU TAKE IT

I would AS-TON-ISH?

DOES THE DAYLIGHT *Astonish?*
OR THE EARLY REDSTART
TWITTERING THROUGH
the WOODS?
{DO I ASTONISH
MORE *than* THEY?}

THIS HOUR I TELL THINGS IN CONFIDENCE,
I MIGHT NOT TELL EVERYBODY
but I WILL TELL YOU.

Who goes There!
HANKERING, GROSS, *Mystical,* NUDE?
HOW IS IT I
EXTRACT
STRENGTH
FROM THE
BEEF I EAT?
WHAT IS A MAN ANYHOW?
WHAT AM I?
AND WHAT ARE YOU?

ALL I MARK AS MY OWN
YOU SHALL OFFSET IT
WITH YOUR OWN, ELSE
IT WERE TIME LOST
LISTENING TO ME.
I DO NOT SNIV~
EL *that* SNIVEL
the WORLD OVER,
THAT MONTHS ARE VACUUMS
and the GROUND BUT
WALLOW *and* FILTH,
THAT LIFE IS A SUCK
and A SELL, *and*
NOTHING REMAINS *at*
the END *but* THREAD
~BARE CRAPE
AND TEARS.

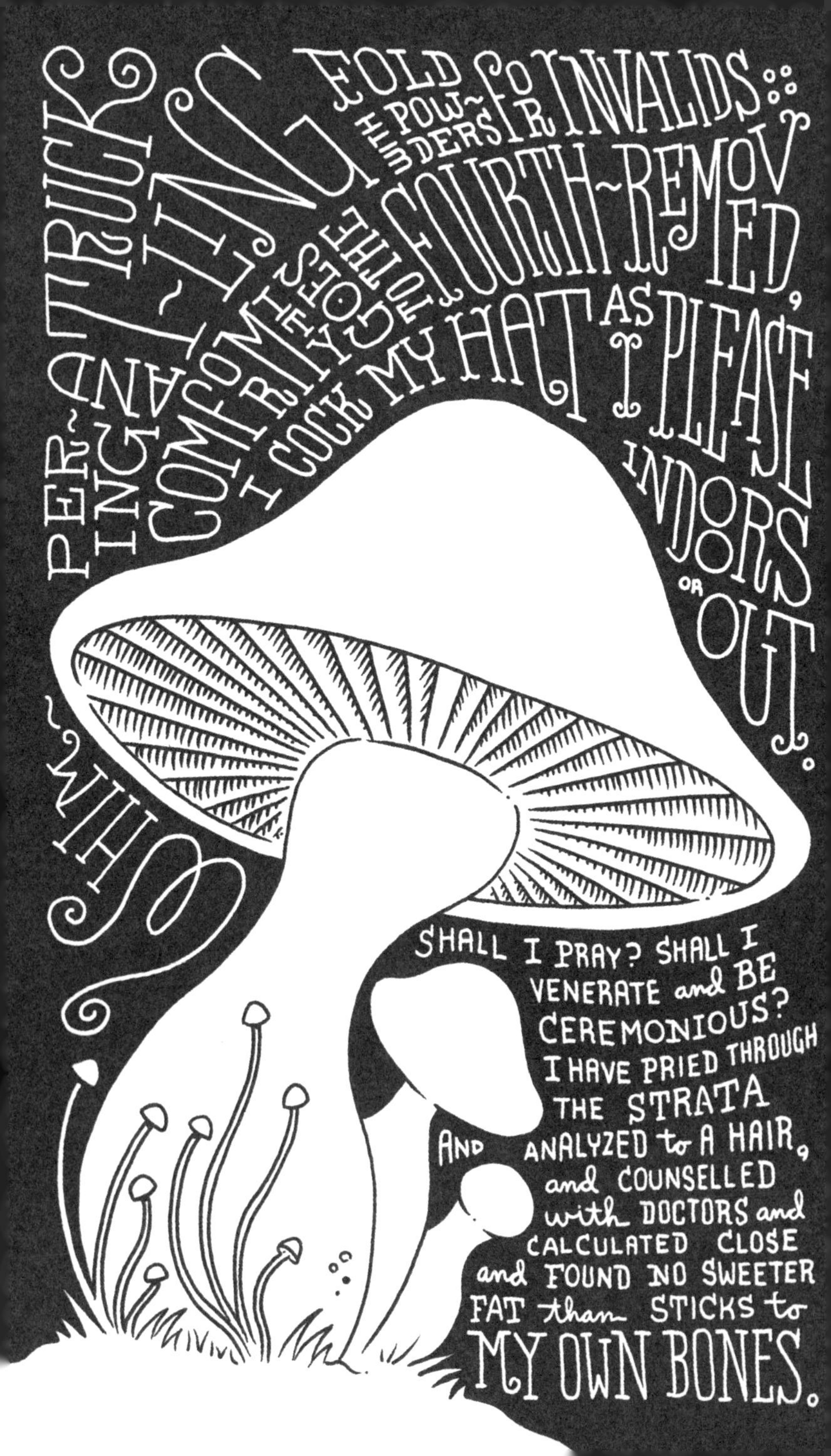
WHIM~PER~ING AND TRUCK~LING FOLD WITH POW~DERS FOR INVALIDS:
CONFORMITY GOES TO THE FOURTH~REMOVED,
I COCK MY HAT AS I PLEASE INDOORS OR OUT.
SHALL I PRAY? SHALL I VENERATE and BE CEREMONIOUS?
I HAVE PRIED THROUGH THE STRATA
AND ANALYZED to A HAIR,
and COUNSELLED with DOCTORS and CALCULATED CLOSE
and FOUND NO SWEETER FAT than STICKS to MY OWN BONES.

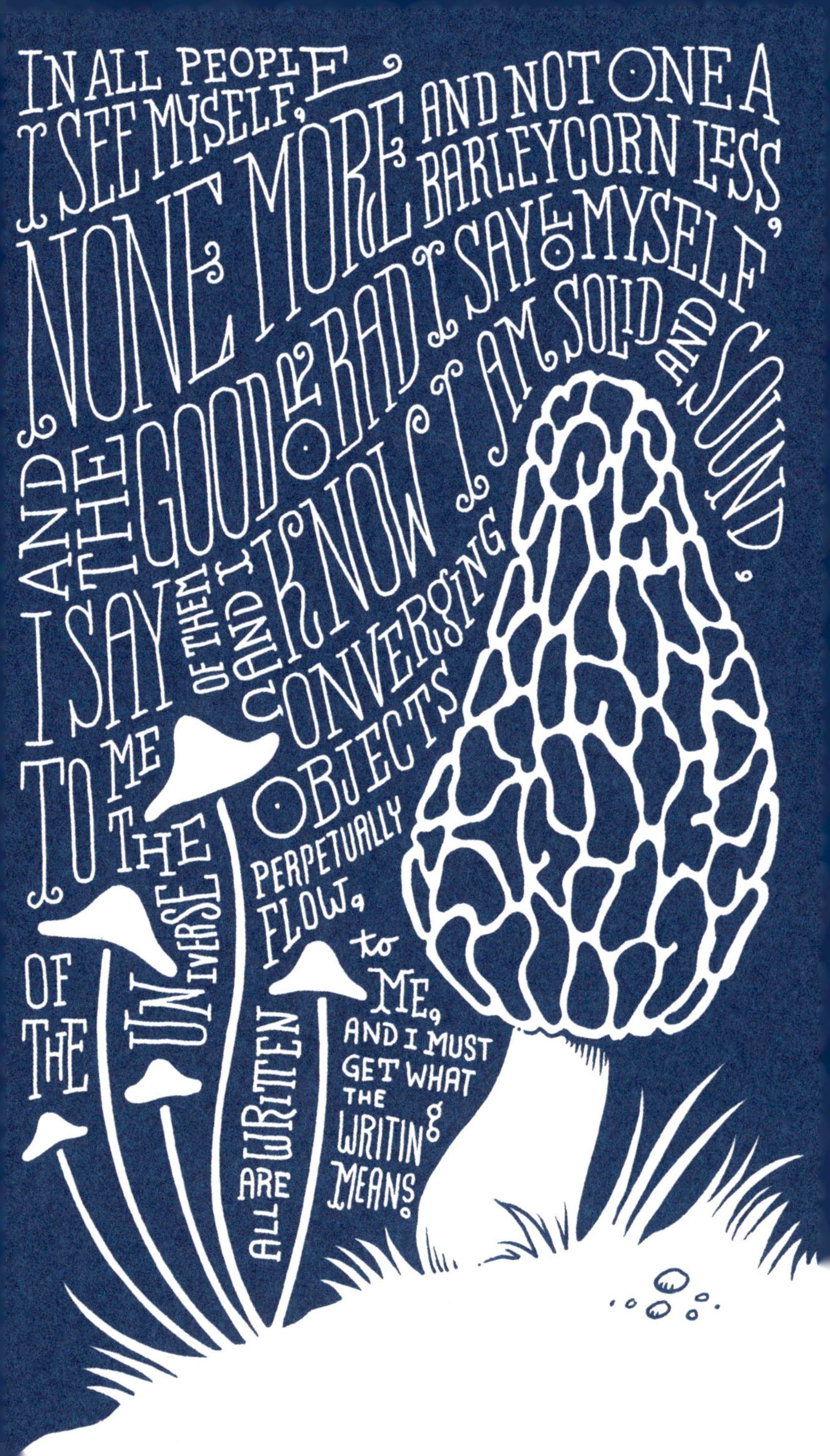
IN ALL PEOPLE
I SEE MYSELF,
NONE MORE AND NOT ONE A
BARLEYCORN LESS,
AND THE GOOD OR BAD I SAY OF MYSELF
I SAY OF THEM
AND I KNOW I AM SOLID AND SOUND,
TO ME THE CONVERGING OBJECTS
OF THE UNIVERSE PERPETUALLY FLOW,
ALL ARE WRITTEN TO ME,
AND I MUST GET WHAT THE WRITING MEANS.

AND I KNOW I AM DEATHLESS, I KNOW THIS ORBIT OF MINE CANNOT BE SWEPT BY A CARPENTER'S COMPASS, I KNOW I SHALL NOT PASS LIKE A CHILD'S CARLACUE CUT WITH A BURNT STICK AT NIGHT.

I KNOW I AM AUGUST, I DO NOT TROUBLE MY SPIRIT TO VINDICATE ITSELF OR BE UNDERSTOOD, I SEE THAT THE ELEMENTARY LAWS NEVER APOLOGIZE, I RECKON I BEHAVE NO PROUDER THAN THE LEVEL I PLANT MY HOUSE BY AFTER ALL.

I EXIST AS I AM, THAT IS ENOUGH, IF NO OTHER IN THE WORLD BE AWARE I SIT CONTENT, AND IF EACH AND ALL BE AWARE I SIT CONTENT.

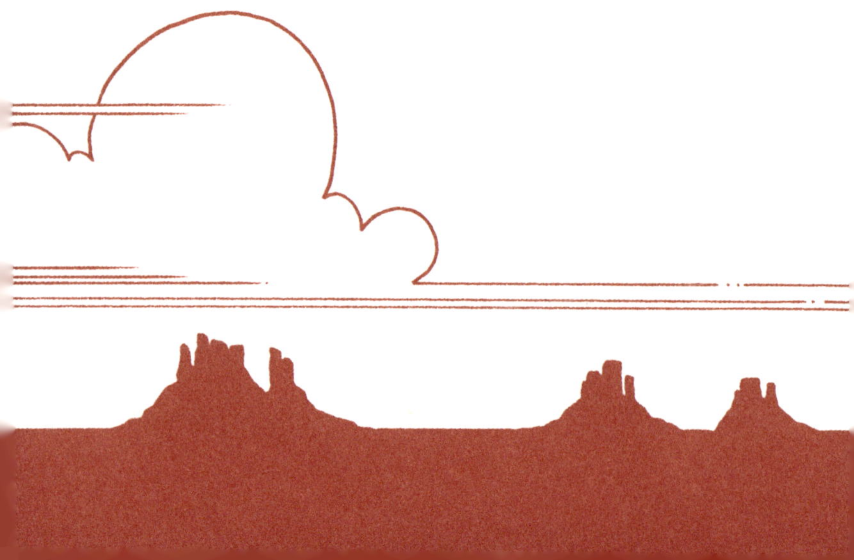

ONE WORLD IS AWARE, AND BY FAR THE LARGEST TO ME, AND THAT IS MYSELF, AND WHETHER I COME TO MY OWN TODAY OR IN TEN MILLION YEARS, I CAN CHEERFULLY TAKE IT NOW, OR WITH EQUAL CHEERFULNESS I CAN WAIT. MY FOOTHOLD IS TENONED AND MORTISED IN GRANITE, I LAUGH AT WHAT YOU CALL DISSOLUTION, AND I KNOW THE AMPLITUDE OF TIME.

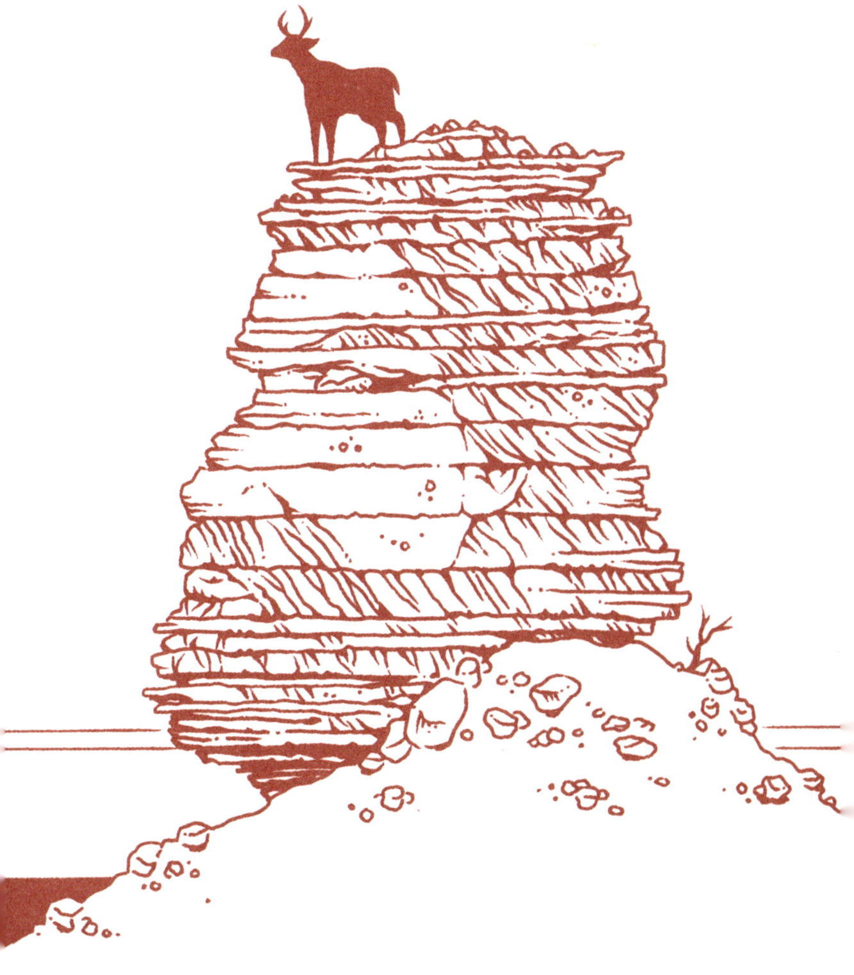

I am the POET of the BODY,
And I am the POET of the SOUL.

The PLEASURES of HEAVEN are with me,
and the PAINS of HELL are with me,

The FIRST I GRAFT and INCREASE
upon MYSELF.... the LATTER I
translate into a NEW TONGUE.

I am the POET of the WOMAN
the same as the MAN,
And I say it is as great to be
a WOMAN as to be a MAN,

And I say there is
NOTHING greater than
the MOTHER of MEN.

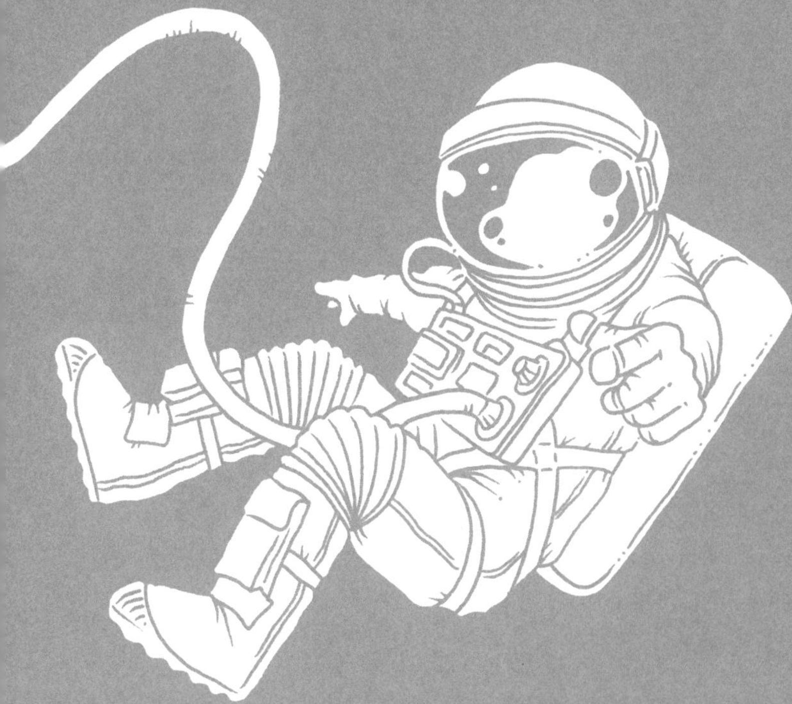

i Chant a New Chant of DILATION OR PRIDE,

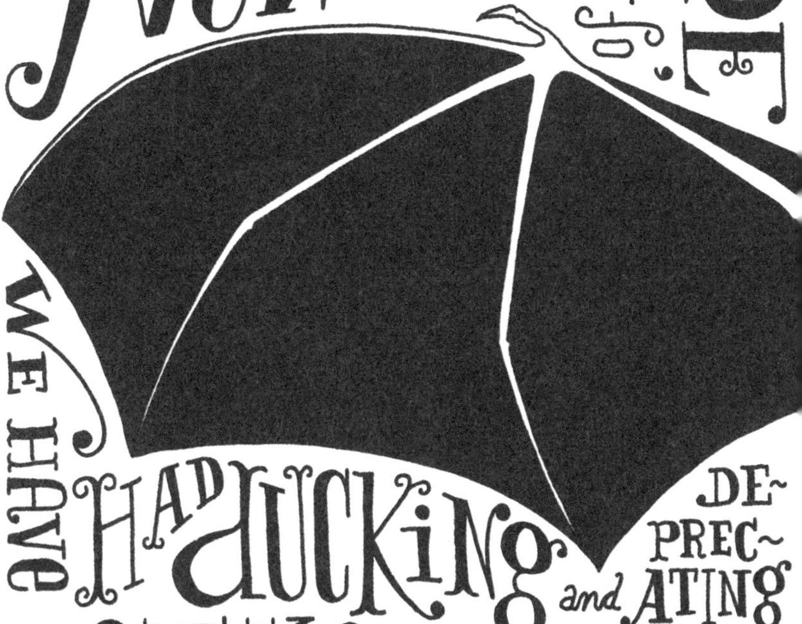

WE HAVE HAD DUCKING and DE~PREC~ATING ABOUT ENOUGH

I SHOW THAT SIZE IS ONLY DEVEL~OPMENT.

HAVE YOU OUT~STRIPT tHe REST? ARE YOU the PRESIDENT?

IT IS A TRIFLE.... they will more THAN arrive there every one, and still Pass On.

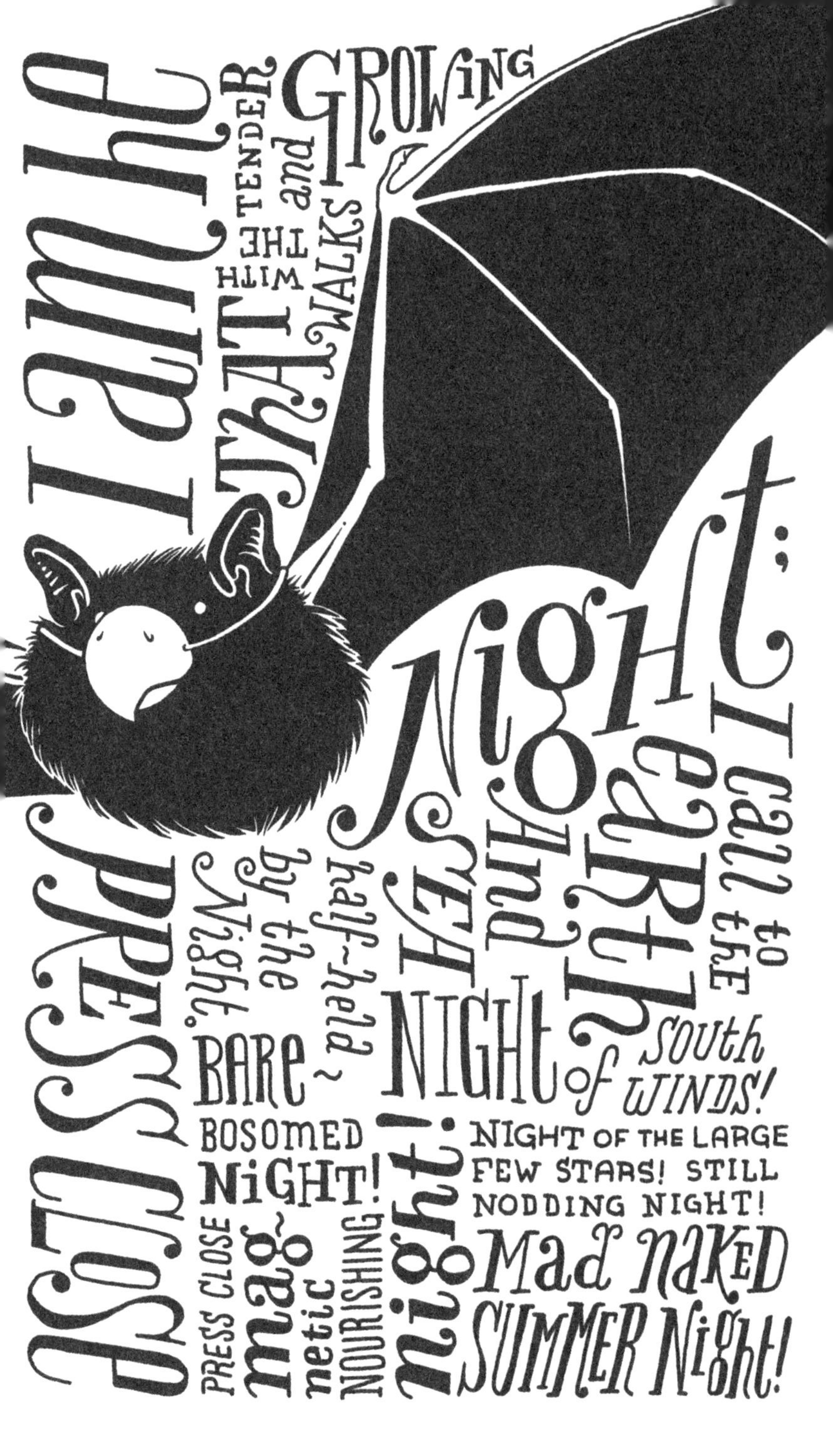

I am he
THAT WALKS WITH THE TENDER and GROWING
Night;
I call to the EARTH And SEA
half-held by the Night.
PRESS CLOSE
BARE-BOSOMED NiGHT!
PRESS CLOSE mag-netic NOURISHING night!
NIGHT of SOUTH WINDS!
NIGHT OF THE LARGE FEW STARS! STILL NODDING NIGHT!
Mad NAKED SUMMER Night!

Smile O voluptuous
Coolbreathed earth!
earth of the slumbering and liquid trees!
earth of departed sunset!
earth of the mountains misty~topt!
earth of the vitreous pour of the full moon just tinged with blue!
earth of shine and dark mottling the tide of the river!
earth of the limpid gray of clouds brighter and clearer for my sake!

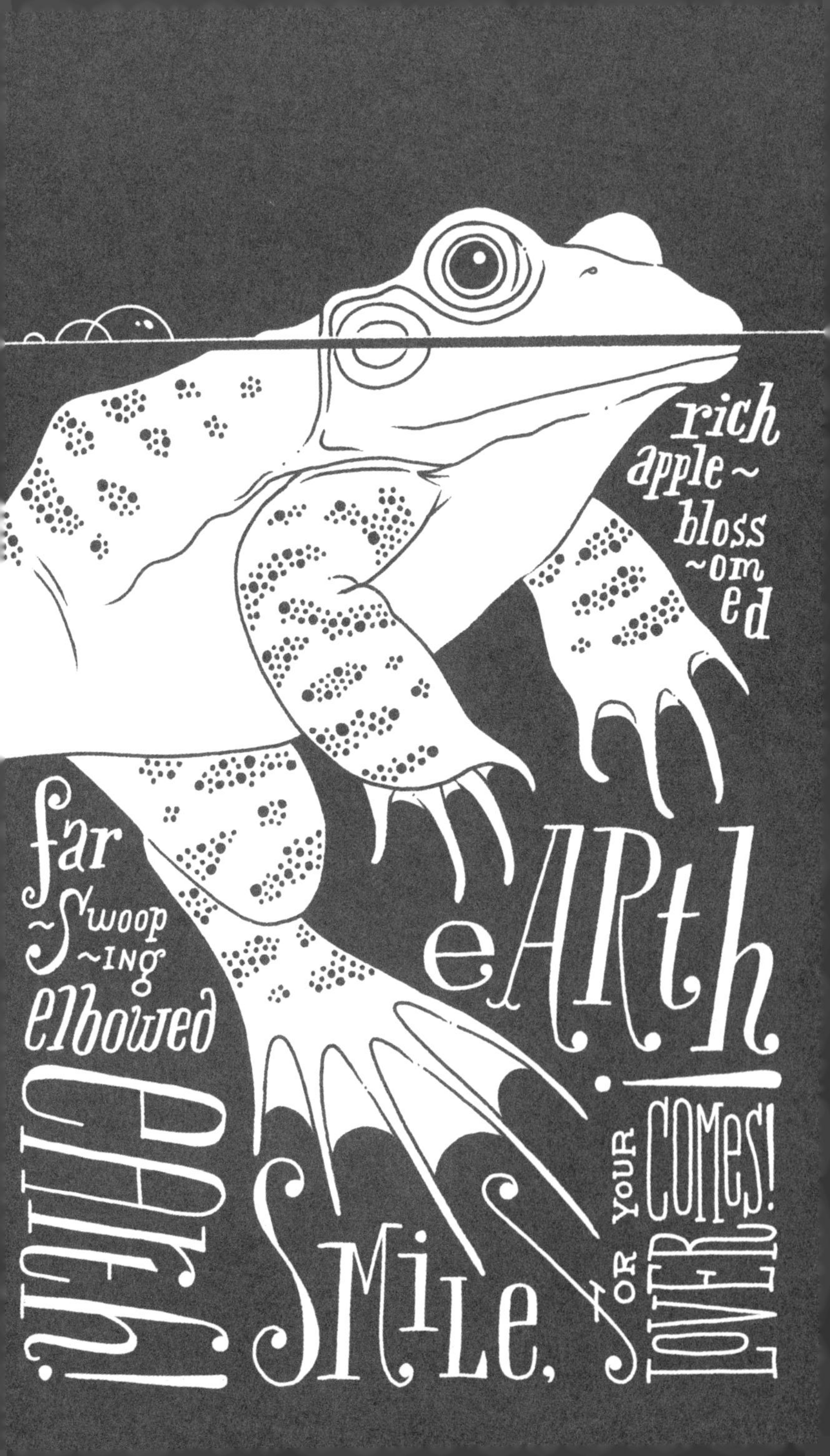

rich apple~bloss~om ed
far ~swoop ~ing elbowed
earth!
earth!
Smile,
for your lover comes!

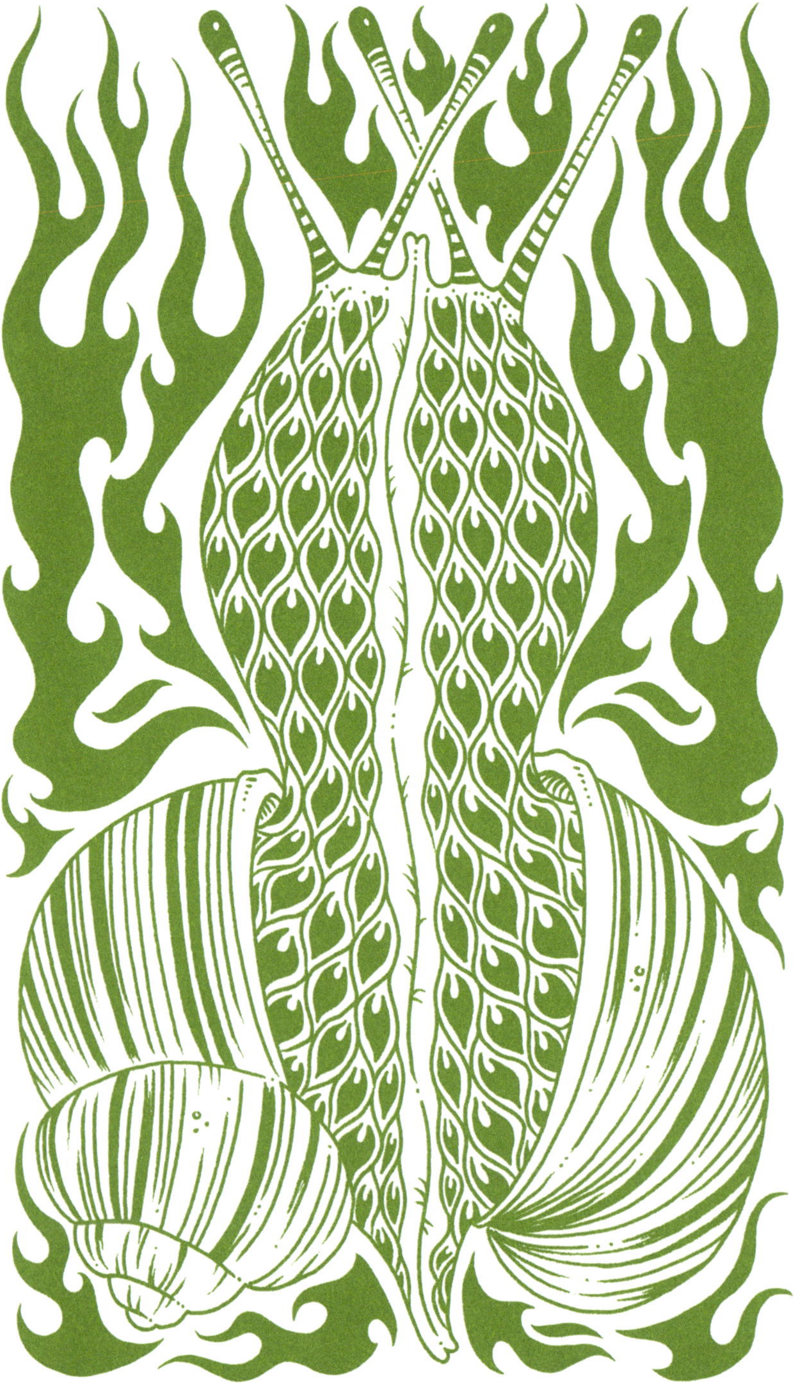

PRODIGAL! YOU HAVE GIVEN ME

LOVE!

THEREFORE I TO YOU GIVE LOVE!

O UNSPEAKABLE PASSIONATE LOVE!

THRUSTER, HOLDING ME TIGHT AND THAT I HOLD TIGHT! WE HURT EACH OTHER AS THE BRIDEGROOM AND THE BRIDE HURT EACH OTHER.

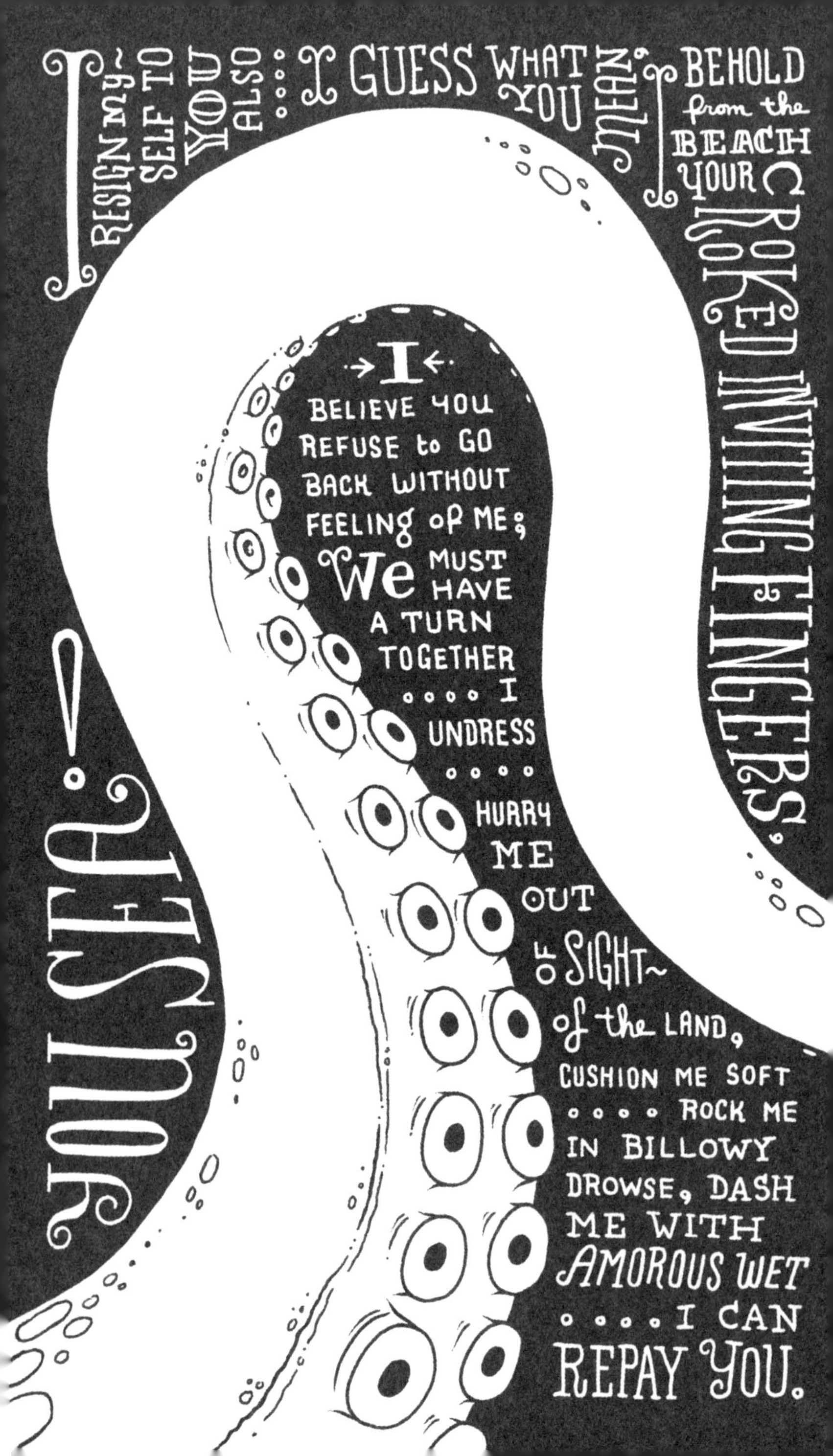
YOU SEA!
I RESIGN MYSELF TO YOU ALSO....
I GUESS WHAT YOU MEAN,
I BEHOLD from the BEACH YOUR CROOKED INVITING FINGERS,
I BELIEVE YOU REFUSE to GO BACK WITHOUT FEELING OF ME;
WE MUST HAVE A TURN TOGETHER
.... I UNDRESS
....
HURRY ME OUT OF SIGHT~ of the LAND,
CUSHION ME SOFT .... ROCK ME IN BILLOWY DROWSE, DASH ME WITH AMOROUS WET
.... I CAN REPAY YOU.

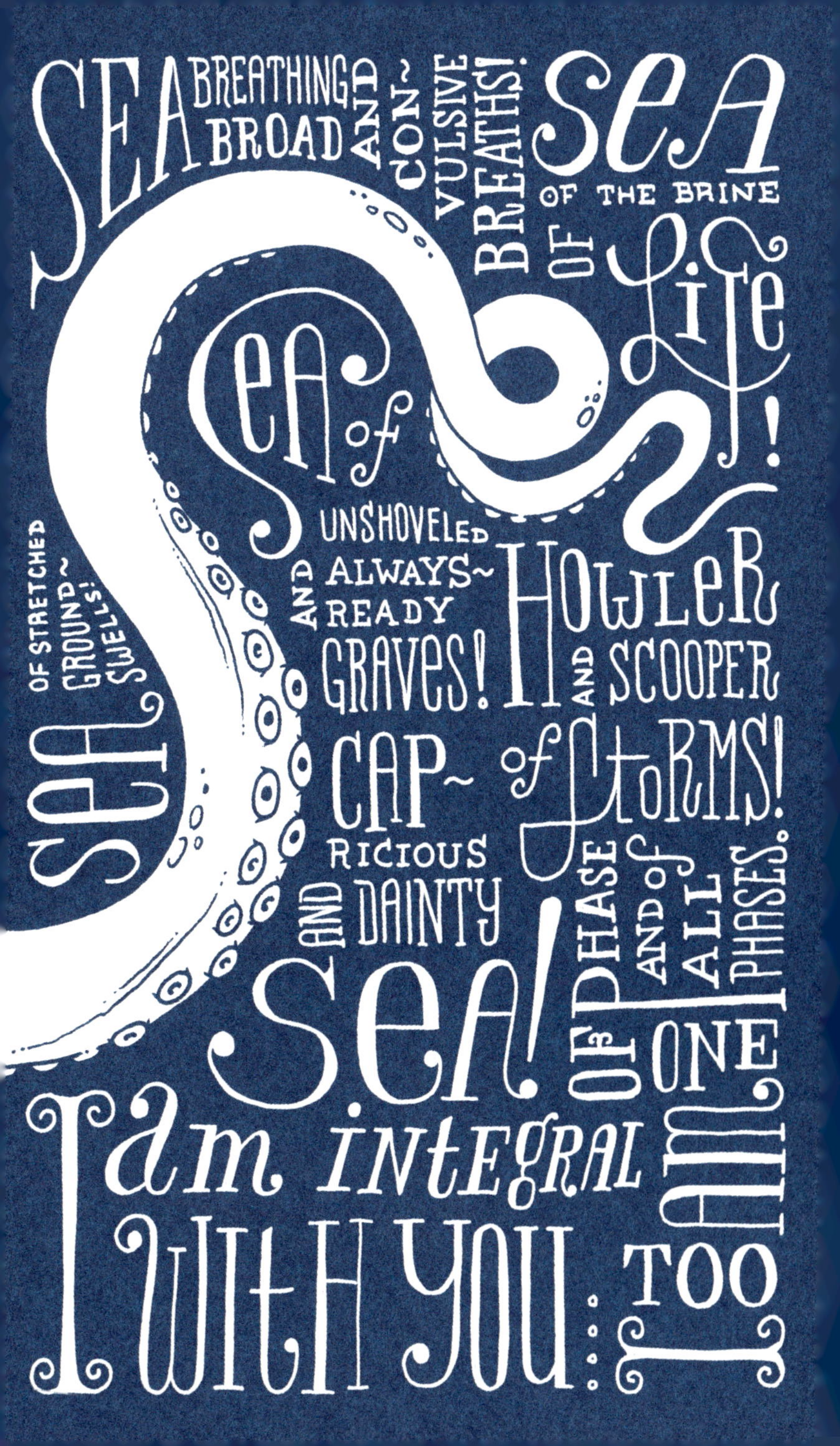
SEA OF STRETCHED GROUND~SWELLS!
SEA BREATHING BROAD AND CON~VULSIVE BREATHS!
SEA OF THE BRINE OF LIFE!
SEA OF UNSHOVELED AND ALWAYS~READY GRAVES!
HOWLER AND SCOOPER OF STORMS!
CAP~RICIOUS AND DAINTY SEA!
I AM INTEGRAL WITH YOU...
I TOO AM OF ONE PHASE AND OF ALL PHASES.

PARTAKER of INFLUX AND EFFLUX ...

I

of HATE AND CONCILIATION,

EX~TOLLER

EXTOLLER OF AMIES and THOSE THAT SLEEP IN EACH OTHERS' ARMS.

I AM HE ATTESTING SYMPATHY; SHALL I MAKE MY list of things in the HOUSE AND SKIP the HOUSE that SUPPORTS them?

I AM the POET OF COMMONSENSE and of the DEMONSTRABLE and of IMMORTALITY; and am NOT the POET of GOODNES ONLY ....

I DO NOT DECLINE to be the POET of WICKEDNESS ALSO.

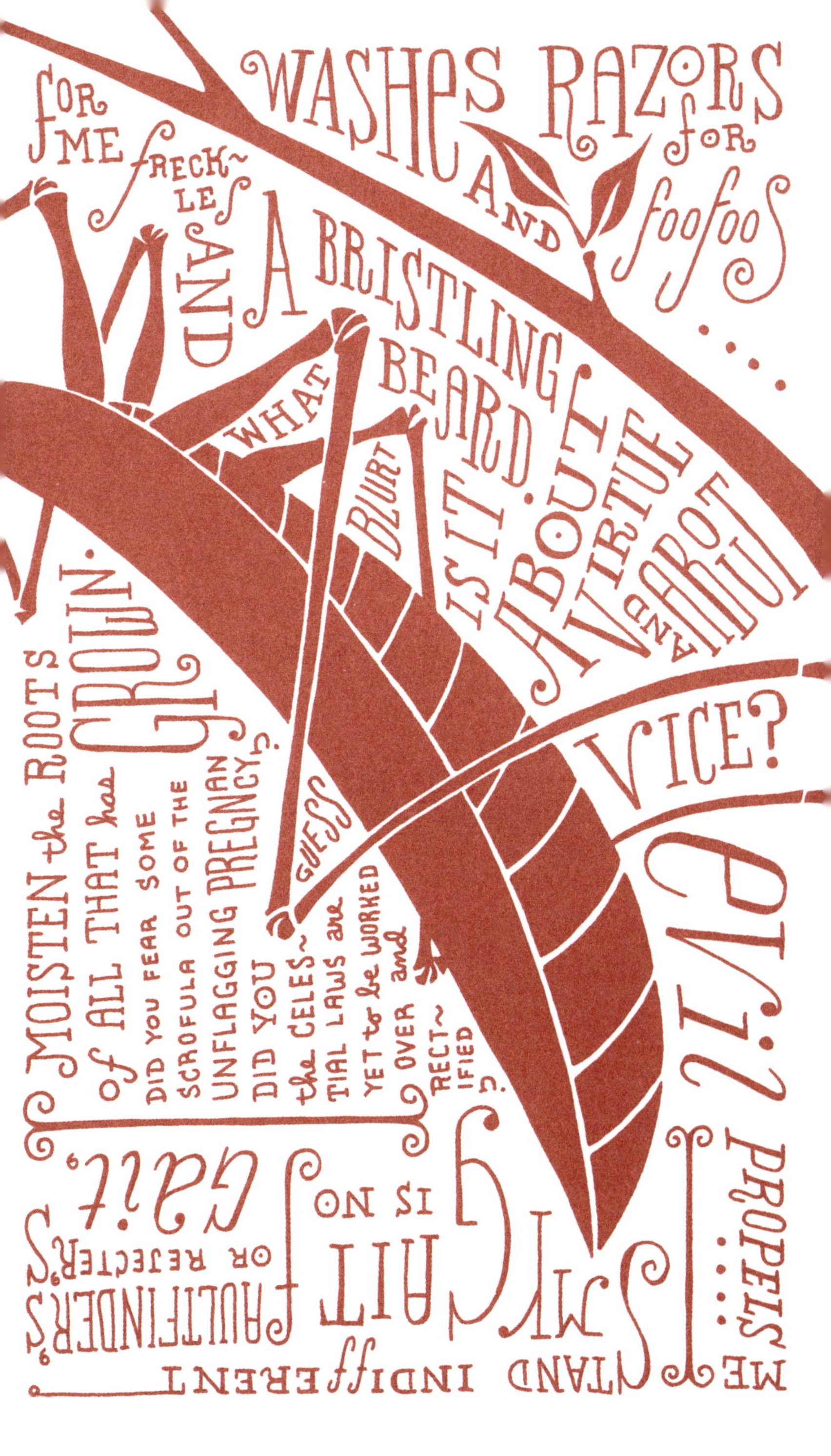
WASHES AND RAZORS FOR foofoos....
FOR ME FRECK~LES AND A BRISTLING BEARD.
WHAT BLURT IS IT ABOUT VIRTUE AND ABOUT VICE?
EVIL PROPELS ME....
I STAND INDIFFERENT,
MY GAIT IS NO FAULTFINDER'S OR REJECTER'S GAIT,
MOISTEN the ROOTS of ALL THAT has GROWN.
DID YOU FEAR SOME SCROFULA OUT OF THE UNFLAGGING PREGNANCY?
DID YOU GUESS the CELES~TIAL LAWS are YET to be WORKED OVER and RECT~IFIED?

I STEP UP TO SAY THAT
WHAT WE DO IS RIGHT
and what we AFFIRM is RIGHT
.... AND SOME IS ONLY the
ORE of RIGHT,
Witnesses of us ....
ONE SIDE A BALANCE AND
THE ANTIPODAL SIDE A
BALANCE,
SOFT DOCTRINE as
STEADY HELP as
Stable doctrine,
thoughts and deeds
of the PRESENT OUR
ROUSE AND EARLY START.

this minute that
comes to me over
the past decillions,
THERE IS NO BETTER
THAN IT AND NOW.
WHAT BEHAVED WELL IN
the PAST or behaves
well TODAY is not such
A WONDER,
the wonder is always
and always how there
can be a MEAN MAN
OR AN
infidel.

END~LESS UNFOLDING of WORDS OF AGES!

AND MINE A WORD of the MODERN
.... A WORD EN MASSE.

A WORD of the faith THAT NEVER BALKS,

ONE TIME AS GOOD AS ANOTHER
.... HERE OR HENCE~FORWARD IT IS ALL THE SAME TO ME.

A WORD of REALITY
.... MATERIALISM FIRST AND LAST IMBUING.

HURRAH FOR POSITIVE SCIENCE!

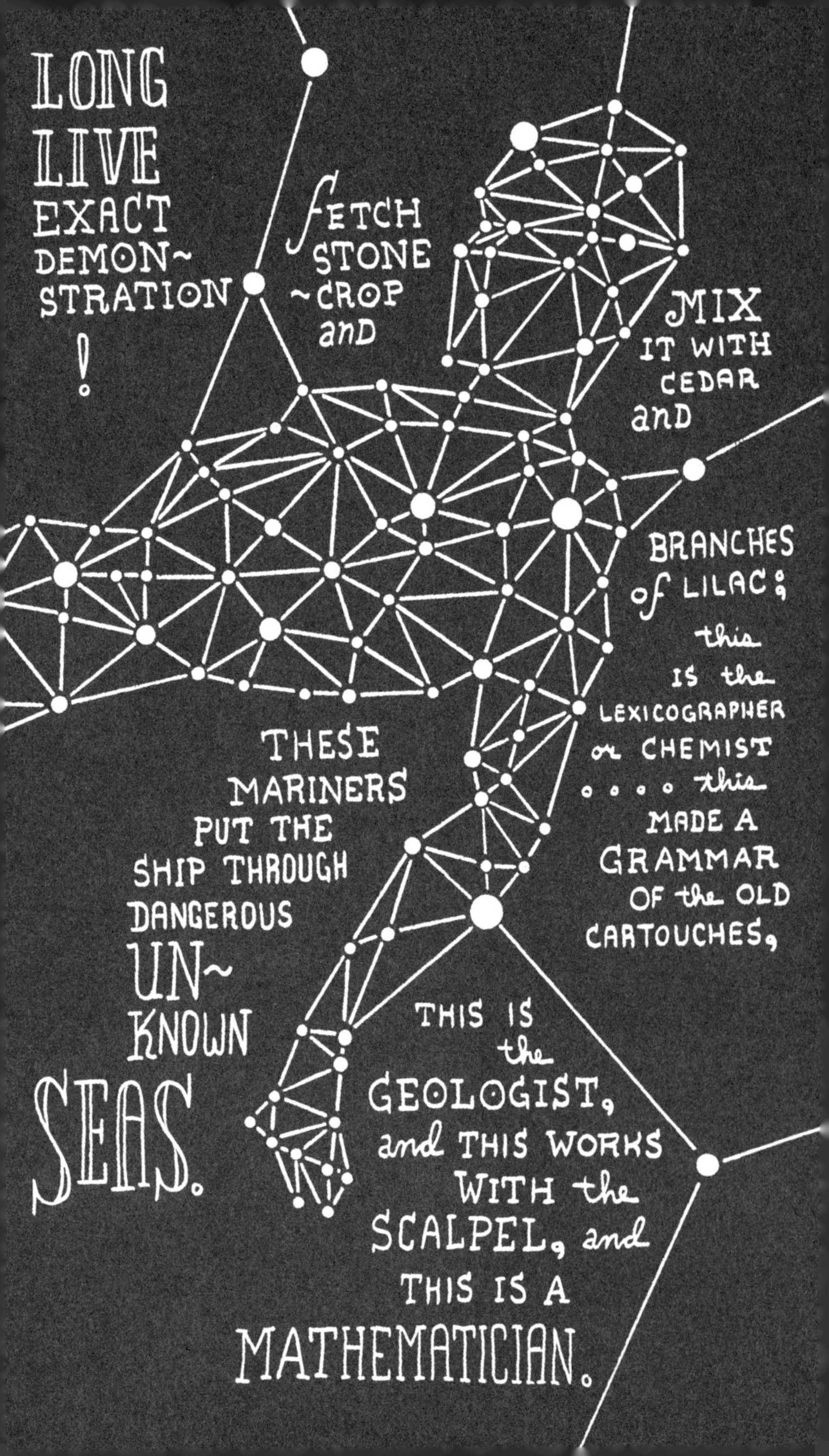

LONG LIVE EXACT DEMON~STRATION !
fETCH STONE ~CROP and
MIX IT WITH CEDAR and
BRANCHES of LILAC; this is the LEXICOGRAPHER or CHEMIST . . . . this MADE A GRAMMAR OF the OLD CARTOUCHES,
THESE MARINERS PUT THE SHIP THROUGH DANGEROUS UN~KNOWN SEAS.
THIS IS the GEOLOGIST, and THIS WORKS WITH the SCALPEL, and THIS IS A MATHEMATICIAN.

GENTLEMEN
I RECEIVE YOU,
and ATTACH and
CLASP HANDS
with YOU,

the FACTS are USEFUL
and REAL . . . . THEY
ARE NOT MY DWELLING
. . . . I ENTER BY
THEM to an AREA OF
the DWELLING.

I am LESS the REMINDER
of PROPERTY or QUALITIES,
and more the
REMINDER of LIFE,

And go on the SQUARE for MY OWN SAKE AND FOR OTHER'S SAKE, and MAKE SHORT ACCOUNT of NEUTERS and GELDINGS, and FAVOR MEN and WOMEN fully EQUIPPED.

AND BEAT the

GONG

of REVOLT, and STOP with FUGITIVES and them that PLOT and CONSPIRE.

Walt Whitman

an AMERICAN,
ONE of the ROUGHS,
a KOSMOS,
DISORDERLY FLESHY
and SENSUAL
∘ ∘ ∘ ∘

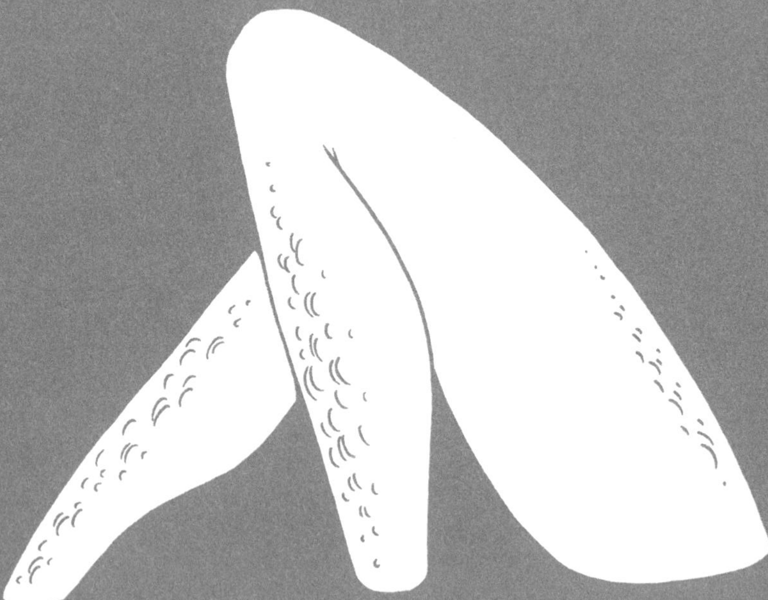

EATING DRINKING
and BREEDING,
NO SENTIMENTALIST
∘ ∘ ∘ ∘

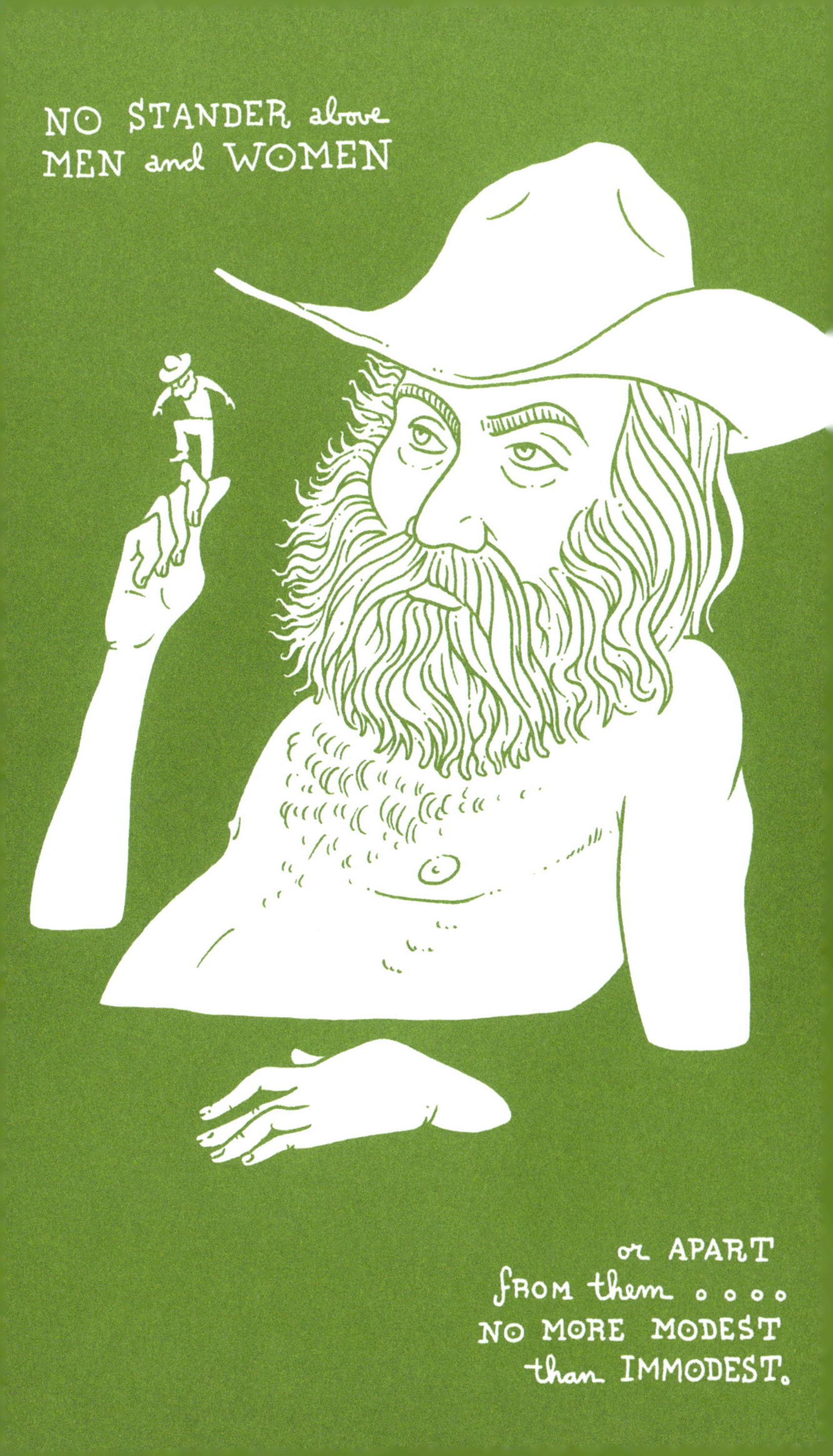
NO STANDER above
MEN and WOMEN
or APART
FROM them ....
NO MORE MODEST
than IMMODEST.

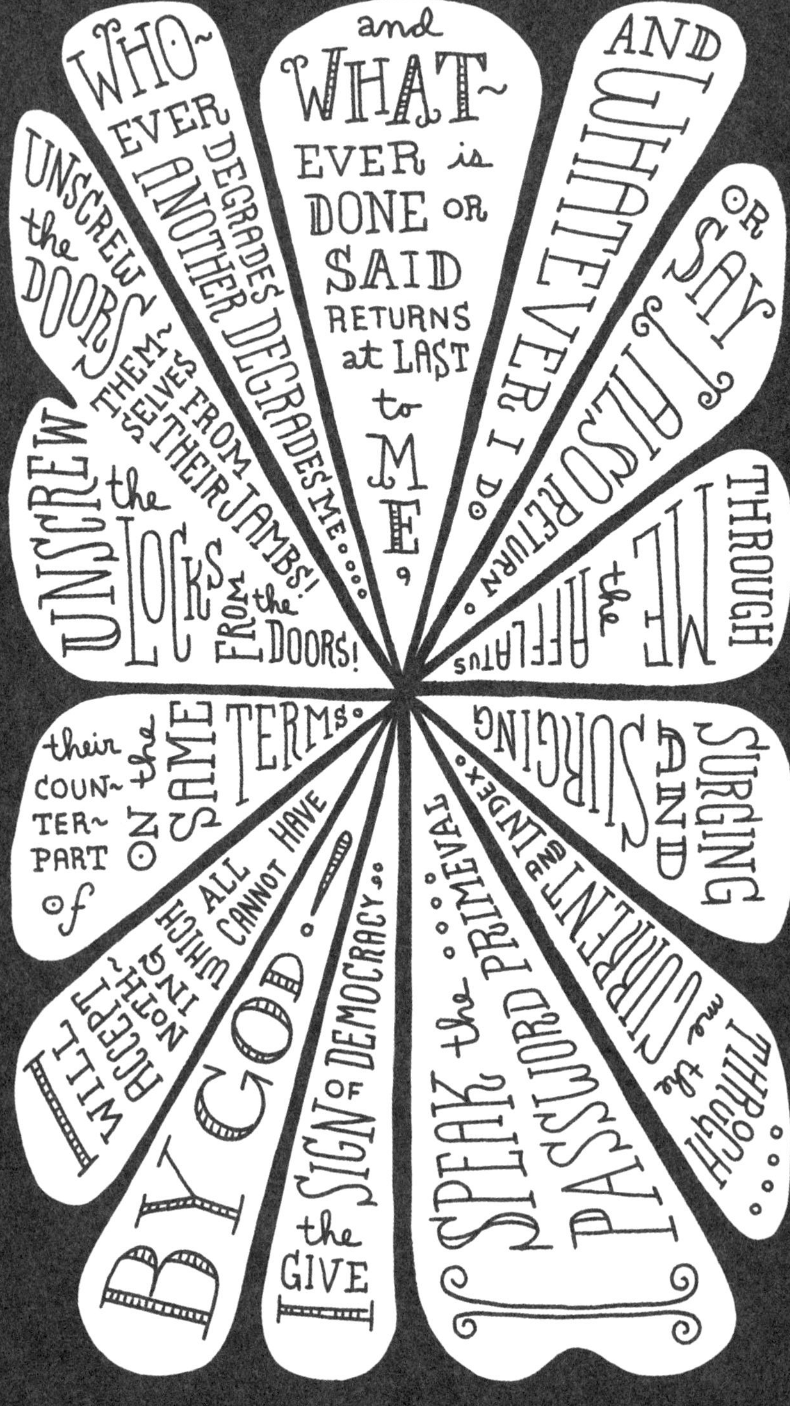
UNSCREW the LOCKS FROM the DOORS!
UNSCREW the DOORS THEM-SELVES FROM THEIR JAMBS!
WHO-EVER DEGRADES ANOTHER DEGRADES ME...
and WHAT-EVER is DONE OR SAID RETURNS at LAST to ME,
AND WHATEVER I DO OR SAY I ALSO RETURN.
THROUGH ME the AFFLATUS SURGING AND SURGING,
THROUGH me the CURRENT AND INDEX.
SPEAK the PASSWORD PRIMEVAL...
GIVE the SIGN OF DEMOCRACY,
BY GOD! I WILL ACCEPT NOTHING WHICH ALL CANNOT HAVE
their COUN-TER-PART of ON the SAME TERMS.

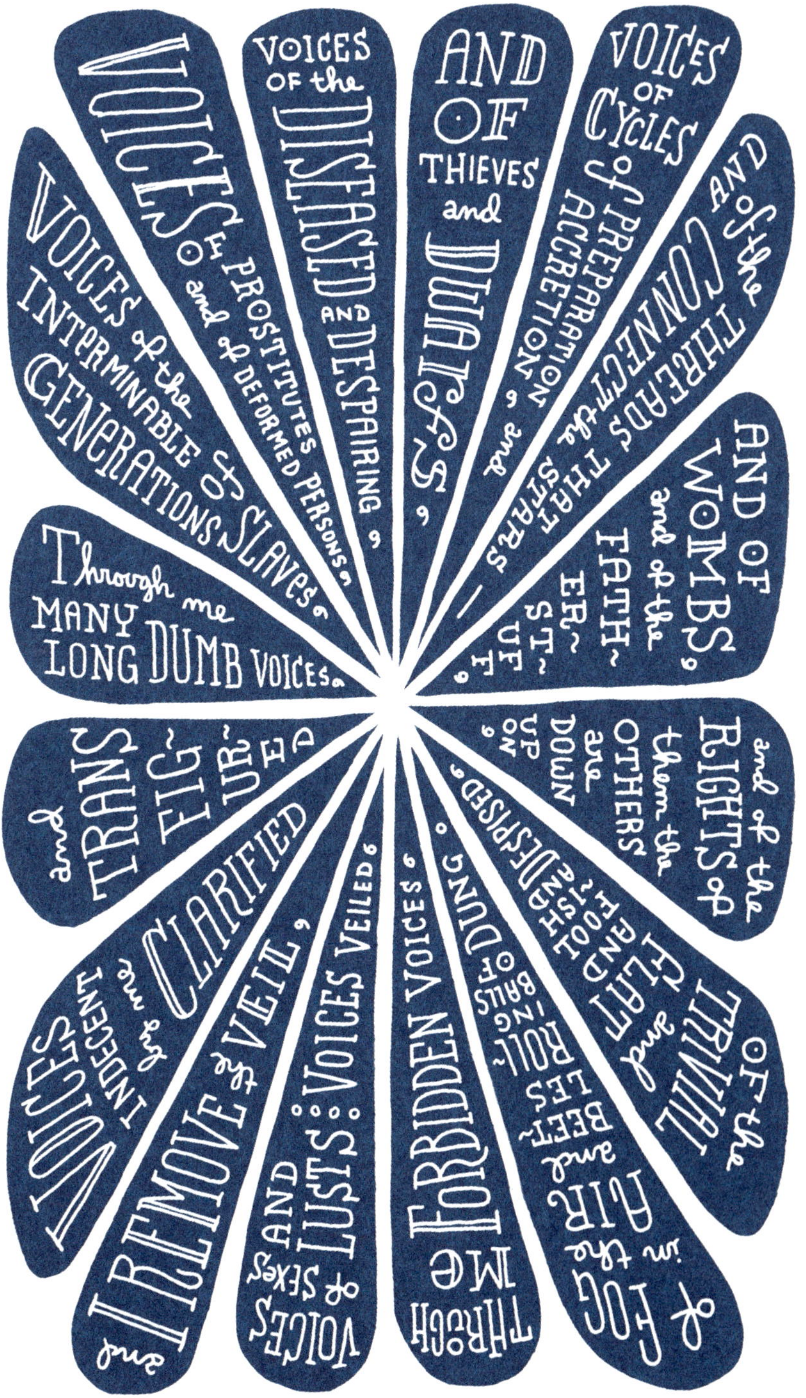

Through me MANY LONG DUMB VOICES,
VOICES of the INTERMINABLE GENERATIONS of SLAVES,
VOICES of PROSTITUTES and of DEFORMED PERSONS,
VOICES OF the DISEASED AND DESPAIRING,
AND OF THIEVES and DWARFS,
VOICES OF CYCLES of PREPARATION and ACCRETION,
AND of the THREADS THAT CONNECT the STARS,
AND OF WOMBS, and of the FATH-ER-STUFF,
and of the RIGHTS of them the OTHERS are DOWN UPON,
OF the TRIVIAL and FLAT AND FOOLISH AND DESPISED,
of FOG in the AIR and BEETLES ROLLING BALLS OF DUNG.
THROUGH ME FORBIDDEN VOICES,
VOICES of SEXES AND LUSTS... VOICES VEILED,
and I REMOVE the VEIL,
VOICES INDECENT by me CLARIFIED and TRANSFIGURED

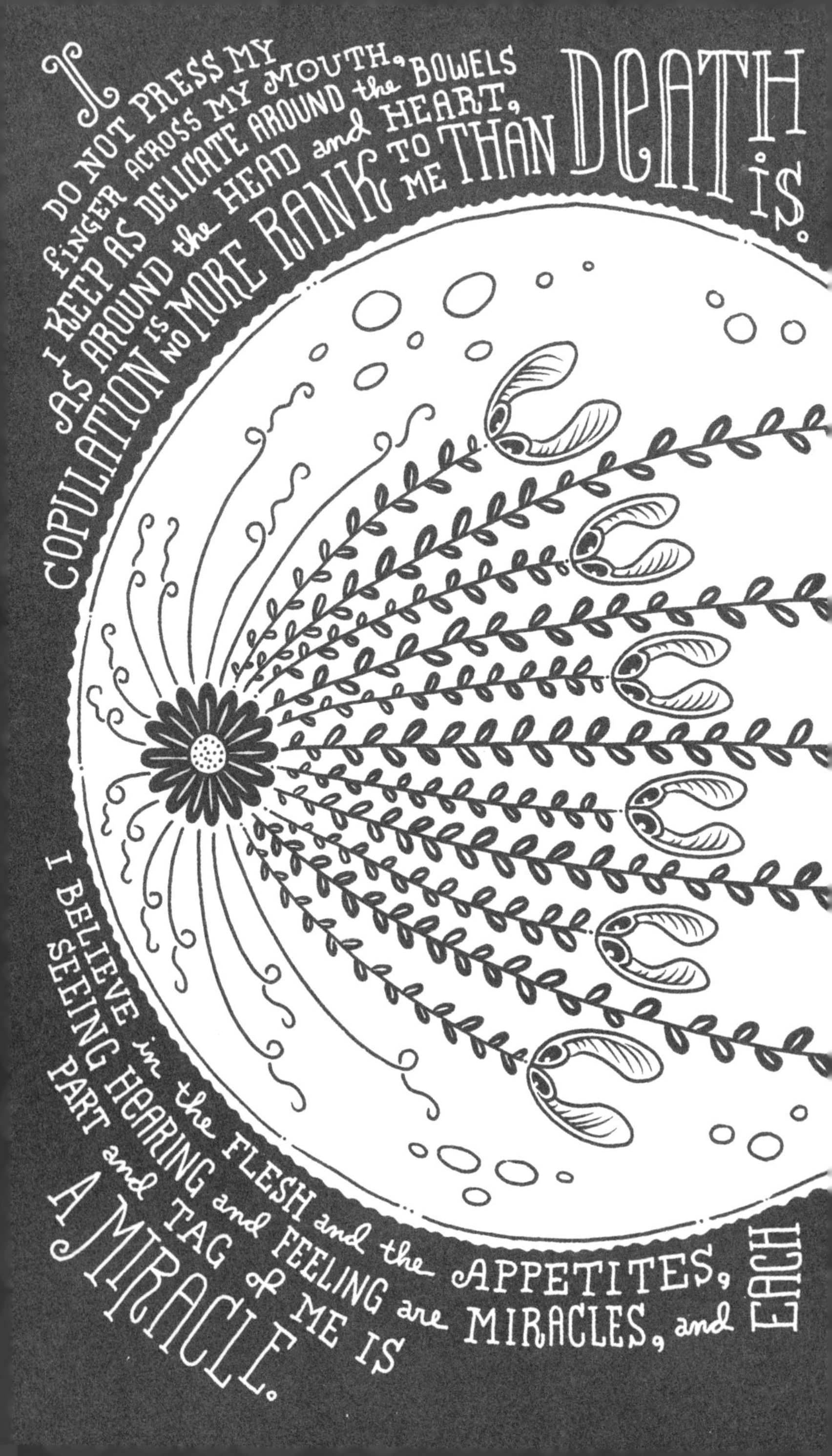
I DO NOT PRESS MY finger ACROSS MY MOUTH,
I KEEP AS DELICATE AROUND the BOWELS AS AROUND the HEAD and HEART,
COPULATION IS NO MORE RANK TO ME THAN DEATH IS.
I BELIEVE in the FLESH and the APPETITES,
SEEING HEARING and FEELING are MIRACLES, and EACH PART and TAG of ME IS
A MIRACLE.

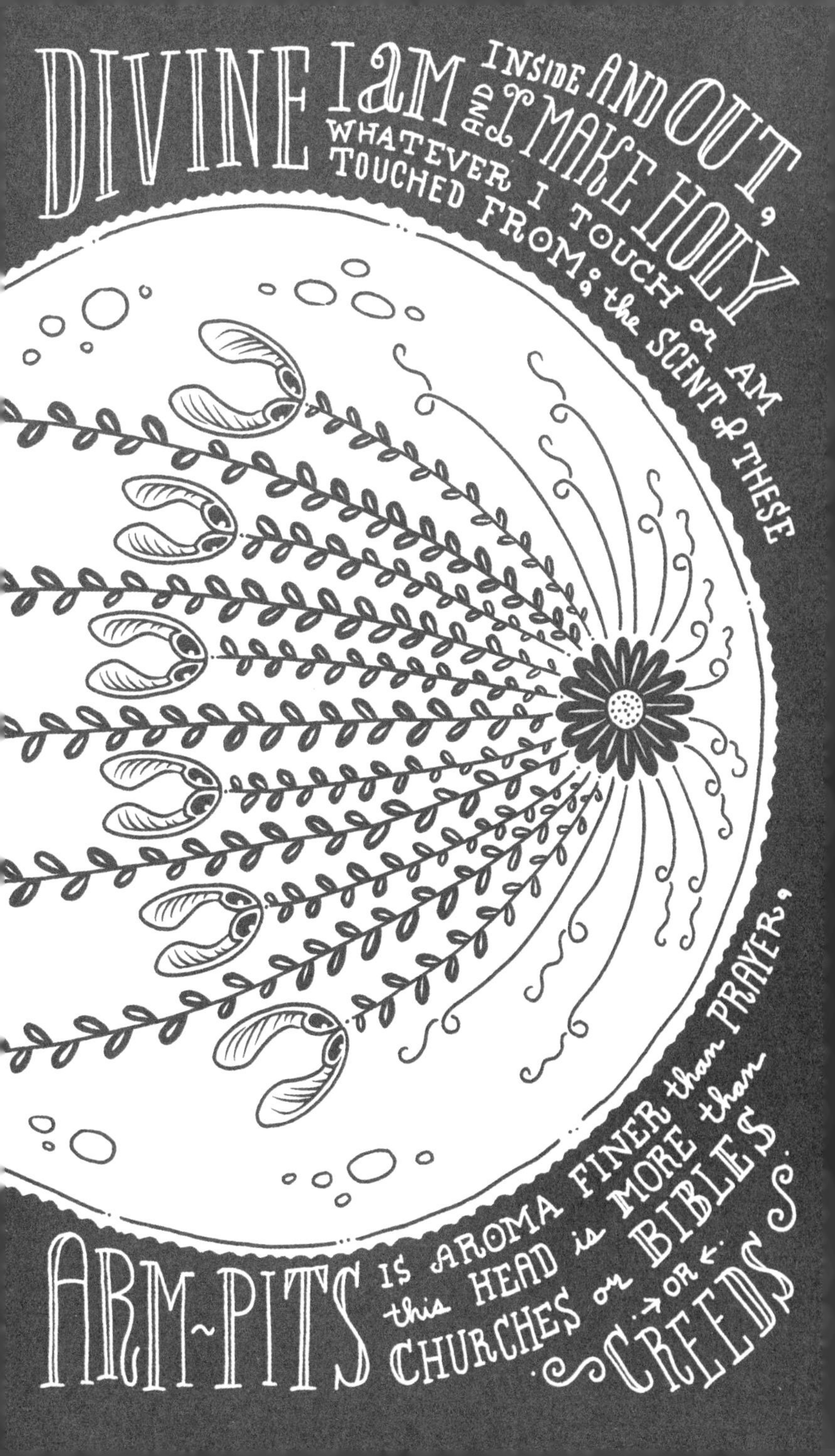
DIVINE I AM INSIDE AND OUT, AND I MAKE HOLY WHATEVER I TOUCH OR AM TOUCHED FROM,
THE SCENT OF THESE
ARM-PITS IS AROMA FINER THAN PRAYER,
THIS HEAD IS MORE THAN CHURCHES OR BIBLES OR CREEDS.

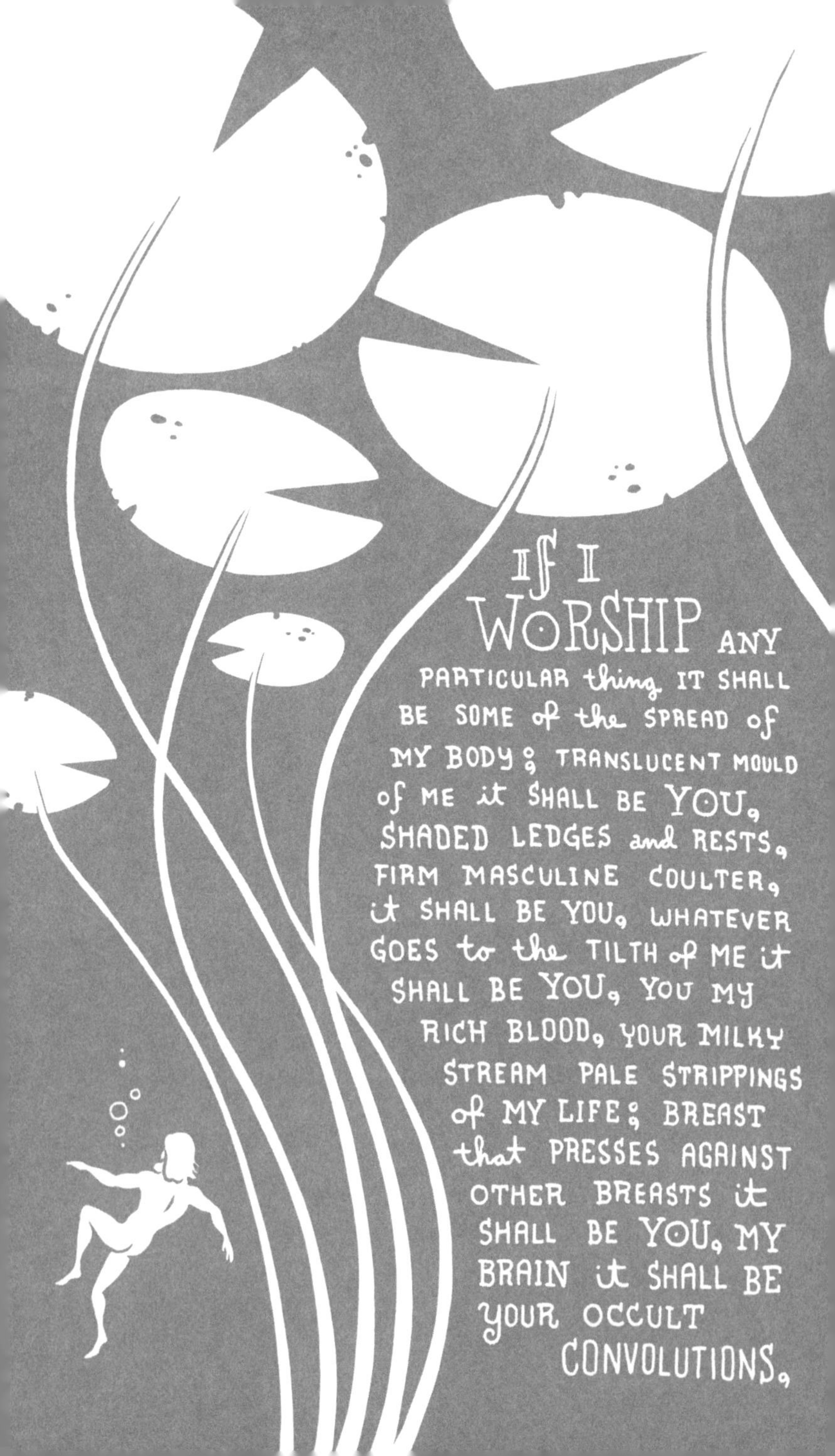
If I
WORSHIP any
particular thing it shall
be some of the spread of
my body; translucent mould
of me it shall be YOU,
shaded ledges and rests,
firm masculine coulter,
it shall be YOU, whatever
goes to the tilth of me it
shall be YOU, You my
rich blood, your milky
stream pale strippings
of my life; breast
that presses against
other breasts it
shall be YOU, my
brain it shall be
your occult
convolutions,

ROOT of WASHED SWEET~FLAG, TIMOR~OUS POND~SNIPE, NEST of GUARDED DUPLICATE EGGS, IT SHALL BE YOU, MIXED TUSSLED HAY of HEAD and BEARD and BRAWN it SHALL BE YOU, TRICKLING SAP of MAPLE, FIBRE of MANLY WHEAT, it SHALL BE YOU;

SUN SO GEN~EROUS it SHALL be YOU, VAPORS LIGHTING and SHADING MY FACE IT SHALL be YOU, YOU SWEATY BROOKS and DEWS it SHALL BE YOU, WINDS WHOSE SOFT~TICKLING GENITALS RUB AGAINST ME it SHALL BE YOU.

BROAD MUSCULAR FIELDS, BRANCHES of LIVEOAK, LOVING LOUNGER in MY WINDING PATHS, it SHALL BE YOU, HANDS I HAVE TAKEN, FACE I HAVE KISSED, MORTAL I HAVE EVER TOUCHED, IT SHALL BE YOU.

I DOTE ON MYSELF :: THERE IS THAT LOT of ME, and ALL SO LUSCIOUS, EACH MOMENT and WHATEVER HAPPENS THRILLS
ME WITH JOY. I CANNOT TELL HOW MY ANKLES BEND :: NOR, WHENCE the CAUSE of MY FAINTEST WISH, NOR the
CAUSE of the FRIENDSHIP I EMIT :: NOR the CAUSE of the FRIENDSHIP I TAKE AGAIN. to WALK UP MY STOOP is
UNACCOUNTABLE :: PAUSE to CONSIDER if it REALLY BE, THAT I EAT and DRINK is SPECTACLE ENOUGH
FOR the GREAT AUTHORS and SCHOOLS, A MORNING~GLORY at MY WINDOW SATISFIES ME
MORE THAN the METAPHYSICS of BOOKS. TO BEHOLD the DAYBREAK! the LITTLE
LIGHT FADES the IMMENSE and DIAPHANOUS SHADOWS, the AIR TASTES
GOOD to MY PALATE. HEFTS of the MOVING WORLD at INNOCENT
GAMBOLS, SILENTLY RISING, FRESHLY EXUDING, SCOOTING
OBLIQUELY HIGH and LOW. SOMETHING I CANNOT
SEE PUTS UPWARD LIBIDINOUS PRONGS, SEAS
OF BRIGHT JUICE SUFFUSE HEAVEN.

THE EARTH BY THE SKY STAID WITH :: THE DAILY CLOSE of THEIR JUNCTION, THE HEAVED CHALLENGE FROM
the EAST that MOMENT OVER MY HEAD. the MOCKING TAUNT, SEE THEN WHETHER YOU SHALL BE MASTER! —
DAZZLING AND TREMENDOUS how QUICK THE SUNRISE OUT of ME. WE ALSO ASCEND DAZZLING AND TREMENDOUS
AS THE SUN, WE FOUND OUR OWN MY SOUL IN the CALM AND COOL of THE DAYBREAK. MY VOICE GOES
AFTER WHAT MY EYES CANNOT REACH, WITH the TWIRL OF MY TONGUE I ENCOMPASS WORLDS
AND VOLUMES of WORLDS. SPEECH IS THE TWIN OF MY VISION :: IT IS UNEQUAL TO
MEASURE ITSELF. IT PROVOKES ME FOREVER, it SAYS SARCASTICALLY,
WALT, YOU UNDERSTAND ENOUGH :: WHY DON'T YOU LET IT
OUT THEN? COME NOW I WILL NOT BE TANTALIZED ::
YOU CONCEIVE TOO MUCH OF ARTICULATION. DO
YOU NOT KNOW HOW THE BUDS BENEATH ARE FOLDED? WAITING
IN GLOOM PROTECTED BY FROST,

the DIRT receding before my pro~phet~ical screams.

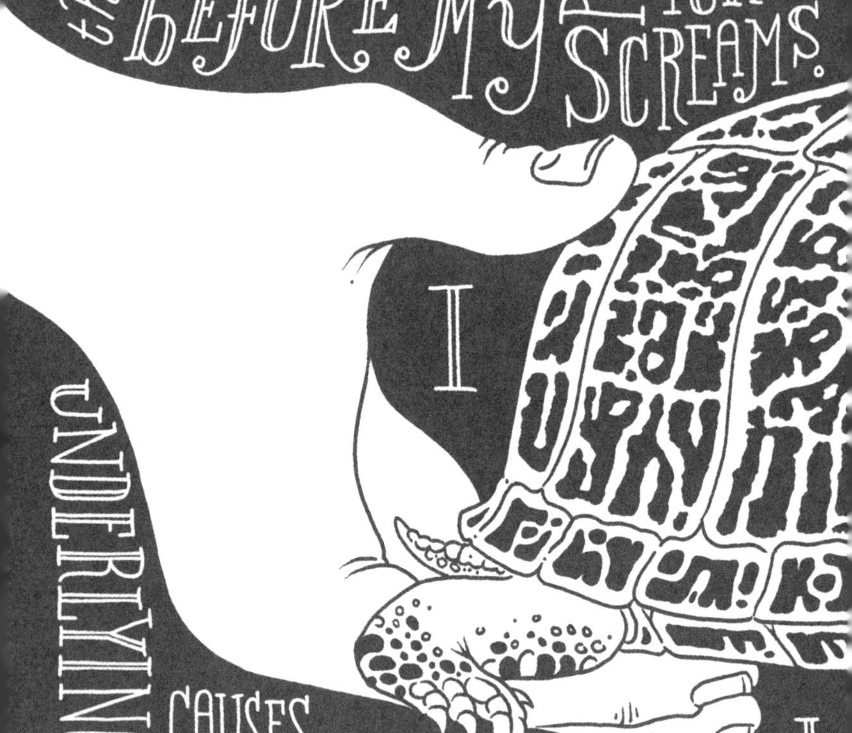

I underlying causes to balance them at last,
My knowledge my live parts . . . .
it keeping tally with the meaning of things,
HAPPINESS . . . which whoever hears me let him or her set out in search of this day.
My final merit I refuse you : : I re~fuse putting from me the best I am.
Encompass worlds but never try to encompass me,
I crowd your noisiest talk by looking toward you.

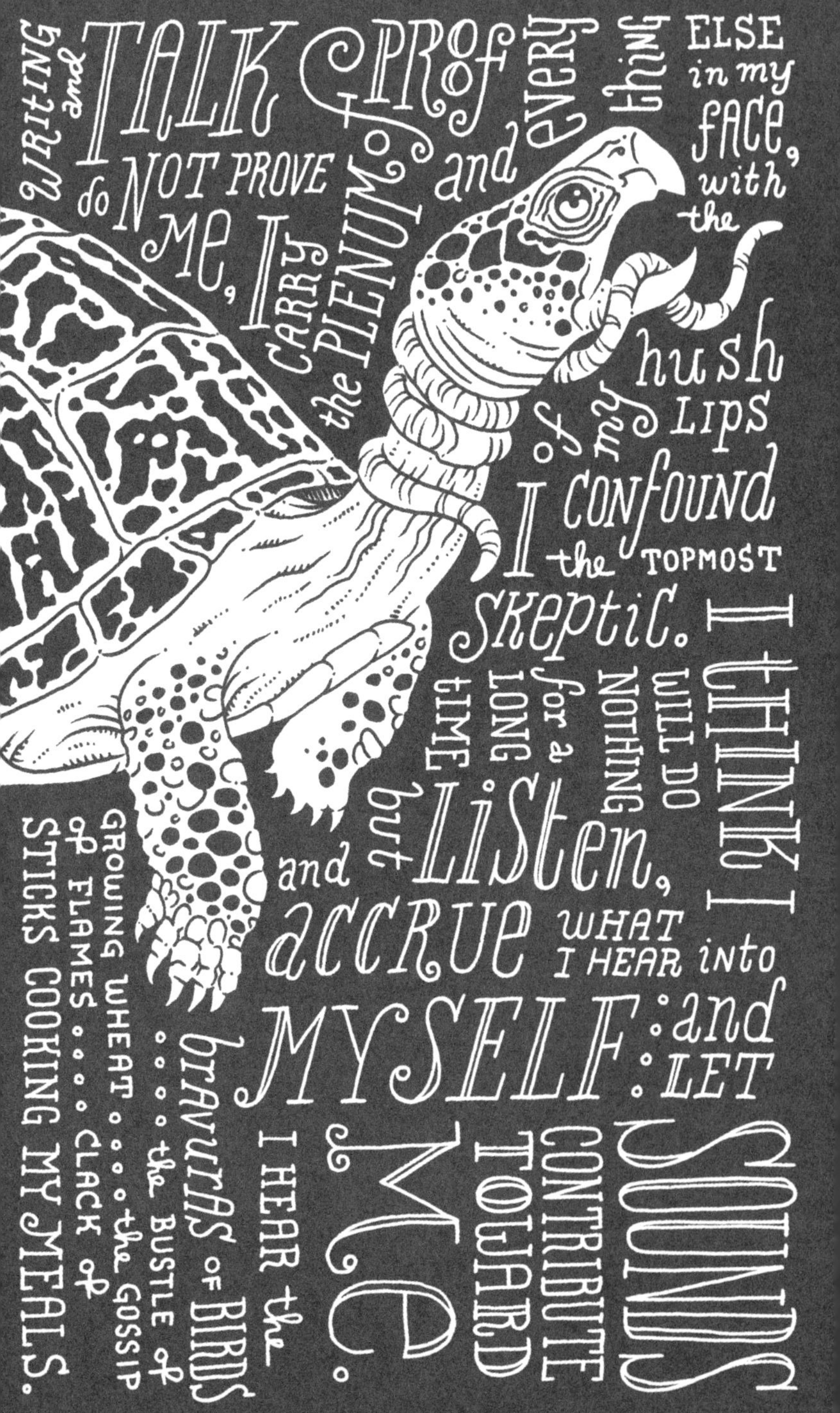

WRITING and TALK do NOT PROVE ME, I CARRY the PLENUM of PROOF and EVERY thing ELSE in my FACE, with the hush of my LIPS I CONFOUND the TOPMOST SKEPTIC.
I THINK I WILL DO NOTHING for a LONG TIME but LISTEN, and ACCRUE WHAT I HEAR into MYSELF: and LET SOUNDS CONTRIBUTE TOWARD ME.
I HEAR the BRAVURAS OF BIRDS . . . the BUSTLE of GROWING WHEAT . . . the GOSSIP of FLAMES . . . CLACK of STICKS COOKING MY MEALS.

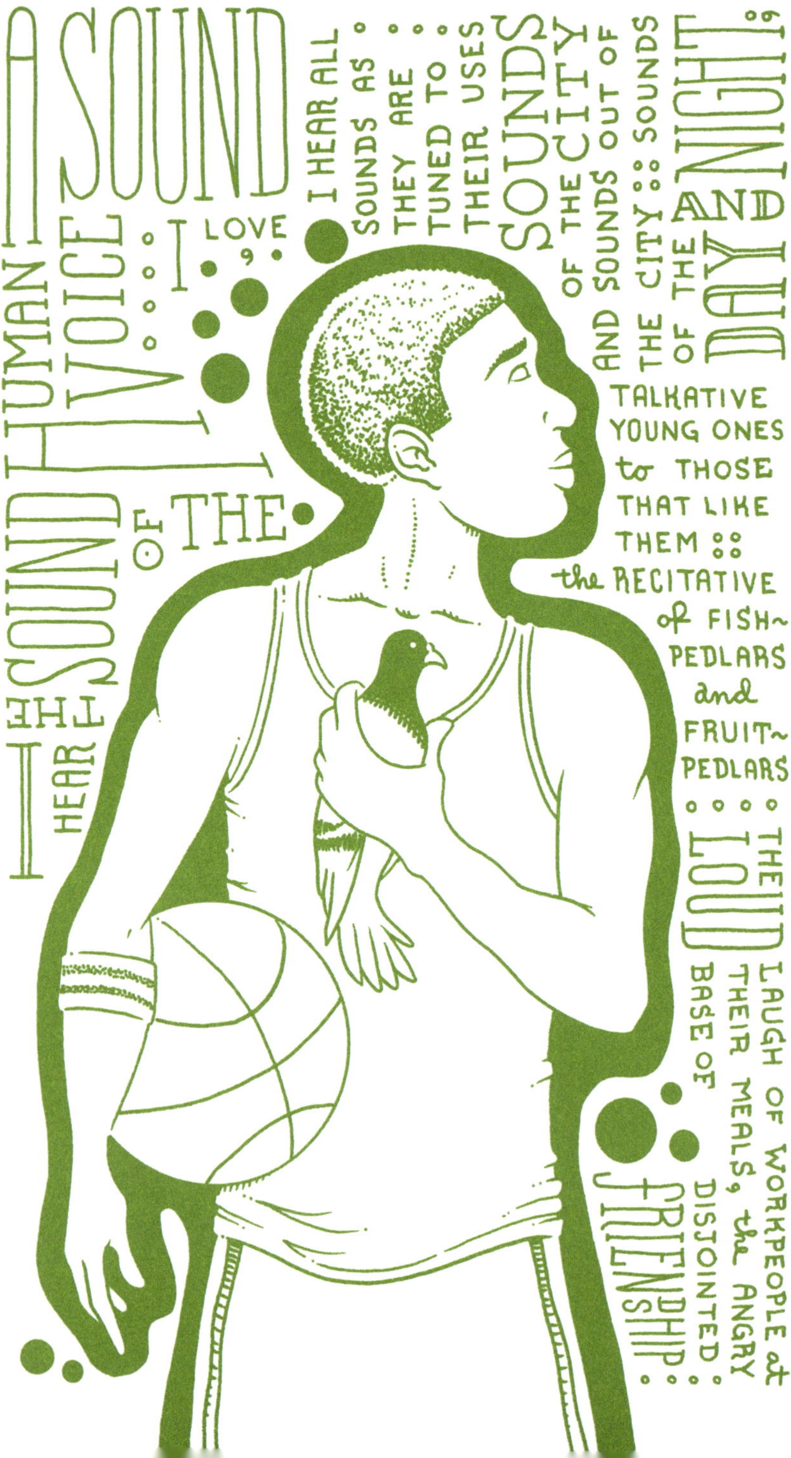

I HEAR THE SOUND I LOVE
THE SOUND OF THE HUMAN VOICE
I HEAR ALL SOUNDS AS THEY ARE TUNED TO THEIR USES
SOUNDS OF THE CITY AND SOUNDS OUT OF THE CITY
SOUNDS OF THE DAY AND NIGHT;
TALKATIVE YOUNG ONES to THOSE THAT LIKE THEM
the RECITATIVE of FISH-PEDLARS and FRUIT-PEDLARS
THE LOUD LAUGH OF WORKPEOPLE at THEIR MEALS, the ANGRY BASE OF DISJOINTED FRIENDSHIP

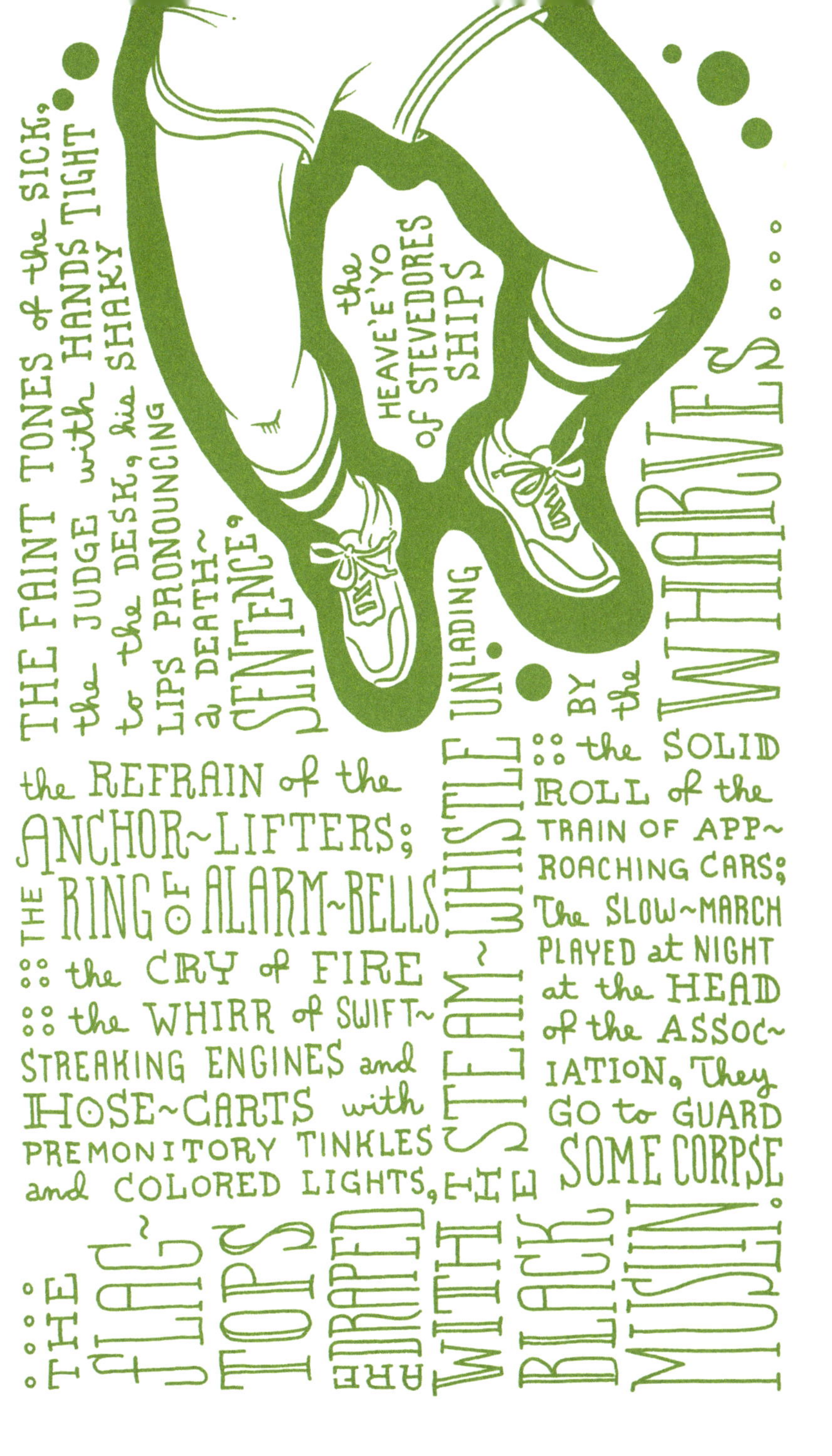
THE FAINT TONES of the SICK,
the JUDGE with HANDS TIGHT
to the DESK, his SHAKY
LIPS PRONOUNCING
a DEATH~
SENTENCE,
the
HEAVE'E'YO
of STEVEDORES
SHIPS
UNLADING
BY
the
WHARVES....
the REFRAIN of the
ANCHOR~LIFTERS;
THE RING OF ALARM~BELLS
:: the CRY of FIRE
:: the WHIRR of SWIFT~
STREAKING ENGINES and
HOSE~CARTS with
PREMONITORY TINKLES
and COLORED LIGHTS, THE
STEAM~WHISTLE
:: the SOLID
ROLL of the
TRAIN OF APP~
ROACHING CARS;
The SLOW~MARCH
PLAYED at NIGHT
at the HEAD
of the ASSOC~
IATION, They
GO to GUARD
SOME CORPSE
:: THE
FLAG~
TOPS
ARE DRAPED
WITH
BLACK
MUSLIN.

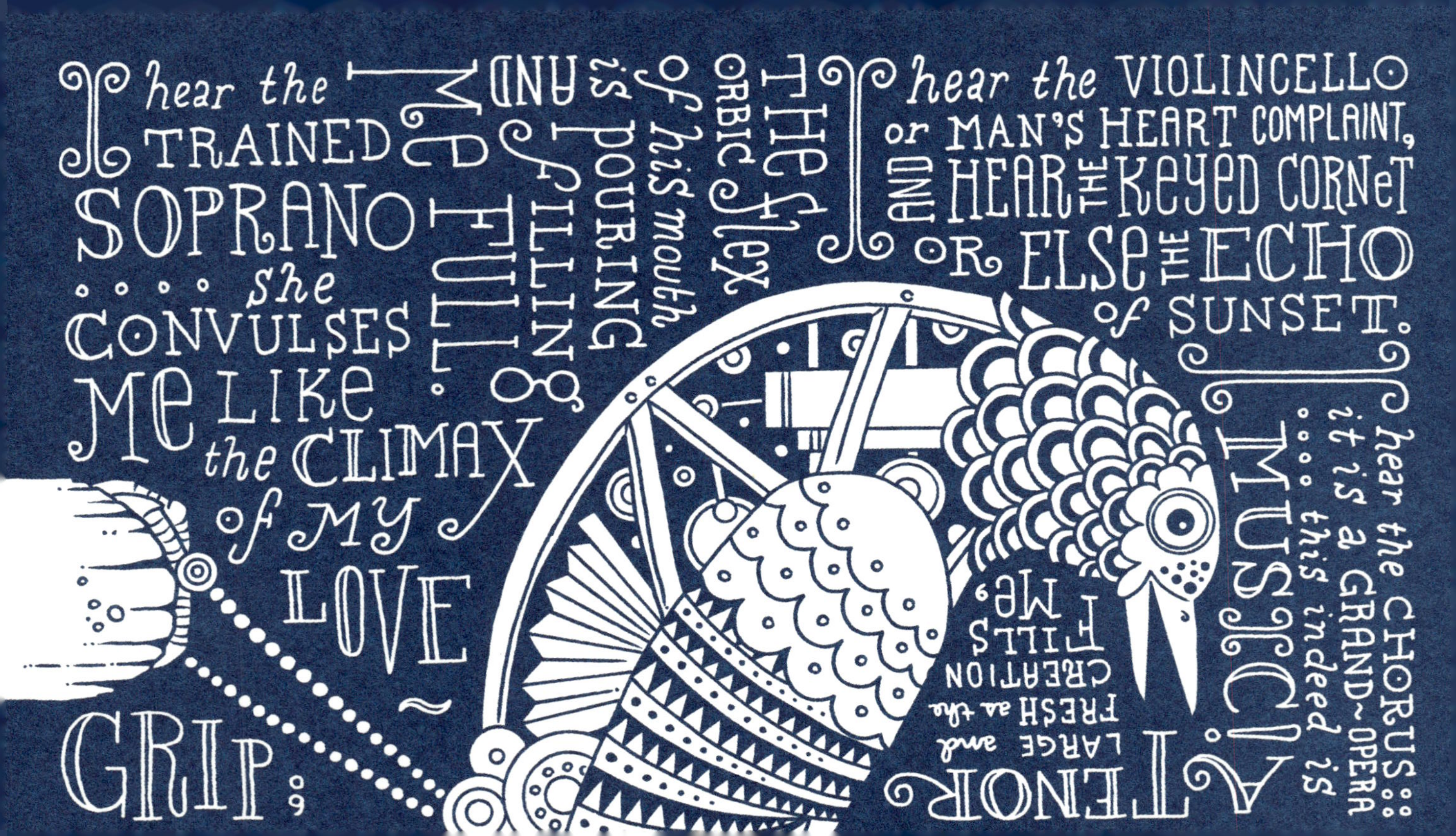
I hear the VIOLINCELLO
or MAN'S HEART COMPLAINT,
AND HEAR THE KEYED CORNET
OR ELSE THE ECHO
of SUNSET.
I hear the CHORUS:::
it is a GRAND~OPERA
.... this indeed is
MUSIC!
A TENOR LARGE and FRESH as the CREATION FILLS ME,
THE ORBIC flex
of his mouth
is POURING
AND FILLING
ME FULL.
I hear the
TRAINED
SOPRANO
.... she
CONVULSES
ME LIKE
the CLIMAX
of MY
LOVE ~
GRIP:

THE ORCHESTRA WHIRLS ME
wider than URANUS flies,
IT WRENCHES UNNAMABLE
ARDORS FROM MY BREAST,

IT THROBS ME TO GULPS
of the FARTHEST DOWN
HORROR,
IT SAILS ME:
I DAB WITH BARE FEET:
THEY ARE LICKED BY THE
INDOLENT WAVES,
I AM EXPOSED....
CUT BY BITTER and
POISONED HAIL,
STEEPED AMID
HONEYED
MORPHINE:...

MY WINDPIPE
SQUEEZED IN THE fakes OF
DEATH, LET UP
AGAIN to FEEL
the PUZZLE
of PUZZLES,
and that
WE call
BEING.

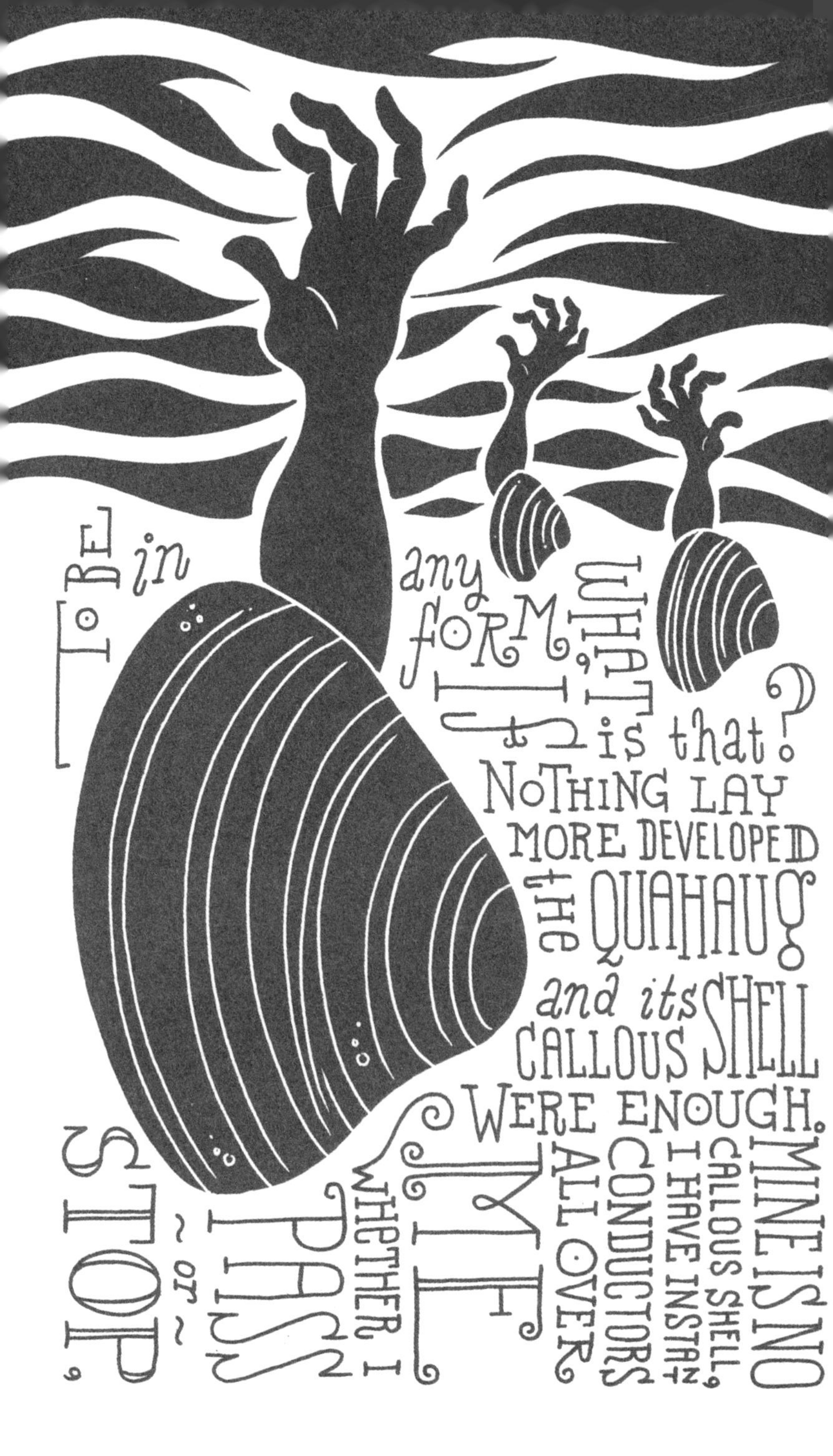
TO BE in
any FORM,
WHAT IT
is that?
NOTHING LAY
MORE DEVELOPED
the QUAHAUG
and its SHELL
CALLOUS SHELL
WERE ENOUGH.
MINE IS NO
CALLOUS SHELL,
I HAVE INSTANT
CONDUCTORS
ALL OVER,
TIME
WHETHER I
PASS
~ or ~
STOP.

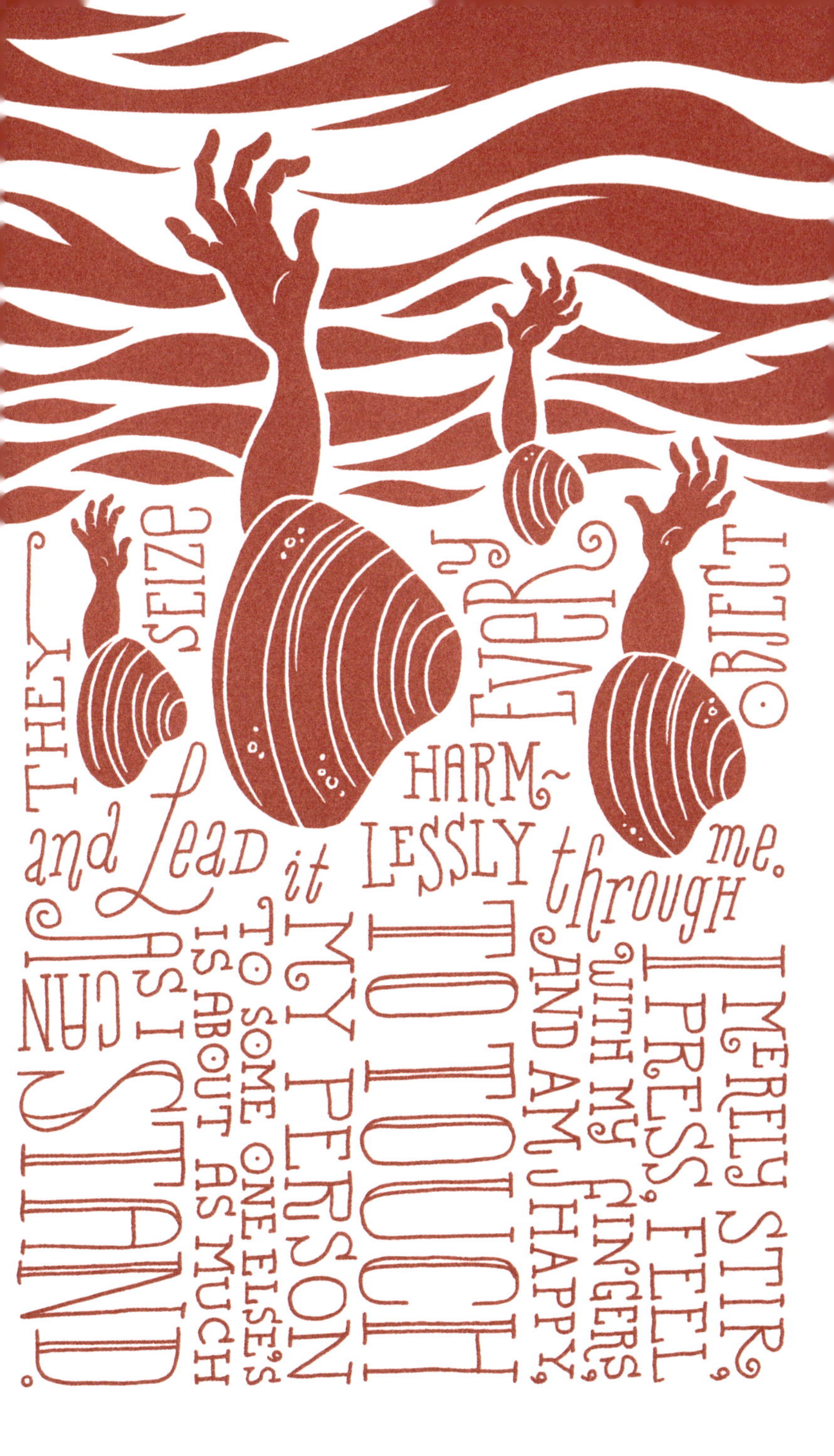

THEY SEIZE EVERY OBJECT
and Lead it HARM-LESSLY through me.
I MERELY STIR,
PRESS, FEEL
WITH MY FINGERS,
AND AM HAPPY,
TO TOUCH
MY PERSON
TO SOME ONE ELSE'S
IS ABOUT AS MUCH
AS I CAN STAND.

IS THIS THEN A TOUCH? . . . QUIVERING ME to A NEW IDENTITY, FLAMES and ETHER MAKING A RUSH FOR MY VEINS, TREACHEROUS TIP OF ME REACH~ING AND CROWDING TO HELP THEM, MY FLESH AND BLOOD PLAYING OUT LIGHTNING, TO STRIKE WHAT IS HARDLY DIFFERENT FROM MYSELF, ON ALL SIDES PUR~IENT PROVOKERS STIFFENING MY LIMBS, STRAIN~ING THE UDDER OF MY HEART FOR ITS WITHHELD DRIP, BEHAVING LICENTIOUS TOWARD ME, TAKING NO DENIAL, DEPRIVING ME OF MY BEST AS FOR A PURPOSE, UNBUTTONING MY CLOTHES AND HOLDING ME BY the BARE WAIST, DELUDING MY CONFUSION WITH the CALM of the SUN~LIGHT AND PASTURE FIELDS, IM~MODESTLY SLIDING the FELLOW ~SENSES AWAY, THEY BRIBED TO SWAP OFF WITH TOUCH, AND GO AND GRAZE AT the EDGES OF ME,

NO CONSIDERATION, NO REGARD FOR MY DRAINING STRENGTH or MY ANGER, FETCHING the REST OF THE HERD AROUND to ENJOY THEM AWHILE, THEN ALL UNITING to STAND ON A HEADLAND AND WORRY ME.

THE SENTRIES DESERT EVERY OTHER PART OF ME, THEY HAVE LEFT ME HELP~LESS to a RED MARAUDER, THEY ALL COME TO THE HEADLAND to WITNESS and ASSIST AGAINST ME.

I AM GIVEN UP BY TRAITORS; I TALK WILDLY :: I HAVE LOST MY WITS :: I AND NOBODY ELSE AM THE GREATEST TRAIT~OR, I WENT MYSELF FIRST TO THE HEADLAND :: MY OWN HANDS CARRIED ME THERE.

YOU VILLAIN TOUCH! WHAT ARE YOU DOING? :: MY BREATH IS TIGHT IN ITS THROAT; UN~CLENCH YOUR FLOODGATES! YOU ARE TOO MUCH FOR ME. BLIND LOVING WRESTLING TOUCH! SHEATHED HOODED SHARPTOOTHED TOUCH!

DID IT MAKE YOU ACHE SO LEAVING ME? PARTING TRACKED BY ARRIVING :: PERPETUAL PAYMENT OF the PERPETUAL LOAN, RICH, SHOWERING RAIN, and RE~COMMENSE RICHER AFTER~WARD. SPROUTS TAKE AND ACCUMULATE :: STAND BY THE CURB PROLIFIC and VITAL, LANDSCAPES PRO~JECTED MASCULINE FULL~SIZED AND GOLDEN.

All truths wait in All things,
they neither hasten their own delivery nor resist it,
they do not need the Obstetric forceps of the surgeon,
The Insignificant is as big to me as any,
What is Less or more than a toucH?
Logic and sermons never convince,
The damp of the NIGht drives deeper into my SOUL.
ONLY what proves itself to Every man and woman is so,
ONLY WHAT NOBODY DENIES is SO.
A minute and a DROP of ME SETTLE MY BRAIN;
I BELIEVE the soggy CLODS SHAll become LOVERS AND LAMPS,

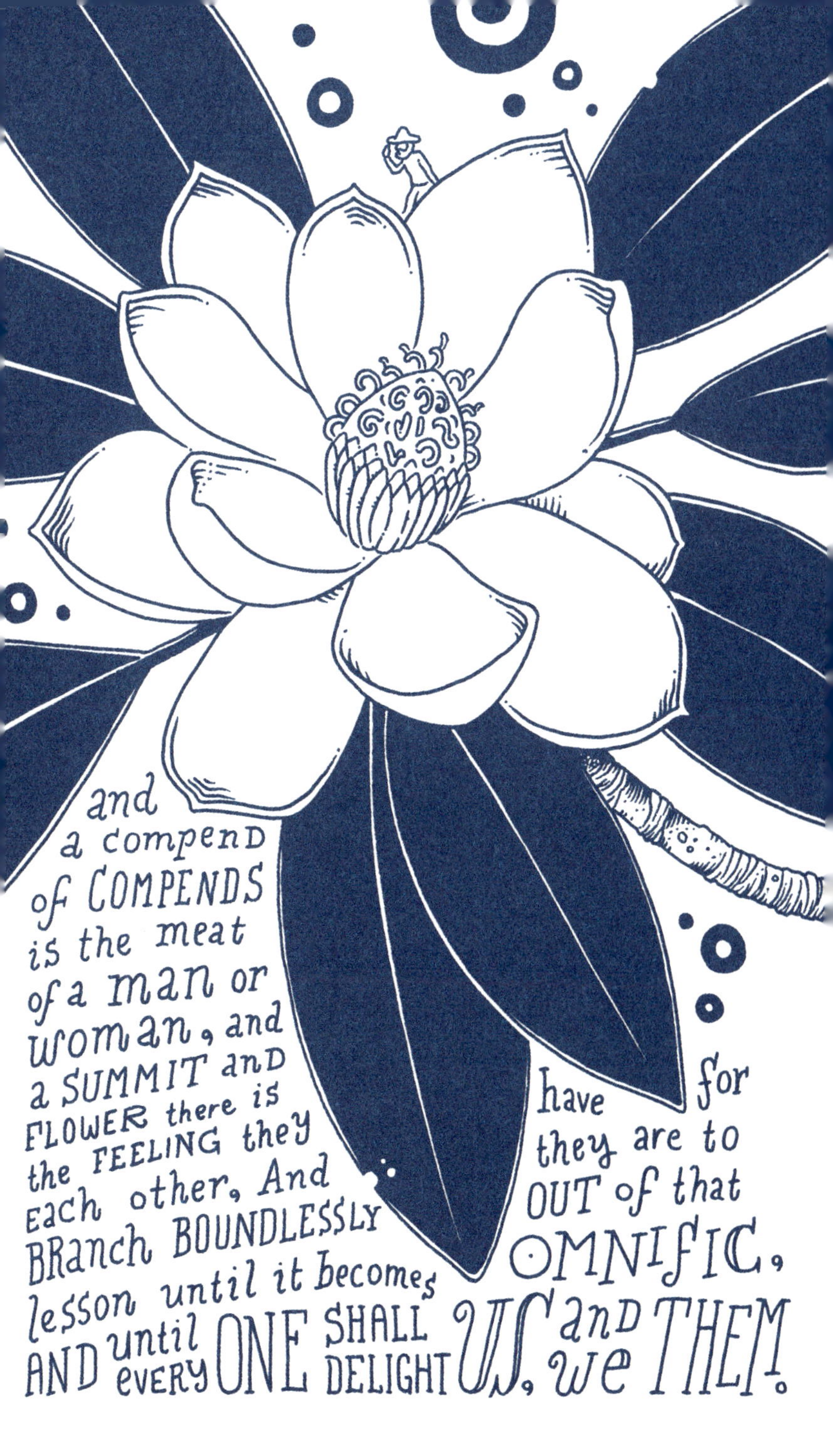
and a compend of COMPENDS is the meat of a man or woman, and a SUMMIT and FLOWER there is the FEELING they have for each other, And they are to BRANCH BOUNDLESSLY OUT of that lesson until it becomes OMNIFIC, AND until EVERY ONE SHALL DELIGHT US, and we THEM.

i Believe
a Leaf of
Grass

is no less than the journey work of the stars,

And the pismire is equally perfect, and a grain of sand, and the egg of the wren,
And the tree-toad is a chef-d'œuvre for the highest,
And the running blackberry would adorn the parlors of heaven,
And the narrowest hinge in my hand puts to scorn all machinery,

And the cow crunching with de-pressed head surpasses any statue,
And a mouse is miracle enough to stagger sextillions of infidels,
And I could come every afternoon of my life to look at the farmer's girl boiling her iron tea-kettle and baking shortcake.

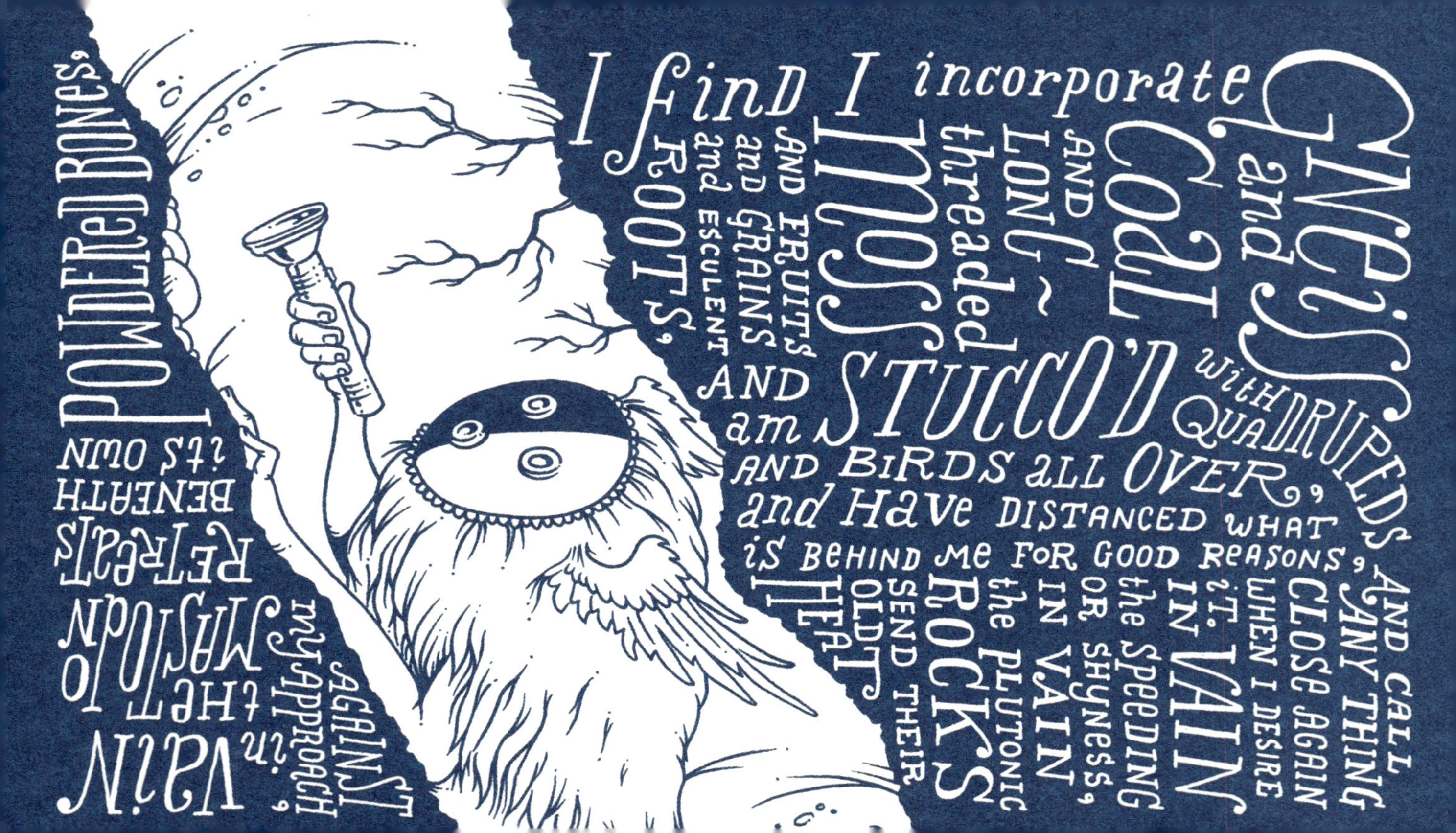

I find I incorporate gneiss and coal and long-threaded moss and fruits and grains and esculent roots,
And am stucco'd with quadrupeds and birds all over,
and have distanced what is behind me for good reasons,
And call any thing close again when I desire it.
In vain the speeding or shyness,
In vain the plutonic rocks send their old heat against my approach,
In vain the mastodon retreats beneath its own powdered bones,

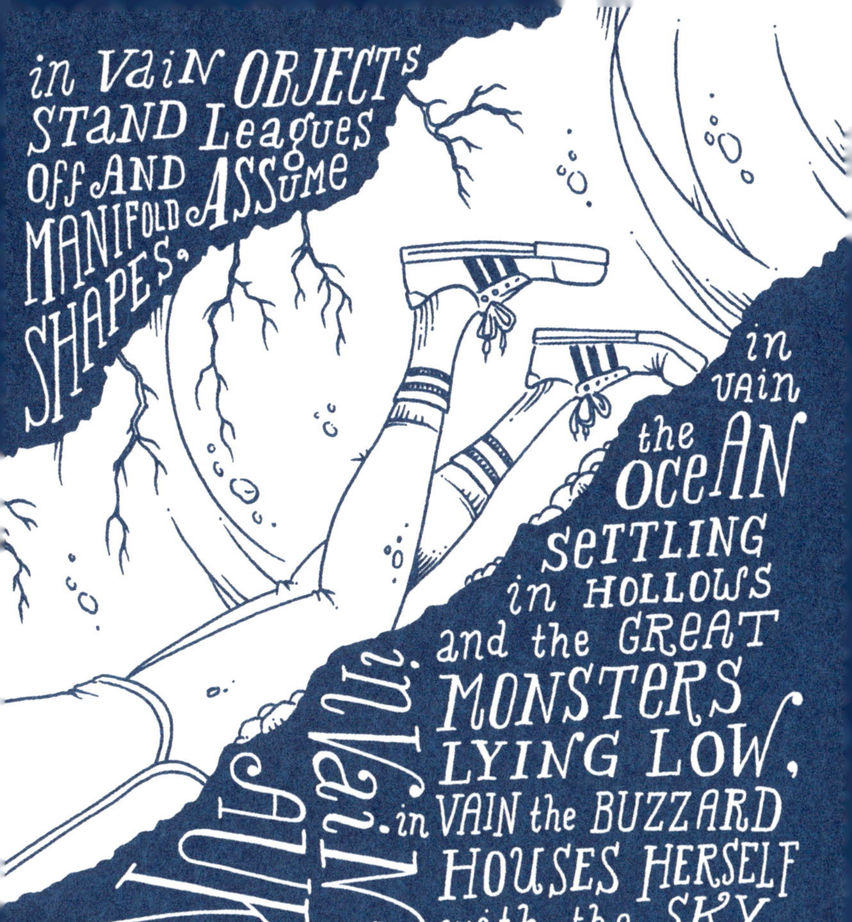

in vain objects stand leagues off and assume manifold shapes,
in vain the ocean settling in hollows and the great monsters lying low,
in vain the buzzard houses herself with the sky,
in vain the snake slides through the creepers and logs,
in vain the elk takes to the inner passes of the woods,
in vain the razorbilled auk sails far north to Labrador,
i follow quickly
I ascend to the nest in the fissure of the cliff.

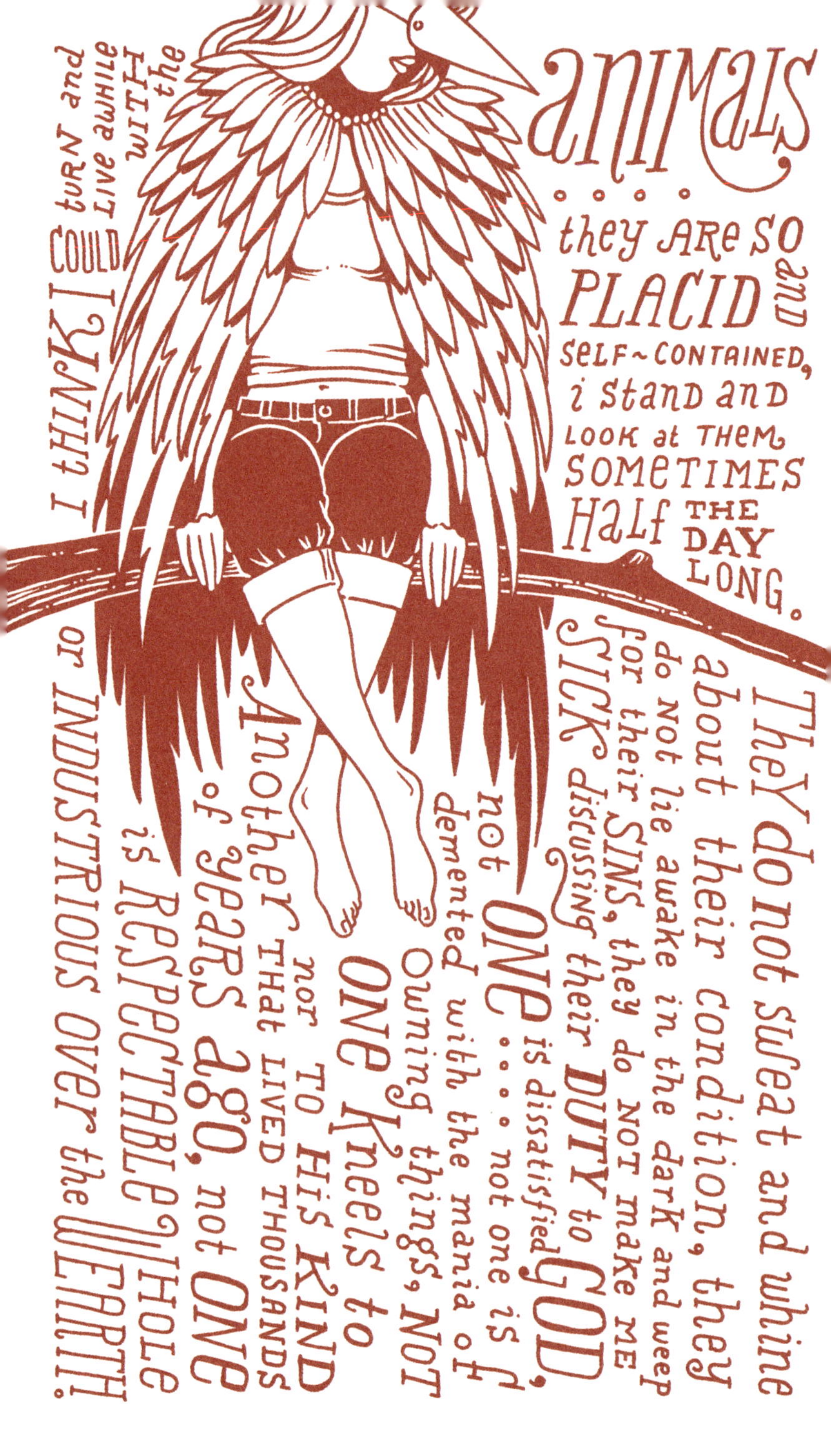

I think I could turn and live awhile with the
animals . . .
they are so placid and self-contained,
i stand and look at them sometimes half the day long.
They do not sweat and whine about their condition, they
do not lie awake in the dark and weep for their sins, they do not make me
sick discussing their duty to GOD,
not one is dissatisfied . . . not one is demented with the mania of owning things, NOT
ONE kneels to Another nor TO HIS KIND THAT LIVED THOUSANDS of YEARS ago, not ONE
is RESPECTABLE or INDUSTRIOUS over the WHOLE EARTH!

So they show their relation to me I accept them; they bring me tokens of myself :: they evince them plainly in their possession. I do not know where they got those tokens, I must have passed that way untold times ago and negligently dropt them, myself moving forward then and now and forever, gathering and showing more always and with velocity, infinite and omnigenous and the like of these among them; not too exclusive toward the reachers of my remembrancers, picking out here one that shall be my amie, choosing to go with him on brotherly terms

A GIGANTIC BEAUTY
of a STALLION, FRESH AND
RESPONSIVE TO MY CARESSES,
HEAD HIGH IN THE FOREHEAD
AND WIDE BETWEEN
the EARS,
LIMBS
glossy
AND
SUPPLE,
TAIL DUSTING
the GROUND,
EYES WELL APART AND FULL of
SPARKLING WICKEDNESS
. . . EARS FINELY CUT
AND FLEXIBLY MOVING.
HIS NOSTRILS DILATE. . . .
MY HEELS EMBRACE HIM. . . .
HIS WELL BUILT LIMBS TREM~
~BLE WITH PLEASURE. . . . WE
SPEED AROUND AND RETURN.
I BUT USE YOU A MOMENT
and THEN I RESIGN YOU
STALLION: AND DO NOT
NEED YOUR
PACES, AND OUTGALLOP
THEM,
AND MYSELF AS I STAND OR
SIT PASS FASTER THAN YOU.

SWIFT WIND! SPACE! MY SOUL!

NOW I KNOW IT IS TRUE WHAT I GUESSED AT;
WHAT I GUESSED WHEN I LOAFED ON THE GRASS,
WHAT I GUESSED WHILE I LAY ALONE IN MY BED
. . . AND AGAIN AS I WALKED THE BEACH
UNDER THE PALING STARS OF THE MORNING.

MY TIES AND BALLASTS LEAVE ME . . . .
I TRAVEL . . . .
I SAIL . . . .
MY ELBOWS REST IN THE SEA-GAPS,
I SKIRT THE SIERRAS . . . .
MY PALMS COVER CONTINENTS
I AM AFOOT WITH MY VISION.

BY THE CITY'S QUADRANGULAR HOUSES, IN LOG-HUTS, OR CAMPING WITH LUMBERMEN, ALONG THE RUTS OF THE TURNPIKE.... ALONG THE DRY GULCH AND RIVULET BED, HOEING MY ONION-PATCH, AND ROWS OF CARROTS AND PARSNIPS: CROSSING SAVANAS: TRAILING IN FORESTS, PROSPECTING, GOLD-DIGGING, GIRDLING the TREES OF A NEW PURCHASE, SCORCHED ANKLE DEEP BY THE HOT SAND.... HAULING MY BOAT DOWN THE SHALLOW RIVER; WHERE the PANTHER WALKS TO and FRO ON A LIMB OVERHEAD: WHERE THE BUCK TURNS FURIOUSLY AT THE HUNTER, WHERE the RATTLESNAKE SUNS HIS FLABBY LENGTH ON A ROCK: WHERE the OTTER IS FEEDING ON FISH,

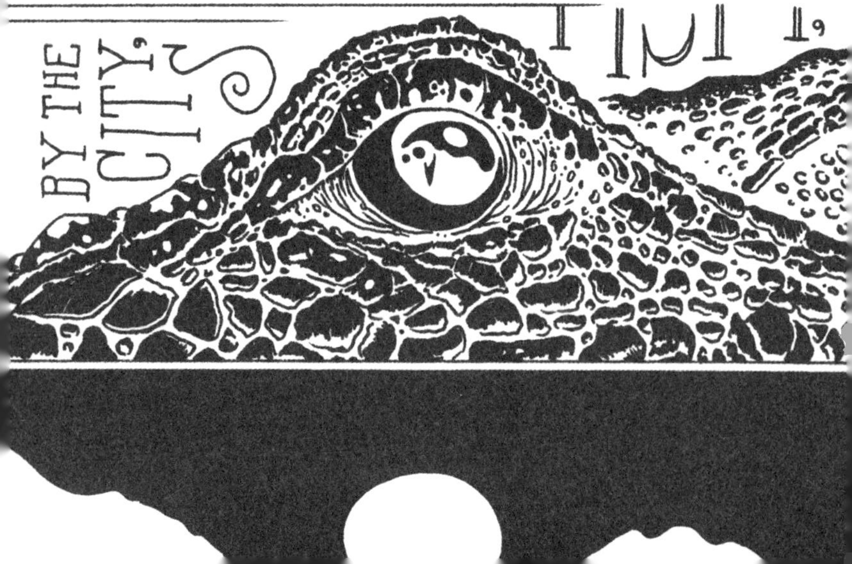

WHERE THE ALLIGATOR IN HIS ROUGH PIMPLES SLEEPS BY THE BAYOU, WHERE THE BLACK BEAR IS SEARCHING FOR ROOTS OR HONEY .... WHERE THE BEAVER PATS THE MUD WITH HIS PADDLE~TAIL; OVER THE GROWING SUGAR .... OVER THE COTTON PLANT .... OVER THE RICE IN ITS LOW MOIST FIELD; OVER THE SHARP~PEAKED FARM~HOUSE WITH ITS SCALLOPED SCUM AND SLENDER SHOOTS FROM THE GUTTERS; OVER THE WESTERN PERSIMMON :: OVER THE LONGLEAVED CORN AND THE DELICATE BLUE~FLOWERED FLAX; OVER THE WHITE AND BROWN BUCK~WHEAT, A HUMMER AND A BUZZER THERE WITH THE REST,

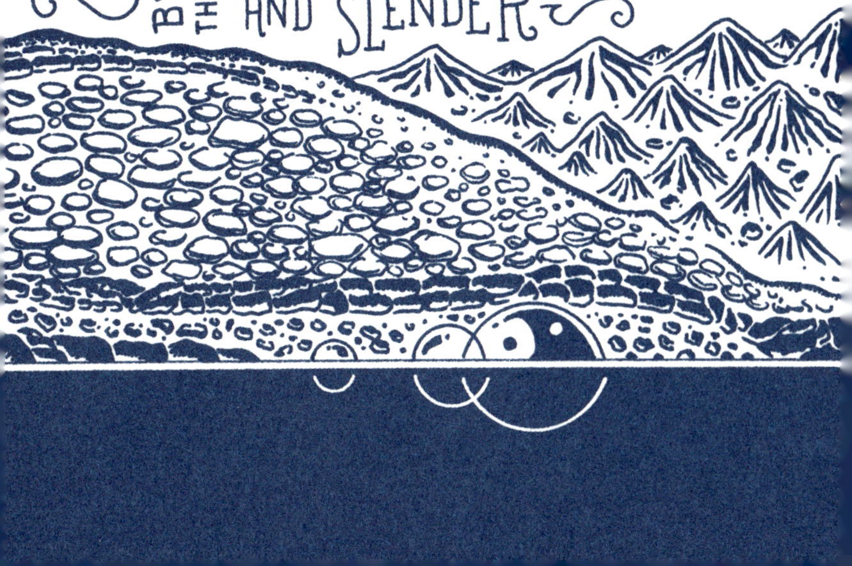

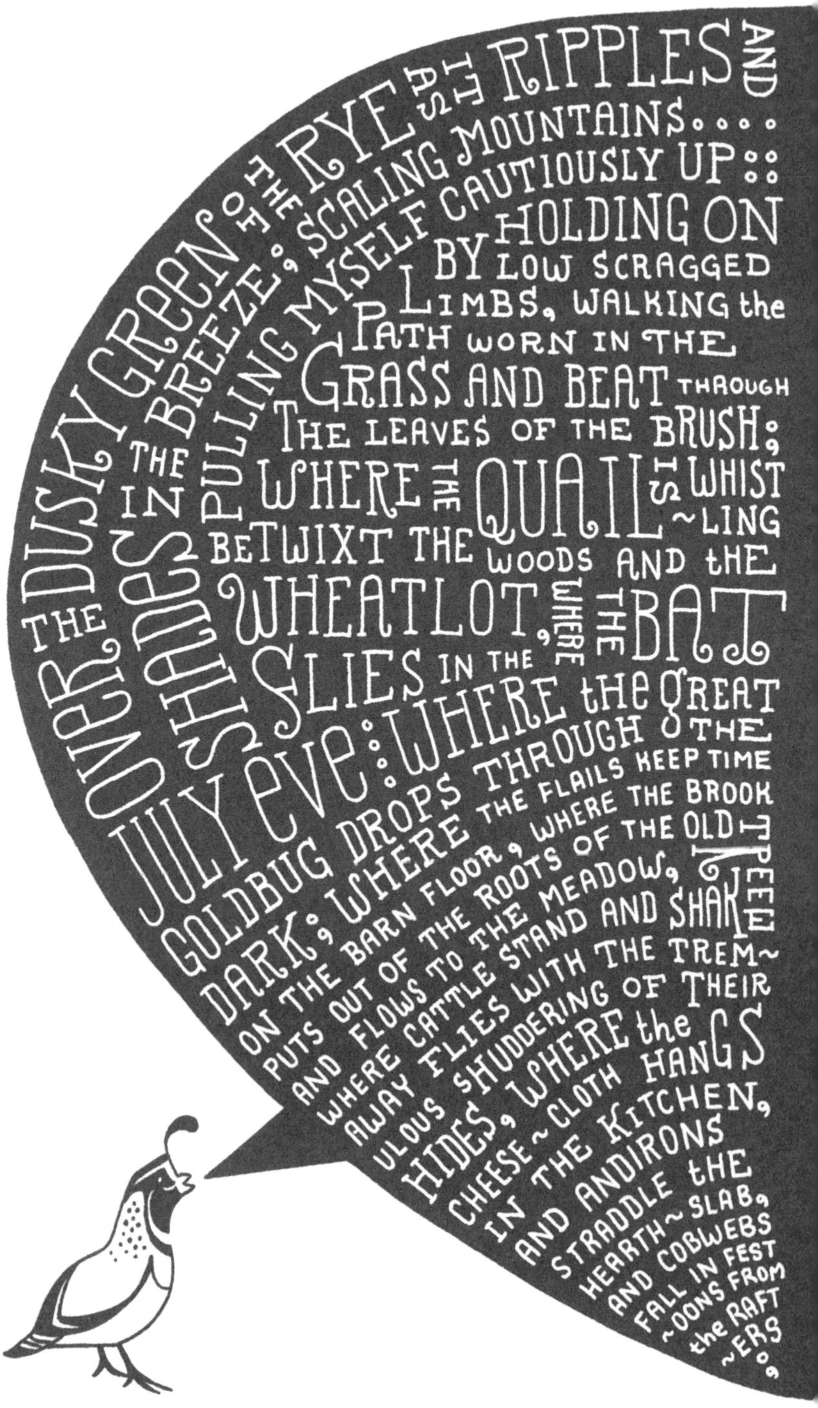
OVER THE DUSKY GREEN OF THE RYE AS IT RIPPLES AND
SHADES IN THE BREEZE, SCALING MOUNTAINS....
PULLING MYSELF CAUTIOUSLY UP::
BY HOLDING ON
LOW SCRAGGED
LIMBS, WALKING the
PATH WORN IN THE
GRASS AND BEAT THROUGH
THE LEAVES OF THE BRUSH,
WHERE THE QUAIL IS WHIST~LING
BETWIXT THE WOODS AND tHE
WHEATLOT, WHERE THE BAT
FLIES IN THE
JULY EVE: WHERE tHE GREAT
GOLDBUG DROPS THROUGH THE
DARK, WHERE THE FLAILS KEEP TIME
ON THE BARN FLOOR, WHERE THE BROOK
PUTS OUT OF THE ROOTS OF THE OLD TREE
AND FLOWS TO THE MEADOW,
WHERE CATTLE STAND AND SHAKE
AWAY FLIES WITH THE TREM~
ULOUS SHUDDERING OF THEIR
HIDES, WHERE the CHEESE~CLOTH HANGS
IN THE KITCHEN,
AND ANDIRONS STRADDLE tHE
HEARTH~SLAB,
AND COBWEBS
FALL IN FEST~OONS FROM
the RAFT~ERS,

WHERE THE PRESS IS WHIRLING ITS CYLINDERS; WHERE TRIPHAMMERS CRASH; WHEREVER THE HUMAN HEART BEATS WITH TERRIBLE THROES OUT OF HIS RIBS; WHERE THE PEAR-SHAPED BALLOON IS FLOATING ALOFT . . . . FLOATING IN IT MYSELF AND LOOKING COMPOSEDLY DOWN; WHERE THE LIFE-CAR IS DRAWN ON THE SLIPNOOSE . . . . WHERE THE HEAT HATCHES PALE-GREEN EGGS IN THE DENTED SAND, WHERE THE SHE-WHALE SWIMS WITH HER CALVES AND NEVER FORSAKES THEM, WHERE THE STEAMSHIP TRAILS HINDWAYS ITS LONG PENNANT OF SMOKE, WHERE THE GROUND-SHARK'S FIN CUTS LIKE A BLACK CHIP OUT OF THE WATER, WHERE THE HALF-BURNED BRIG IS RIDING ON UNKNOWN CURRENTS, WHERE SHELLS GROW TO HER SLIMY DECK, AND THE DEAD ARE CORRUPTING BELOW; WHERE THE STRIPED AND STARRED FLAG IS BORNE AT THE HEAD OF THE REGIMENTS

APPROACHING MANHATTAN,

UP BY THE LONG~STRETCHING ISLAND,
UNDER NIAGARA, THE CATARACT FALLING
LIKE A VEIL OVER MY COUNTENANCE, UPON
A DOOR~STEP:: UPON THE HORSE~BLOCK
OF HARDWOOD OUTSIDE, UPON THE RACE~
COURSE, OR ENJOYING PIC~NICS OR
JIGS OR A GOOD GAME OF BASE~
BALL, AT HE~FESTIVALS
WITH BLACKGUARD JIBES
AND IRONICAL LIC~
ENSE AND BULL~
DANCES AND
DRINKING
AND LAUGHTER,

AT THE CIDER~MILL, TASTING THE SWEET OF THE BROWN
SQUSH:: SUCKING THE JUICE THROUGH A STRAW, AT
APPLE~PEELINGS, WANTING KISSES FOR ALL THE RED
FRUIT I FIND, AT MUSTERS AND BEACH~PARTIES AND
FRIENDLY BEES AND HUSKINGS AND HOUSE~RAISINGS;
WHERE THE MOCKINGBIRD SOUNDS HIS DELICIOUS
GURGLES, AND CACKLES AND SCREAMS AND
WEEPS, WHERE THE HAY~RICK STANDS IN THE
BARNYARD, AND THE DRY~STALKS ARE SCATTERED, AND
THE BROOD COW WAIT IN THE HOVEL, WHERE THE BULL
ADVANCES TO DO HIS MASCULINE WORK, AND THE

STUD TO THE MARE, AND THE COCK IS TREADING THE HEN, WHERE THE HEIFERS BROWSE, AND THE GEESE NIP THEIR FOOD WITH SHORT JERKS;

WHERE THE SUNDOWN SHADOWS LENGTHEN OVER THE LIMITLESS AND LONESOME PRAIRIE, WHERE THE HERDS OF BUFFALO MAKE A CRAWLING SPREAD OF THE SQUARE MILES FAR AND NEAR,

WHERE THE HUMMINGBIRD SHIMMERS:: WHERE THE NECK OF THE LONGLIVED SWAN IS CURVING AND WINDING; WHERE THE LAUGHING-GULL SCOOTS BY THE SLAPPY SHORE AND LAUGHS HER NEAR-HUMAN LAUGH; WHERE BEEHIVES RANGE ON A GRAY BENCH IN THE GARDEN HALF-HID BY THE HIGH WEEDS; WHERE THE BAND-NECKED PARTRIDGES ROOST IN A RING ON THE GROUND WITH THEIR HEADS OUT;

WHERE BURIAL COACHES ENTER THE ARCHED GATES OF A CEMETERY, WHERE WINTER WOLVES BARK AMID WASTES OF SNOW AND ICICLED TREES, WHERE THE YELLOW-CROWNED HERON COMES TO THE EDGE OF THE MARSH AT NIGHT AND FEEDS UPON SMALL CRABS; WHERE THE SPLASH OF SWIMMERS AND DIVERS COOLS THE WARM NOON;

WHERE THE KATYDID WORKS HER CHROMATIC REED ON THE WALNUT-TREE OVER THE WELL;

Through patches of citrons and cucumbers with silver~wired leaves, through the salt~lick or orange glade .... or under conical firs; through the gymnasium .... through the curtained saloon .... through the office or public hall; pleased with the native and pleased with the foreign .... pleased with the new and old, pleased with the women the homely as well as the handsome, pleased with the quakeress as she puts off her bonnet and talks melo-dio-us-ly, pleased with the primitive tunes of the choir of the white~wash'd church; pleased with the earnest words of the sweating Methodist preacher, or any preacher, looking in at the shop~windows in Broad~way the whole fore~noon .... pressing the flesh of my nose to the thick plate~glass, wandering the same afternoon with my face turned up to the clouds;

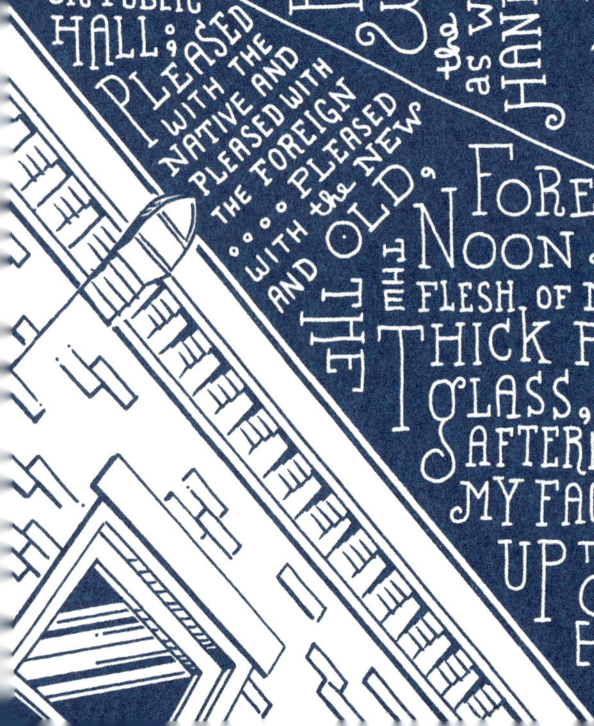

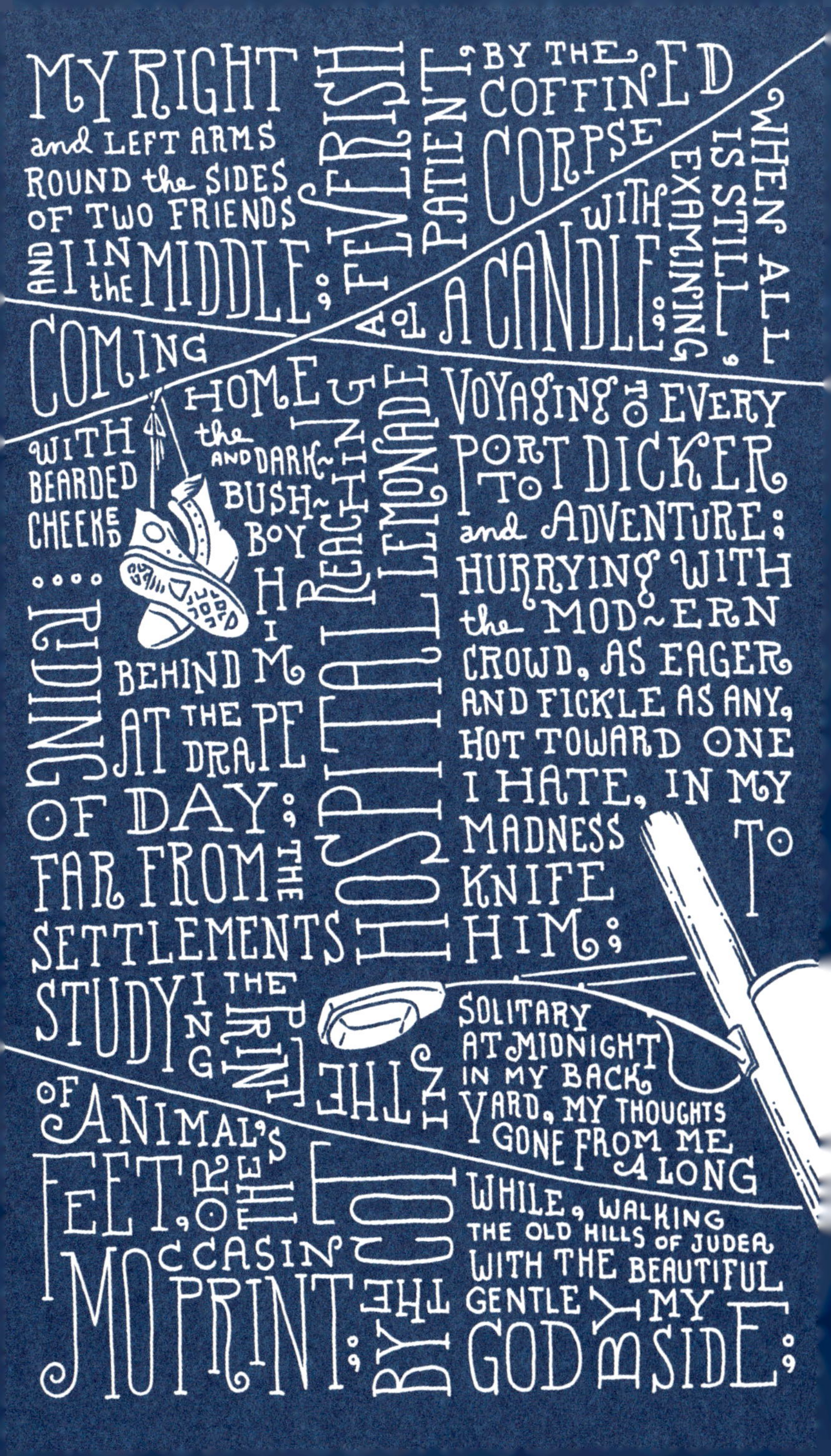
MY RIGHT and LEFT ARMS ROUND the SIDES OF TWO FRIENDS AND I IN the MIDDLE;
COMING HOME WITH the BEARDED AND DARK~CHEEKED BUSH~BOY ... RIDING BEHIND HIM AT THE DRAPE OF DAY;
FAR FROM THE SETTLEMENTS STUDYING THE PRINT OF ANIMAL'S FEET, OR THE MOCCASIN PRINT;
BY THE COT IN THE HOSPITAL REACHING LEMONADE TO A FEVERISH PATIENT,
BY THE COFFINED CORPSE WHEN ALL IS STILL, EXAMINING WITH A CANDLE;
VOYAGING TO EVERY PORT TO DICKER and ADVENTURE;
HURRYING WITH the MOD~ERN CROWD, AS EAGER AND FICKLE AS ANY,
HOT TOWARD ONE I HATE, IN MY MADNESS TO KNIFE HIM;
SOLITARY AT MIDNIGHT IN MY BACK YARD, MY THOUGHTS GONE FROM ME A LONG WHILE,
WALKING THE OLD HILLS OF JUDEA WITH THE BEAUTIFUL GENTLE GOD BY MY SIDE;

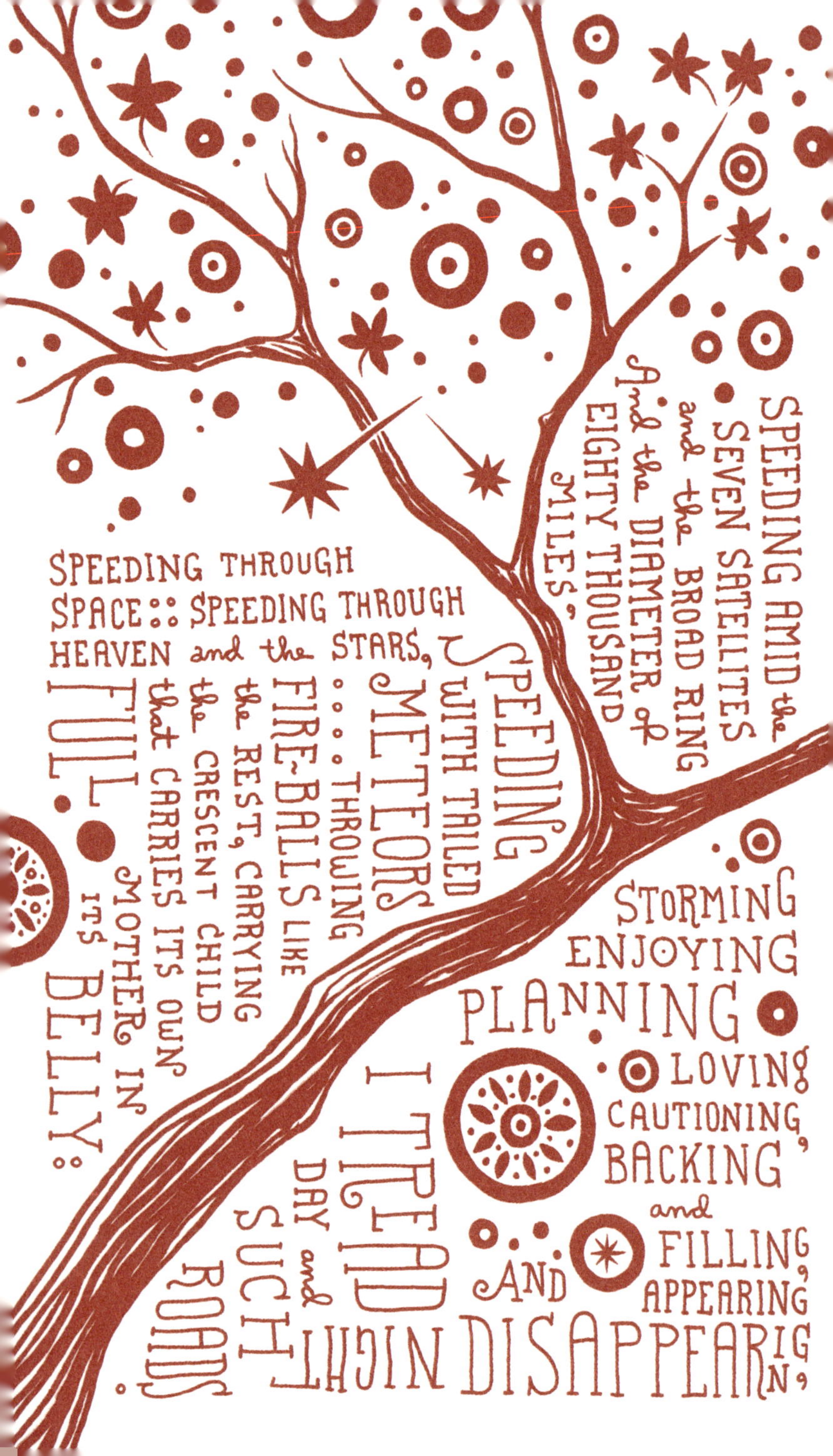
SPEEDING THROUGH SPACE :: SPEEDING THROUGH HEAVEN and the STARS,
SPEEDING AMID the SEVEN SATELLITES and the BROAD RING And the DIAMETER of EIGHTY THOUSAND MILES,
SPEEDING WITH TAILED METEORS ::: THROWING FIRE-BALLS LIKE the REST, CARRYING the CRESCENT CHILD that CARRIES ITS OWN FULL MOTHER IN ITS BELLY:
STORMING ENJOYING PLANNING LOVING CAUTIONING, BACKING and FILLING, APPEARING AND DISAPPEARING,
I TREAD DAY and NIGHT SUCH ROADS.

I

VISIT
THE ORCHARDS
OF GOD and LOOK
at the SPHERIC
PRODUCT, and
LOOK at QUIN-
TILLIONS RIPENED,
and LOOK at
QUINTILLIONS
GREEN.

I FLY the
FLIGHT of
the FLUID and
SWALLOWING SOUL,
MY COURSE RUNS
BELOW the SOUNDINGS
of PLUMMETS

I HELP MYSELF
TO MATERIAL and
IMMATERIAL, NO
GUARD CAN SHUT ME
OFF, NO LAW CAN
PREVENT ME.

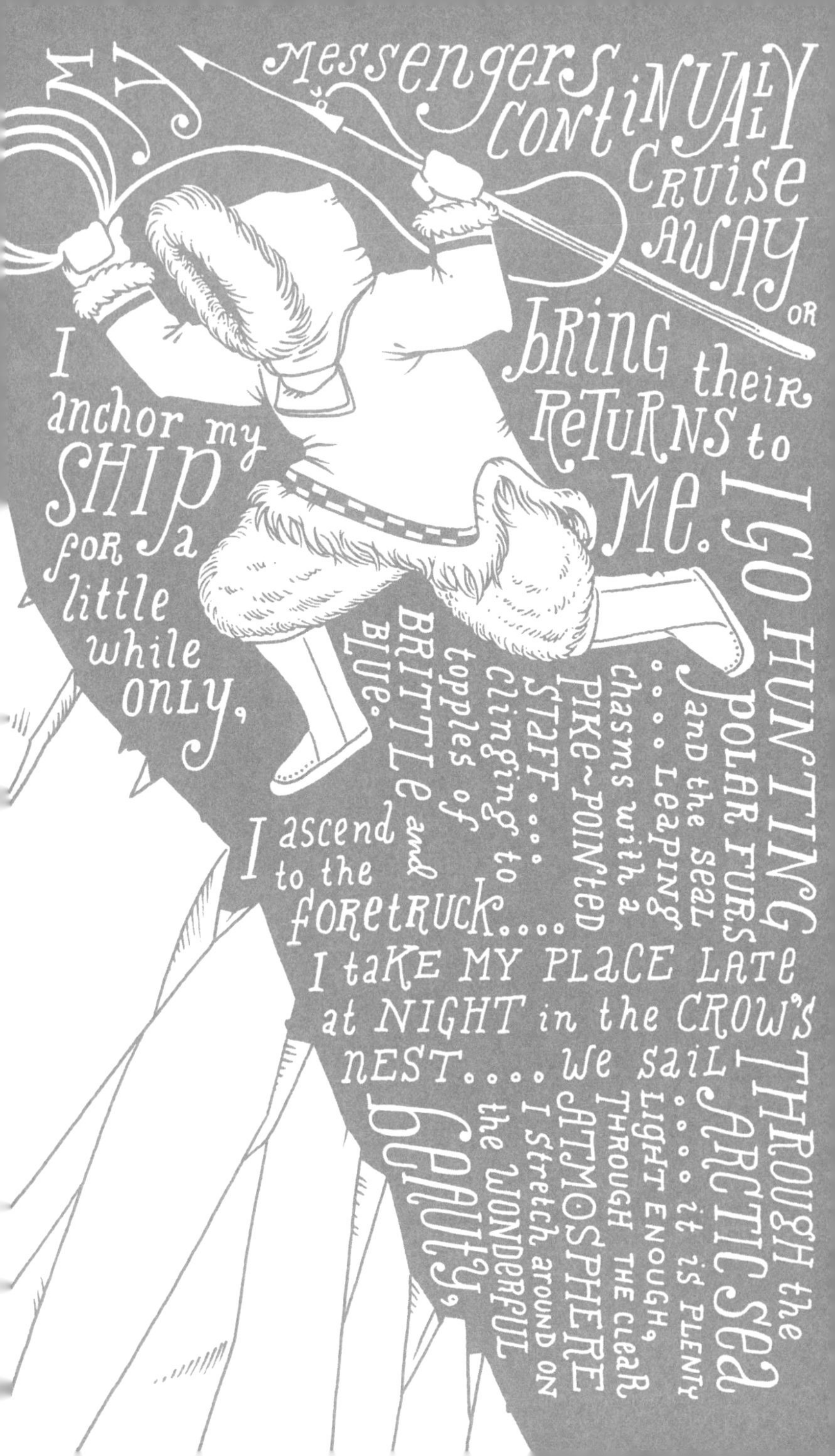

I anchor my SHIP for a little while ONLY,
MY Messengers CONTINUALLY CRUISE AWAY OR bRING their RETURNS to ME.
I GO HUNTING POLAR FURS and the SEAL .... LEAPING chasms with a PIKE-POINTED STAFF.... clinging to topples of BRITTLE and BLUE.
I ascend to the foRETRUCK....
I taKE MY PLACE LATE at NIGHT in the CROW'S NEST.... We saiL THROUGH the ARCTIC SEA.... it is PLENTY LIGHT ENOUGH, THROUGH THE CLEAR ATMOSPHERE I stretch around ON the WONDERFUL bEAUTY,

the ENORMOUS masses of ice PASS me and I PASS THEM.... the scenery is plain in all directions, The WHITE~TOPPED MOUNTAINS POINT UP in the DISTANCE.... i FLING OUT my FANCIES TOWARD them; we are about approaching some great BATTLEFIELD in which we are soon to be ENGAGED, we pass the colossal OUTPOSTS OF THE ENCAMPMENT: we PASS with still feet AND CAUTION: or we are entering by the SUBURBS some vast and RUINED CITY .... the BLOCKS and fallen ARCHITECTURE more than all the living cities of THE GLOBE.

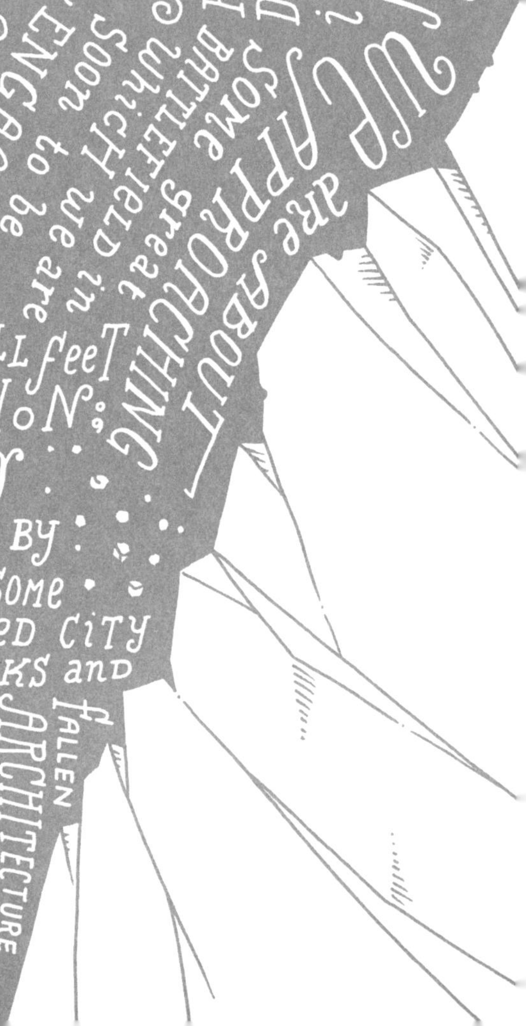

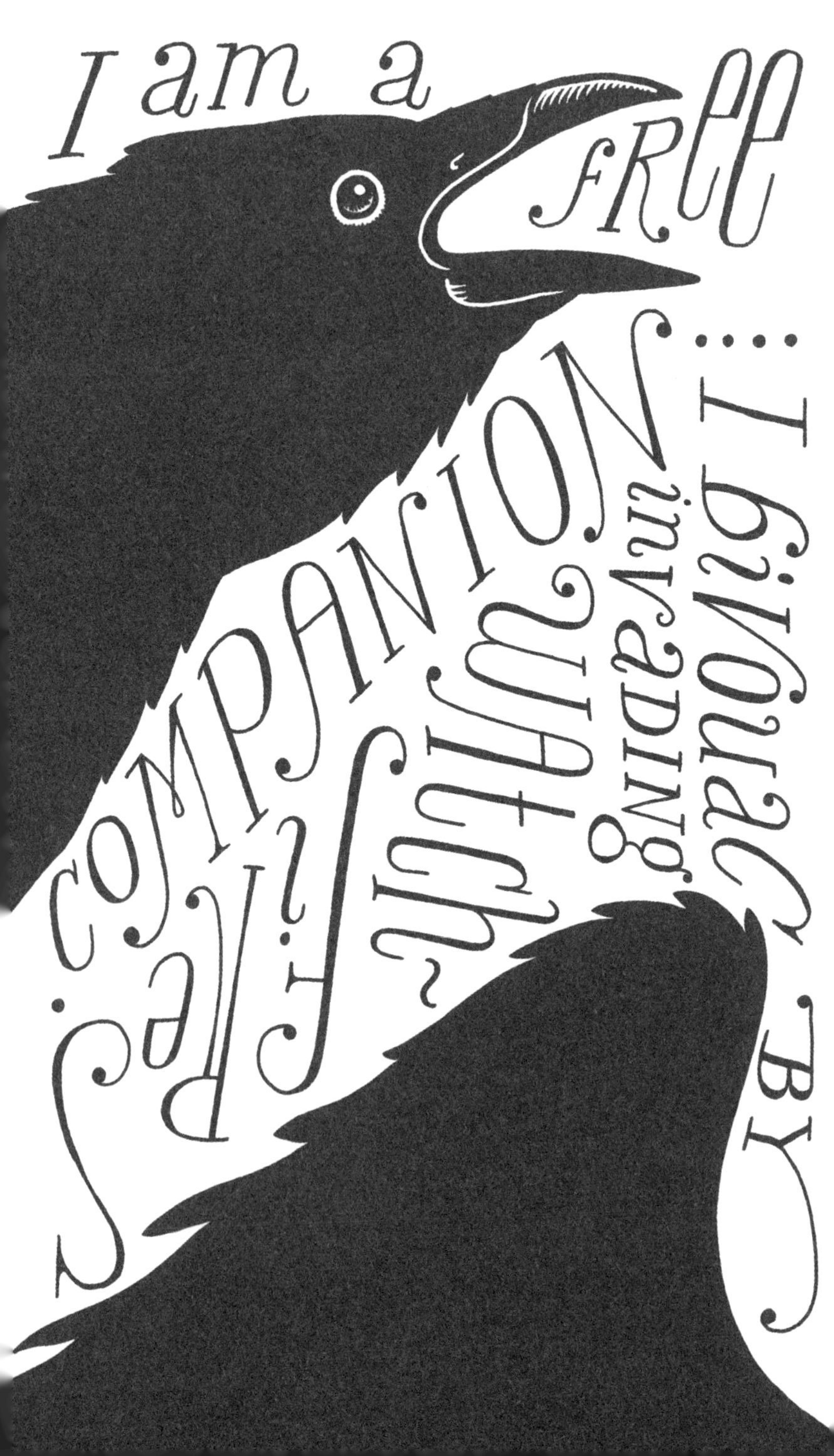

I am a free
companion…
I bivouac
by
invading
watchfires

I turn the bridegroom
out of bed and stay with
the bride myself,
and tighten
her all night to my thighs
and lips. My
voice is the wife's
voice, the screech by the
rail of the stairs,
They fetch my man's
body up
dripping
and
drowned

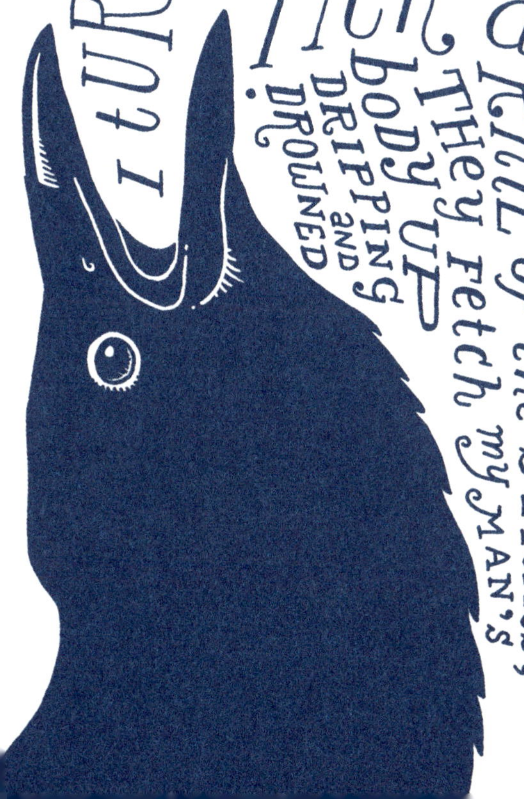

I understand the large hearts of heroes,
the courage of present times and all times,
how the skipper saw the crowded and rudderless wreck of the steamship, and death chasing it up and down the storm,
how he knuckled tight and gave not back one inch, and was faithful of days and faithful of nights,
and chalk'd in large letters on a board, be of good cheer, we will not desert you;
how he saved the drifting company at last,

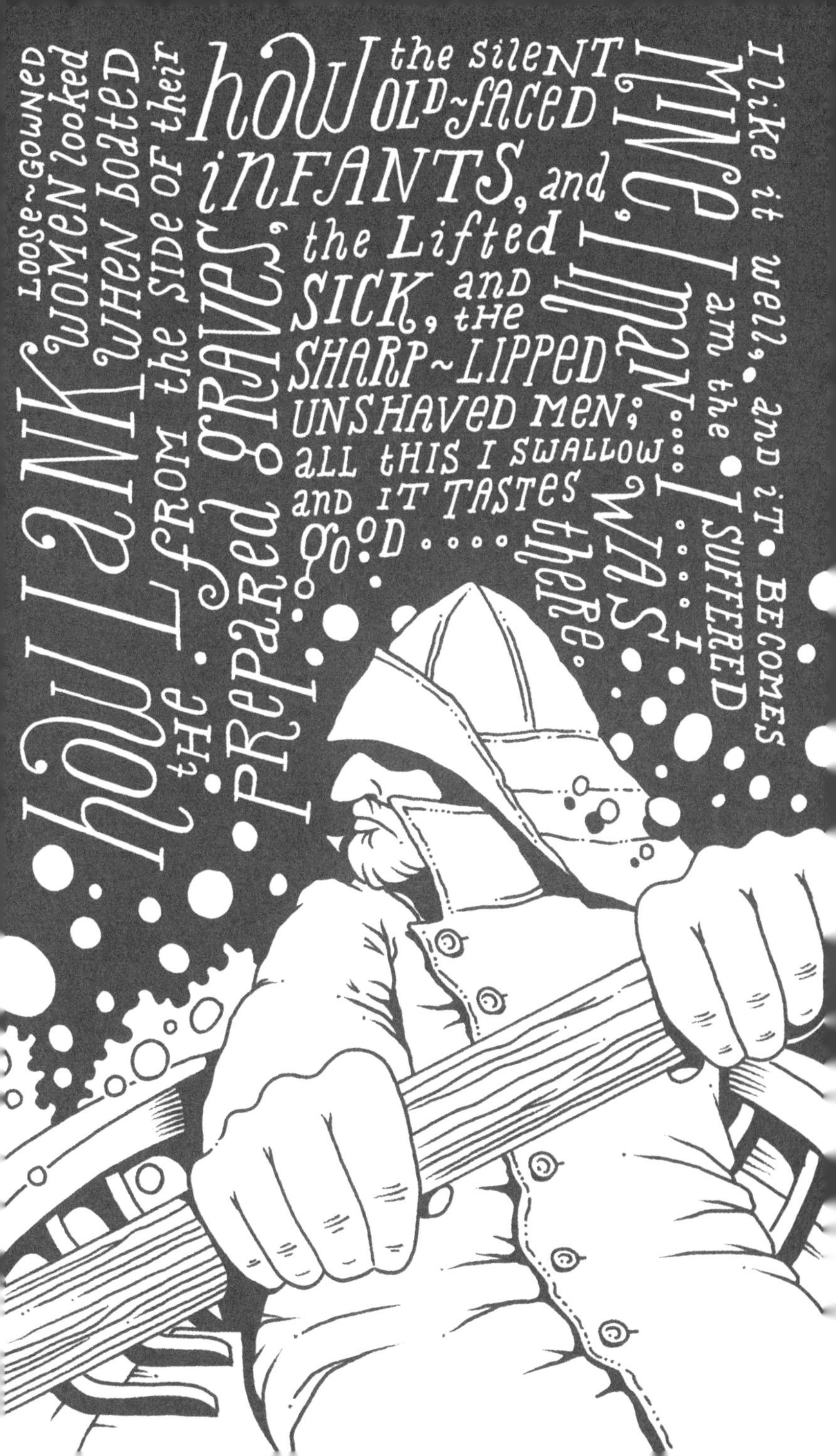
how lank loose-gowned women looked when boated from the side of their prepared graves,
how the silent old-faced infants, and the lifted sick, and the sharp-lipped unshaved men;
all this I swallow and it tastes good....
I like it well, and it becomes mine, I am the man.... I suffered.... I was there.

the DiSdain and calmness of martyrs, the mother condemned for a witch and burnt with dry wood, and her children gazing on, the hounded slave that flags in the race and leans by the fence, blowing and covered with sweat, the twinges that sting like needles his legs and neck, the murderous buckshot and the bullets, all these I feel or am.

I am the hounded slave . . . I wince at the bite of the dogs, hell and despair are upon me, . . . crack and again crack the marksmen,

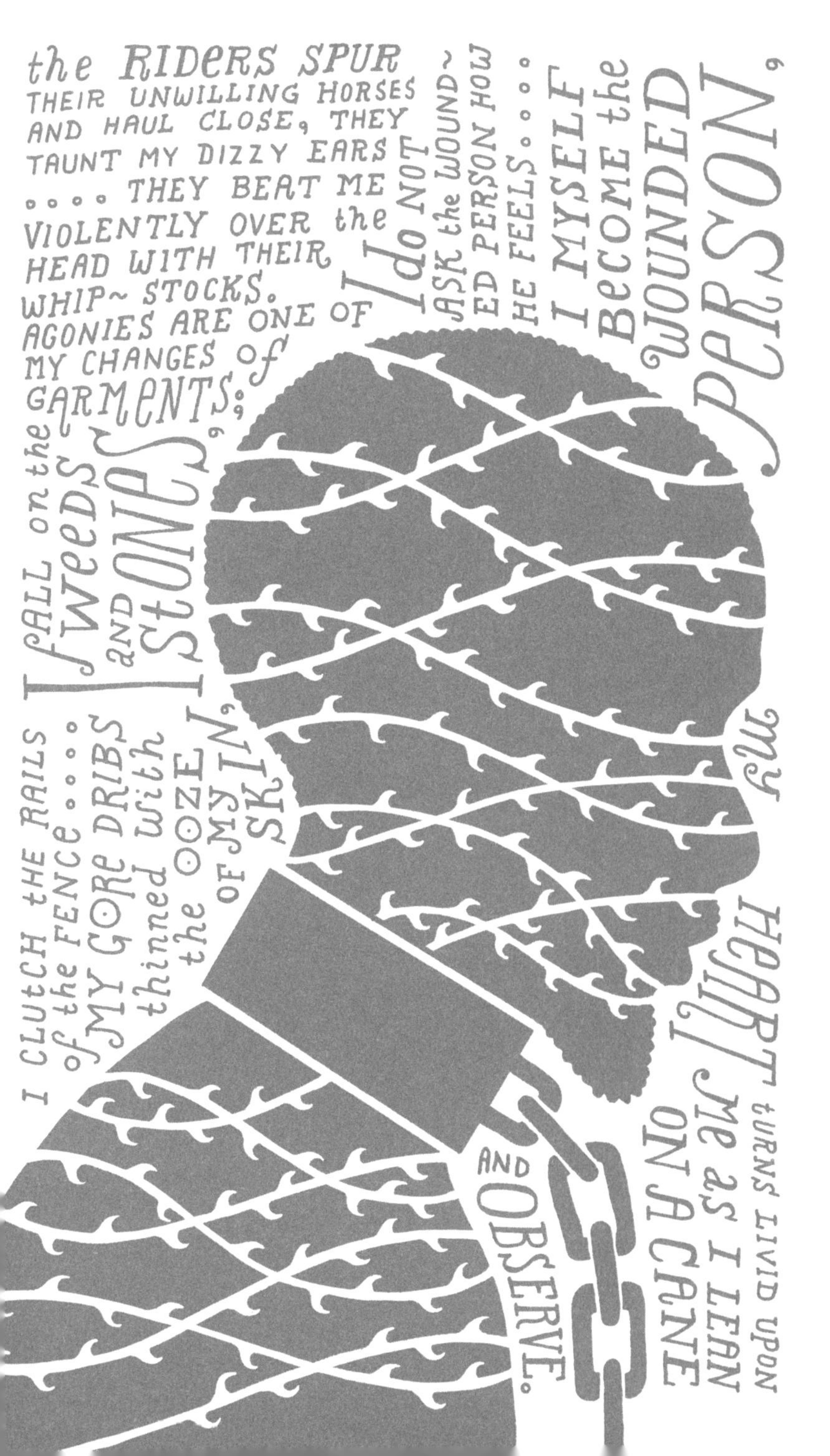
the RIDERS SPUR
THEIR UNWILLING HORSES
AND HAUL CLOSE, THEY
TAUNT MY DIZZY EARS
.... THEY BEAT ME
VIOLENTLY OVER the
HEAD WITH THEIR
WHIP~ STOCKS.
AGONIES ARE ONE OF
MY CHANGES of
GARMENTS;
I FALL on the
WEEDS
AND
STONES,
I CLUTCH tHE RAILS
of the FENCE....
MY GORE DRIBS
thinned with
the OOZE
OF MY
SKIN,
I do NOT
ASK the WOUND~
ED PERSON HOW
HE FEELS....
I MYSELF
Become the
WOUNDED
PERSON,
my
HEART turns LIVID UPON
Me as I LEAN
ON A CANE
AND
OBSERVE.

I am the MASHED FIREMAN with breastbone broken. . . . tumbling walls buried me in their debris,
heat and smoke I inspired. . . . I heard the yelling shouts of my comrades,
I heard the distant click of their picks and shovels;
They have cleared the beams away. . . . they tenderly lift me forth.
I lie in the NIGHT air my RED SHIRT. . . . the pervading hush is for my sake,
Painless after all I lie, exhausted but not so unhappy,
White and beautiful are the faces around me. . . . the heads are bared of their fire-caps,
The kneeling crowd fades with the light of the torches.

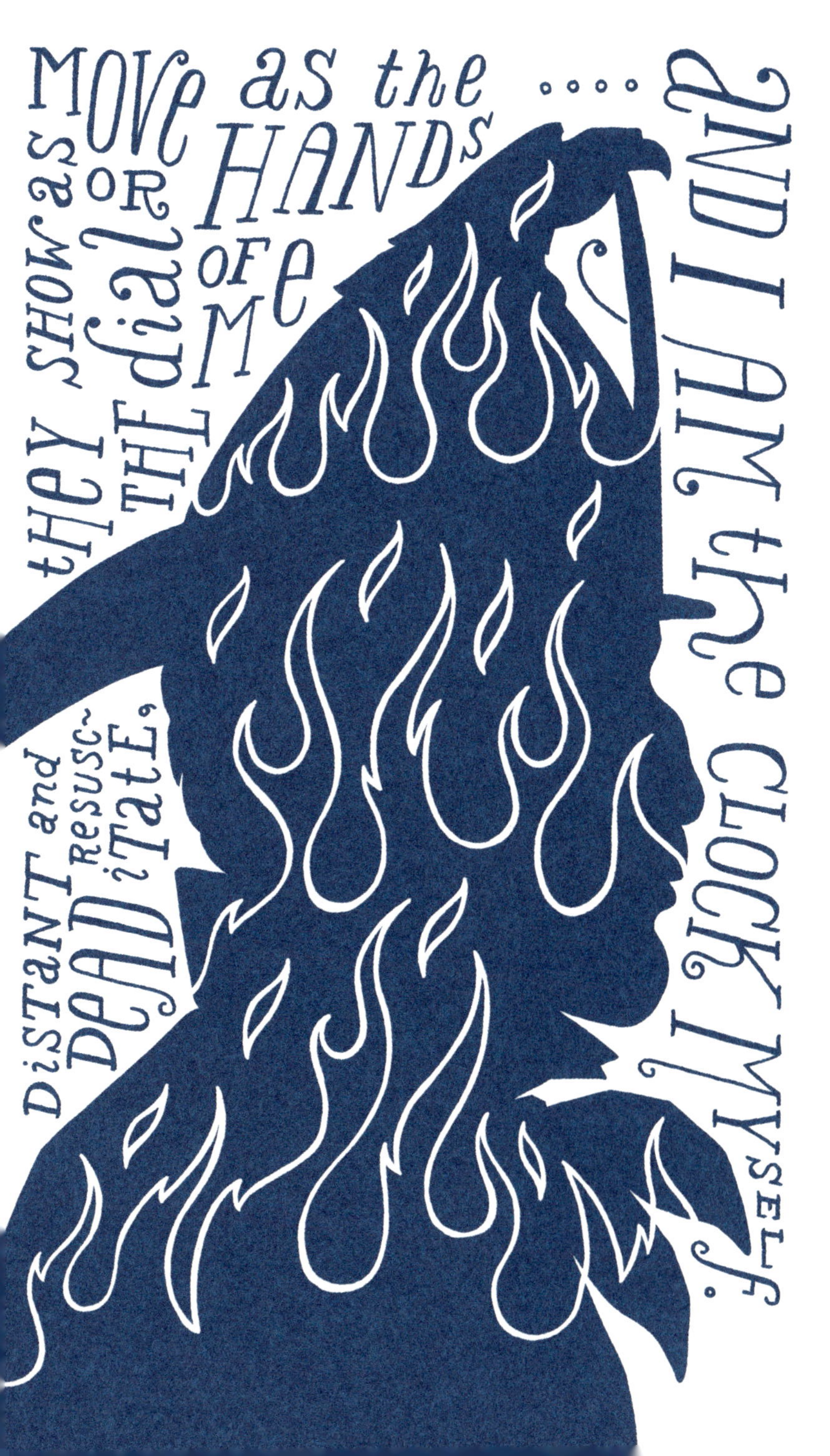
Distant and dead resusc-itate,
they show as the dial or move as the hands of me
....and I am the clock myself.

I am an old artillerist, and tell of some fort's bombardment, and am there again.

again the reveille of drummers.... again the attacking cannon and mortars and howitzers,

Again the attacked send their cannon responsive:

I take part, I see and hear the whole, the cries and curses and roar.... the plaudits for well aimed shots, the ambulanza slowly passing trailing its red drip, workmen searching after damages and to make indispensable repairs, the fall of grenades through the rent roof.... the fan~shaped explosion,

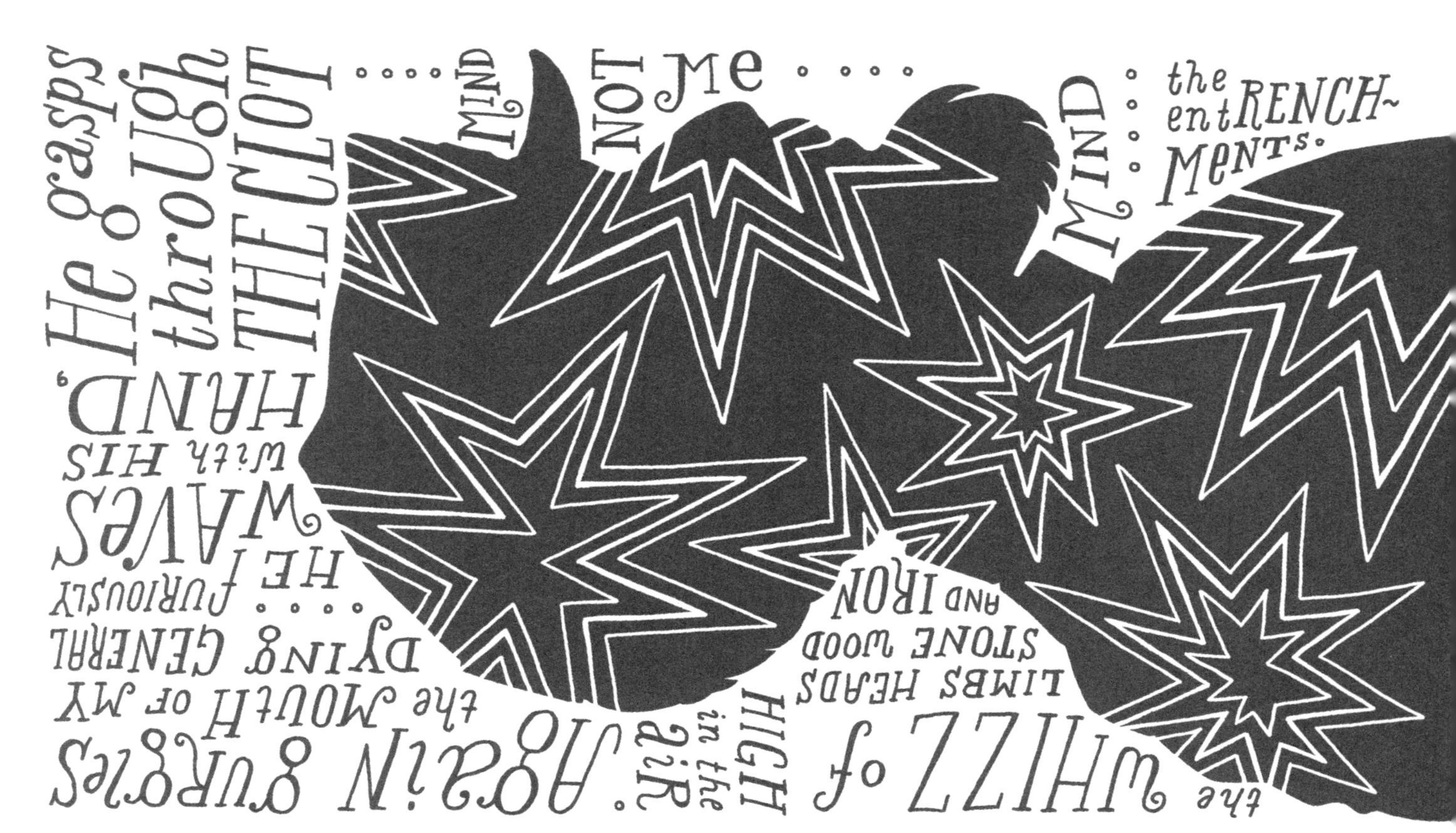
the WHIZZ of LIMBS HEADS STONE WOOD AND IRON
HIGH in the air.
Again gurgles the MOUTH OF MY DYING GENERAL....
HE furiously WAVES with HIS HAND,
He gasps through THE CLOT....
MIND
NOT ME....
MIND....
the entRENCH-MENTS.

I TELL NOT the FALL of

ALAMO . . . . NOT ONE ESCAPED to TELL the FALL of ALAMO, the HUNDRED and FIFTY are ARE DUMB YET at ALAMO. HEAR NOW the TALE OF A JET BLACK SUNRISE,

HEAR OF THE MURDER IN COLD BLOOD OF FOUR HUNDRED AND TWELVE YOUNG MEN. RETREATING THEY HAD FORMED IN A HOLLOW SQUARE WITH THEIR BAGGAGE FOR BREASTWORKS, NINE HUNDRED LIVES OUT OF THE SURROUNDING ENEMY'S NINE TIMES THEIR NUMBER WAS THE PRICE THEY TOOK IN ADVANCE, THEIR COLONEL WAS WOUNDED and THEIR AMMUNITION GONE, THEY TREATED FOR AN HONORABLE CAPITULATION, RECEIVED WRITING AND SEAL, GAVE UP THEIR ARMS AND MARCHED BACK PRISONERS OF WAR. THEY WERE THE GLORY OF THE RACE OF RANGERS, MATCHLESS WITH A HORSE, A RIFLE, A SONG, A SUPPER, OR A COURTSHIP, LARGE, TURBULENT, BRAVE, HANDSOME, GENEROUS, PROUD AND AFFECTIONATE, BEARDED, SUNBURNT, DRESSED IN the FREE COSTUME OF HUNTERS, NOT A SINGLE ONE OVER THIRTY YEARS of AGE.

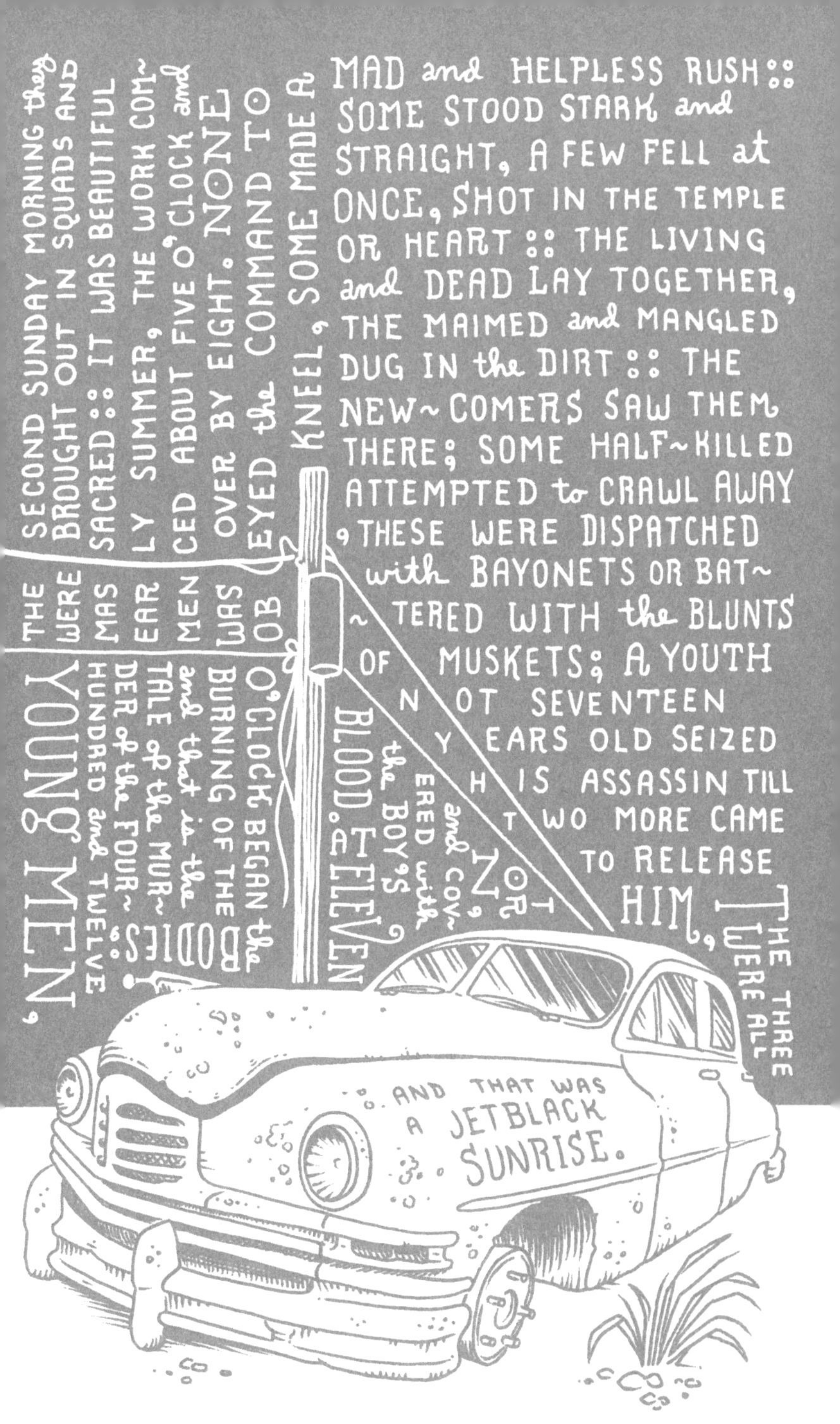
THE SECOND SUNDAY MORNING they WERE BROUGHT OUT IN SQUADS AND MASSACRED :: IT WAS BEAUTIFUL EARLY SUMMER, THE WORK COMMENCED ABOUT FIVE O'CLOCK and WAS OVER BY EIGHT. NONE OBEYED the COMMAND TO KNEEL, SOME MADE A MAD and HELPLESS RUSH :: SOME STOOD STARK and STRAIGHT, A FEW FELL at ONCE, SHOT IN THE TEMPLE OR HEART :: THE LIVING and DEAD LAY TOGETHER, THE MAIMED and MANGLED DUG IN the DIRT :: THE NEW~COMERS SAW THEM THERE; SOME HALF~KILLED ATTEMPTED to CRAWL AWAY, THESE WERE DISPATCHED with BAYONETS OR BAT~TERED WITH the BLUNTS OF MUSKETS; A YOUTH NOT SEVENTEEN YEARS OLD SEIZED HIS ASSASSIN TILL TWO MORE CAME TO RELEASE HIM. THE THREE WERE ALL TORN, and COVERED with the BOY'S BLOOD. AT ELEVEN O'CLOCK BEGAN the BURNING OF THE BODIES: and that is the TALE of the MURDER of the FOUR HUNDRED and TWELVE YOUNG MEN.
AND THAT WAS A JETBLACK SUNRISE.

Did you read in the seabooks of the OLDFASHIONED fight?

Did you Learn wHO WON BY The Light of the moon and stars?

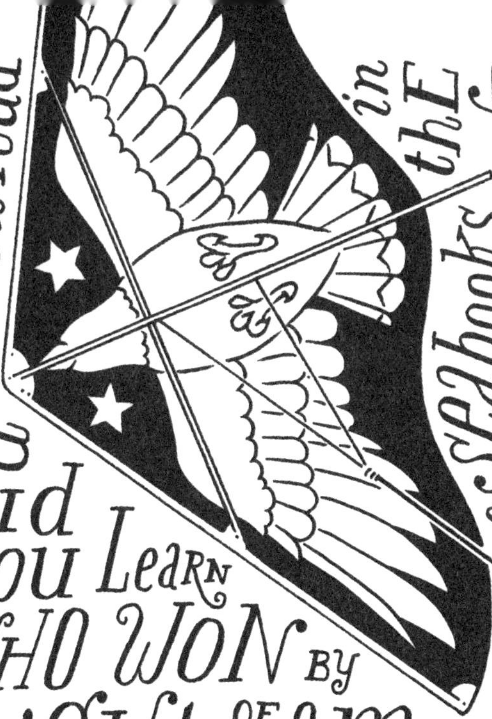

Our foe was no skulk in his ship, i tell you, his was the ENGLISH PLUCK, and there is no tougher or truer, and never was, and never will be; along the Lowered eve he came, horribly Raking us. We closed with him... the yards entangled... the CANNON touched, MY CAPTAIN Lashed fast with his OWN HANDS.

We had received some eighteen~pound shots under the water, on our lower~gun~deck two large pieces had burst at the first fire, killing all around and blowing up over~head.

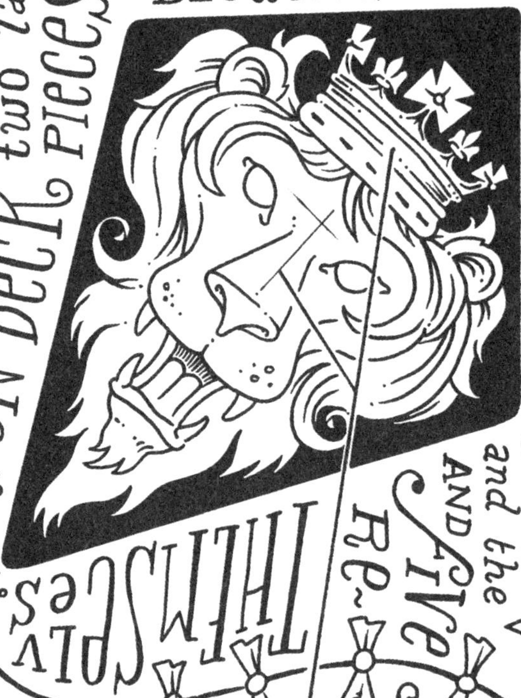

Ten o'clock at night, and the full moon shining, and the leaks on the gain, and five feet of water re~ported, the master~at~arms loosing the pris'oners confined in the after hold to give them a chance for themselves.

the transit to and FROM the MAGAZINE was now stopped by the SENTINELS, they saw so many strange faces they DID NOT KNOW WHOM TO TRUST.

OUR FRIGATE was AFIRE.... the other ASKED if WE demanded QUARTERS? OUR COLORS STRUCK WERE AND the fighting DONE?

I laughed content when i heard the voice of my little captain, we have NOT STRUCK, HE COMPOSEDLY CRIED, WE have JUST BEGUN OUR PART OF THE FIGHTING. ONLY three GUNS WERE in USE, ONE WAS DIRECTED HIMSELF against the ENEMY'S MAINMAST,

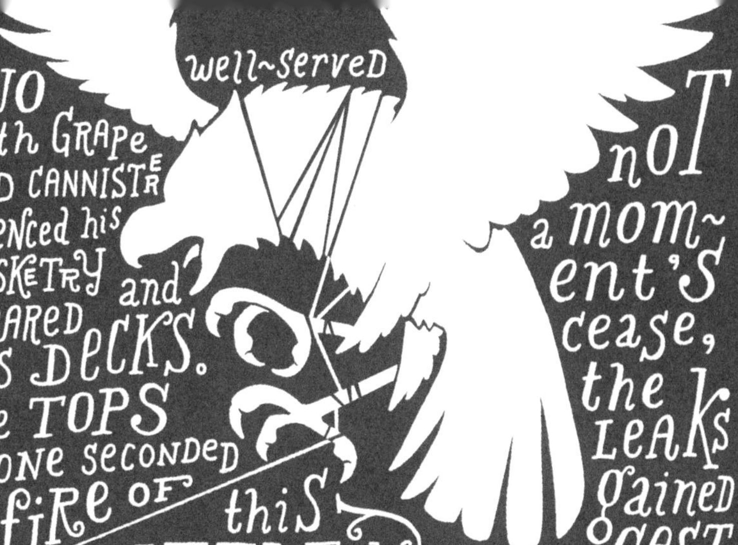

two with grape and cannistre silenced his musketry and cleared his decks. the tops alone seconded the fire of this little battery, especially the maintop; they all held out bravely during the whole of the action.

not a moment's cease, the leaks gained fast on the pumps. the fire eat toward the powder-magazine, one of the pumps was shot away. . . It was generally thought we were sinking. Serene stood the little captain, He was not hurried. . . His voice 'twas neither high nor low, His eyes gave more light to us than our battle-lanterns. toward twelve at night, there in the beams of the moon they surrendered to us.

Stretched and still lay the midnight, two great hulls motionless on the breast of the darkness, our vessel riddled and slowly sinking.... preparations to pass to the one we had conquered, the Captain on the quarter deck coldly giving his orders through a countenance white as a sheet, near by the corpse of the child that served in the cabin, the dead face of an old salt with long white hair and carefully curled whiskers, the flames spite of all that could be done flickering aloft and below, the husky voices of the two or three officers yet fit for duty.

FORM-LESS STACKS OF BODIES AND BODIES BY THEMSELVES :: DABS OF FLESH UPON THE MASTS AND SPARS, THE CUT OF CORDAGE AND DANGLE OF RIGGING.... THE SLIGHT SHOCK OF THE SOOTHE OF WAVES, BLACK AND IMPASSIVE GUNS, AND LITTER OF POWDER-PARCELS, AND THE STRONG SCENT, DELICATE SNIFFS OF THE SEA BREEZE :: SMELLS OF SEDGY GRASS AND FIELDS BY THE SHORE.... DEATH-MESSAGES GIVEN IN CHARGE TO SURVIVORS, THE HISS OF THE SURGEON'S KNIFE AND THE GNAWING TEETH OF HIS SAW, THE WHEEZE, THE CLUCK, THE SWASH OF FALLING BLOOD.... THE SHORT WILD SCREAM, THE LONG DULL TAPERING GROAN, THESE SO.... THESE IRRETRIEVABLE.

O CHRIST! MY FIT IS MASTERING ME!

& WHAT the REBEL SAID GAILY ADJUSTING His throat to the ROPE~NOOSE,

& What the SAVAGE at the Stump, his EYe~SocKets empty, his MOUTH SPIRTING WHOOPS and DEFIANCE,

WHAT Stills the TRAVELER come to the VAULT at MOUNT VERNON,

What SOBERS the BROOKLYN BOY as HE LOOKS DOWN the SHORES OF the WALLABOUT AND REMEMBERS the PRISON SHIPS,

WHAT BURNT the GUMS OF the REDCOAT at SARATOGA WHEN HE SURRENDERED HIS BRIGADES,

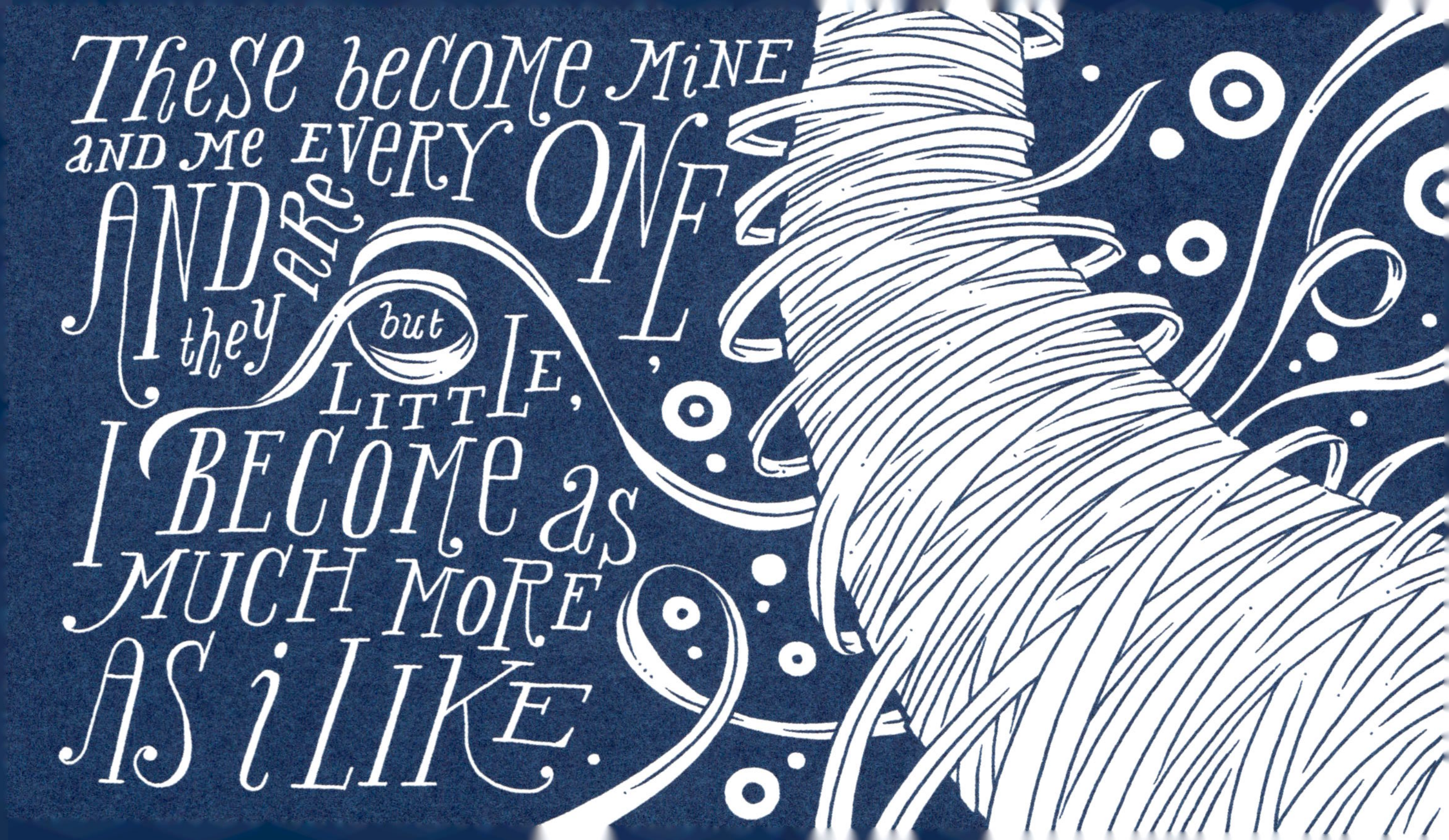
These become mine
and me every one,
And they are but little,
I become as
much more
as i like.

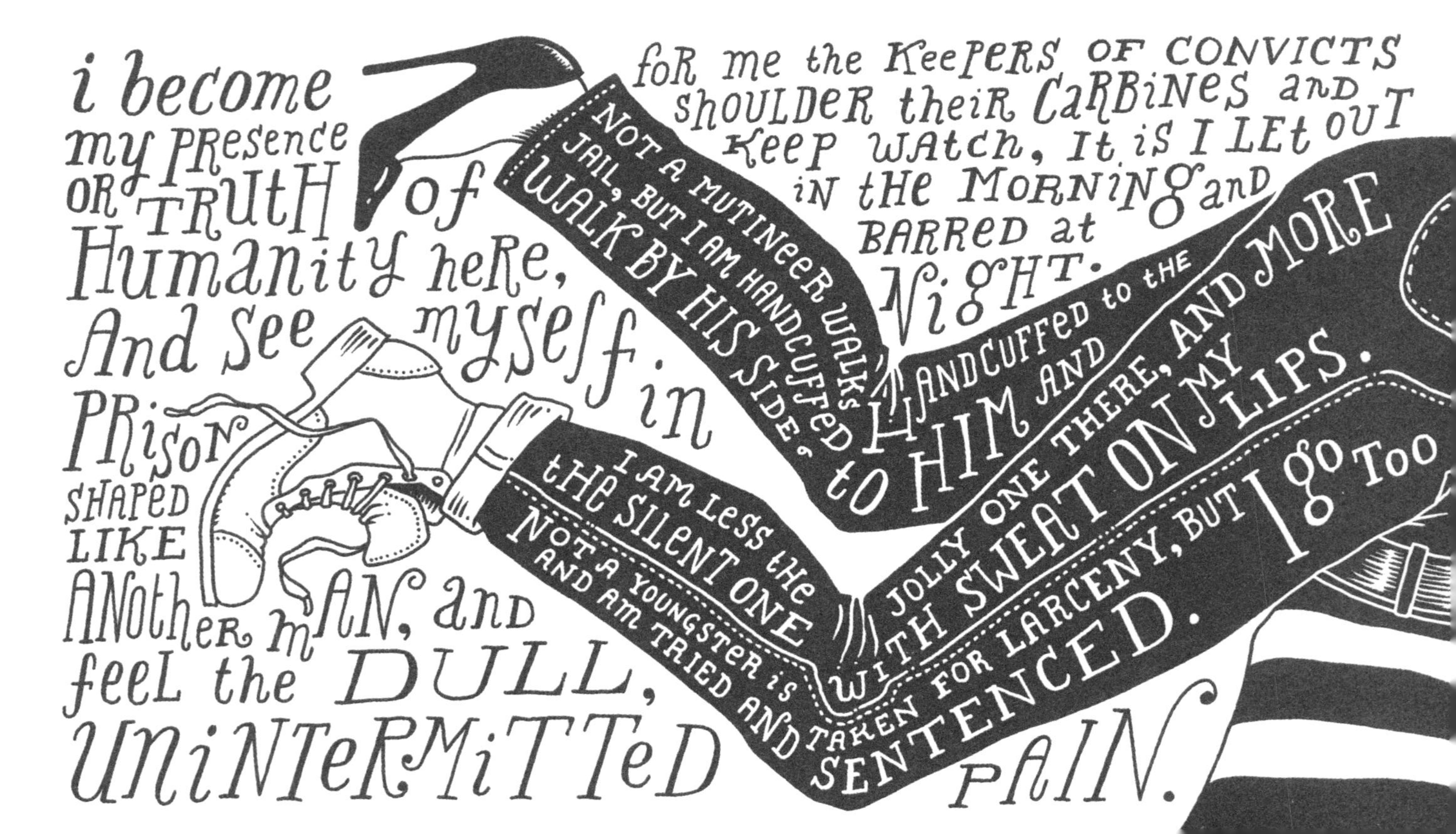
i become my presence or truth of humanity here, and see myself in prison shaped like another man, and feel the dull, unintermitted pain.
for me the keepers of convicts shoulder their carbines and keep watch, it is I let out in the morning and barred at night.
Not a mutineer walks handcuffed to the jail, but I am handcuffed to him and walk by his side,
I am less the jolly one there, and more the silent one with sweat on my lips.
Not a youngster is taken for larceny, but I go too and am tried and sentenced.

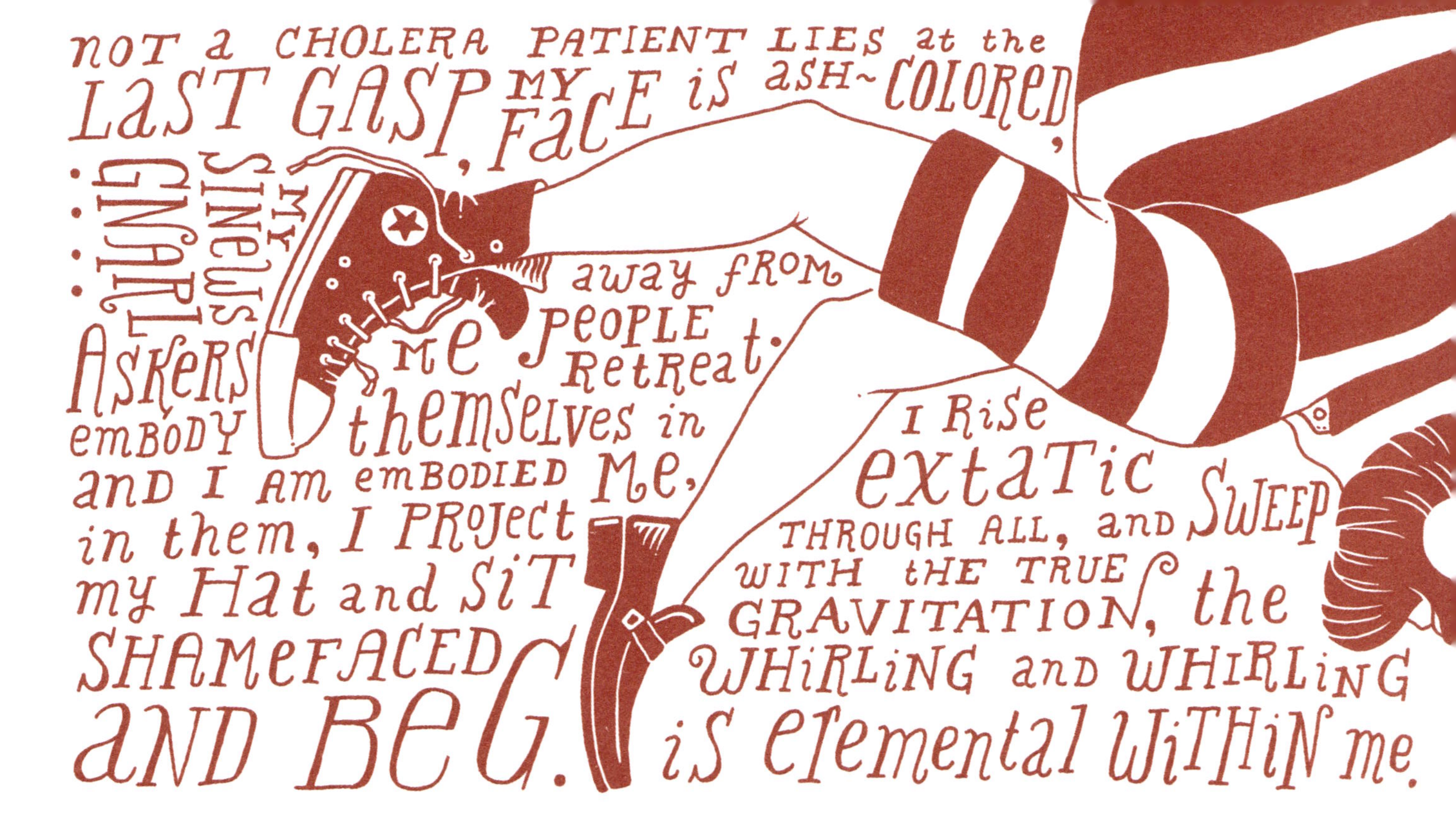
not a CHOLERA PATIENT LIES at the
LAST GASP, MY FACE is ash~COLORED,
MY SINEWS GNARL...
ASKERS embody
me
away from PEOPLE Retreat.
themselves in
and I am embodied me,
in them, I project
my Hat and sit
SHAMEFACED
AND BEG.
I Rise extatic
THROUGH ALL, and SWEEP
WITH tHE TRUE
GRAVITATION, the
WHIRLING and WHIRLING
is elemental WiTHiN me.

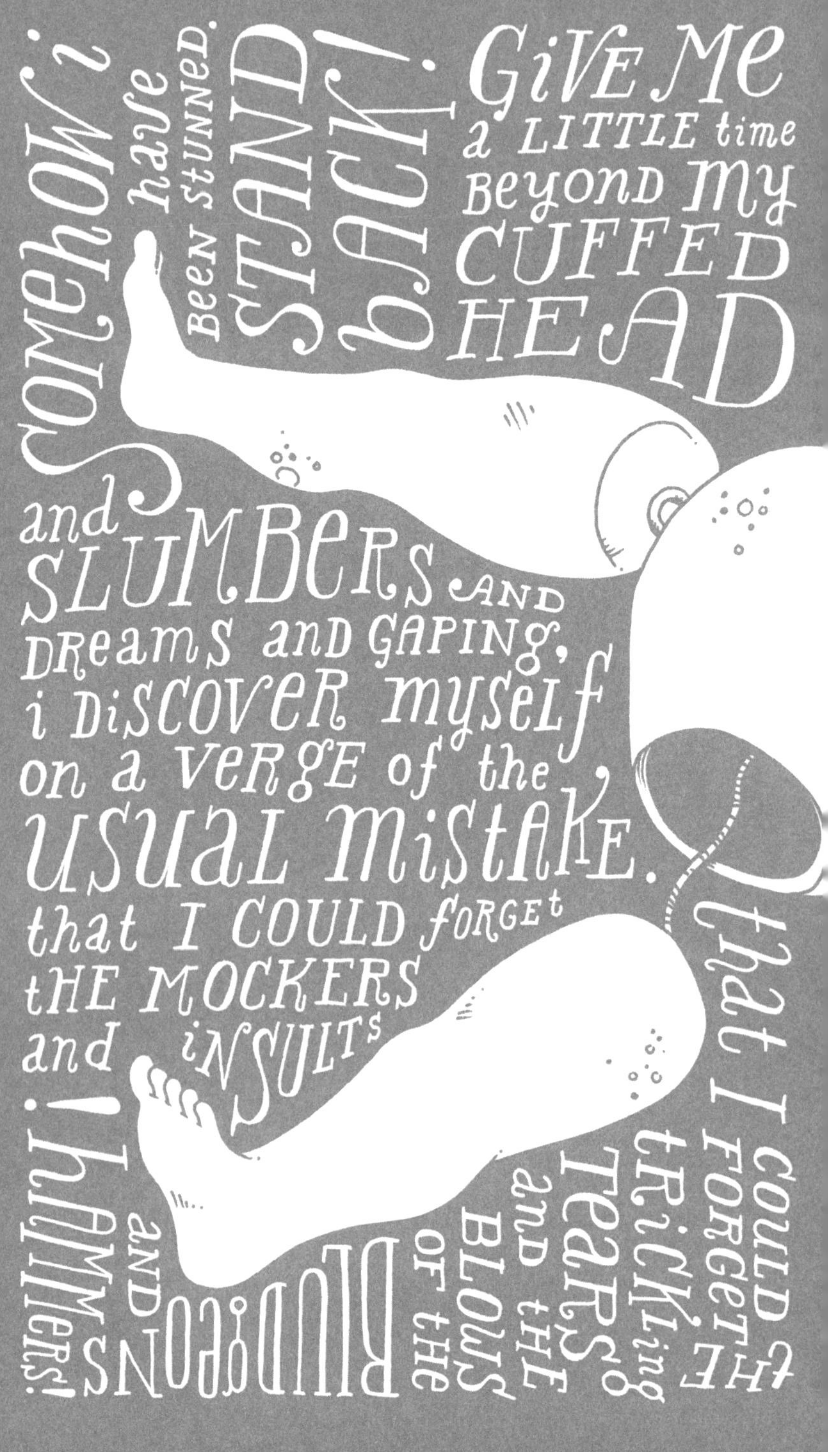

Somehow i have been stunned. Stand back!
Give me a little time beyond my cuffed head
and slumbers and dreams and gaping,
i discover myself on a verge of the usual mistake.
that I could forget the mockers and insults and
that I could forget the trickling tears and the blows of the bludgeons and hammers!

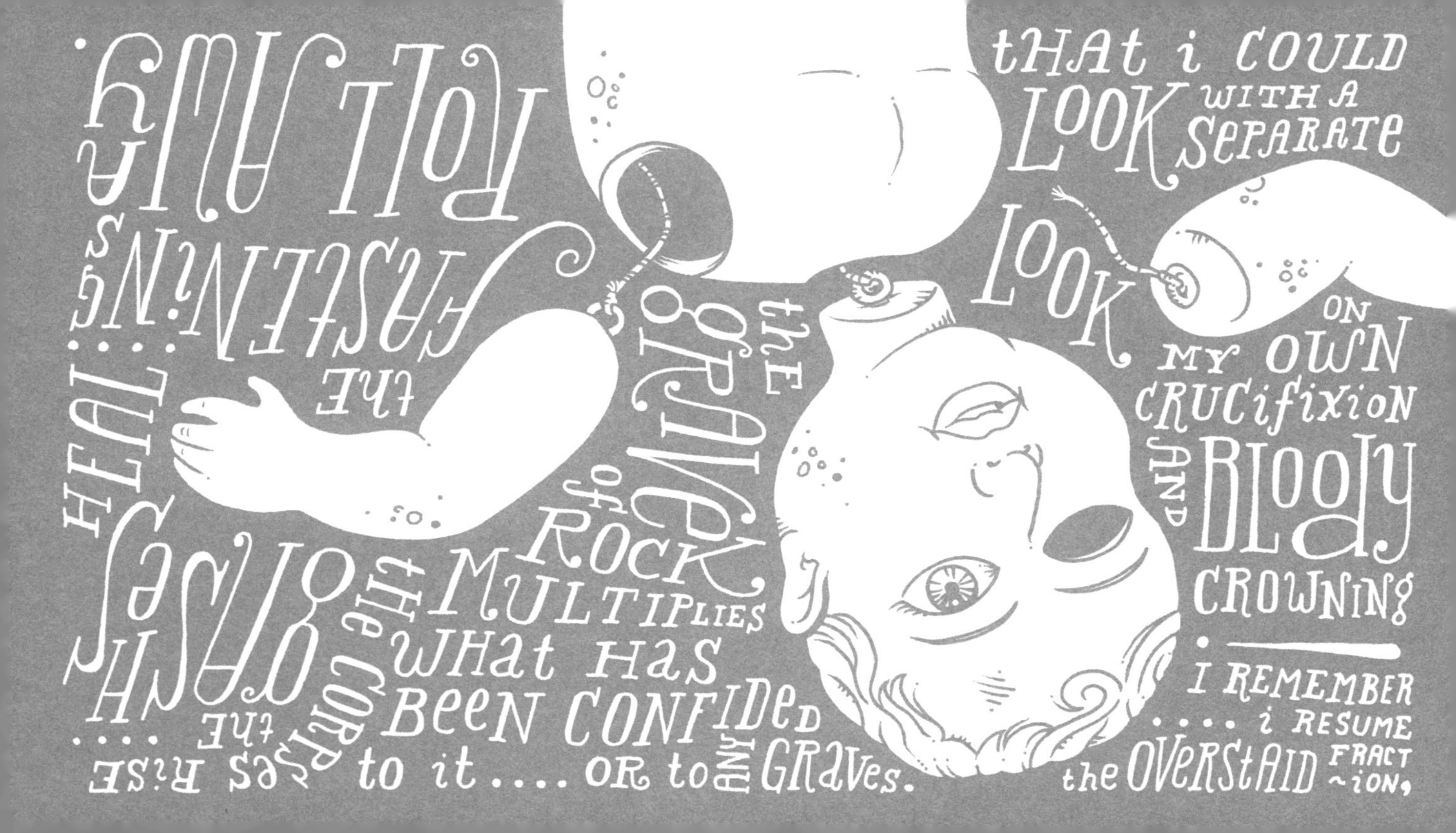

that i could look with a separate look on my own crucifixion and bloody crowning!
I remember.... i resume the overstaid fraction,
the grave of rock multiplies what has been confided to it.... or to any graves.
.... the corpses rise
the gashes heal:....
the fastenings roll away.

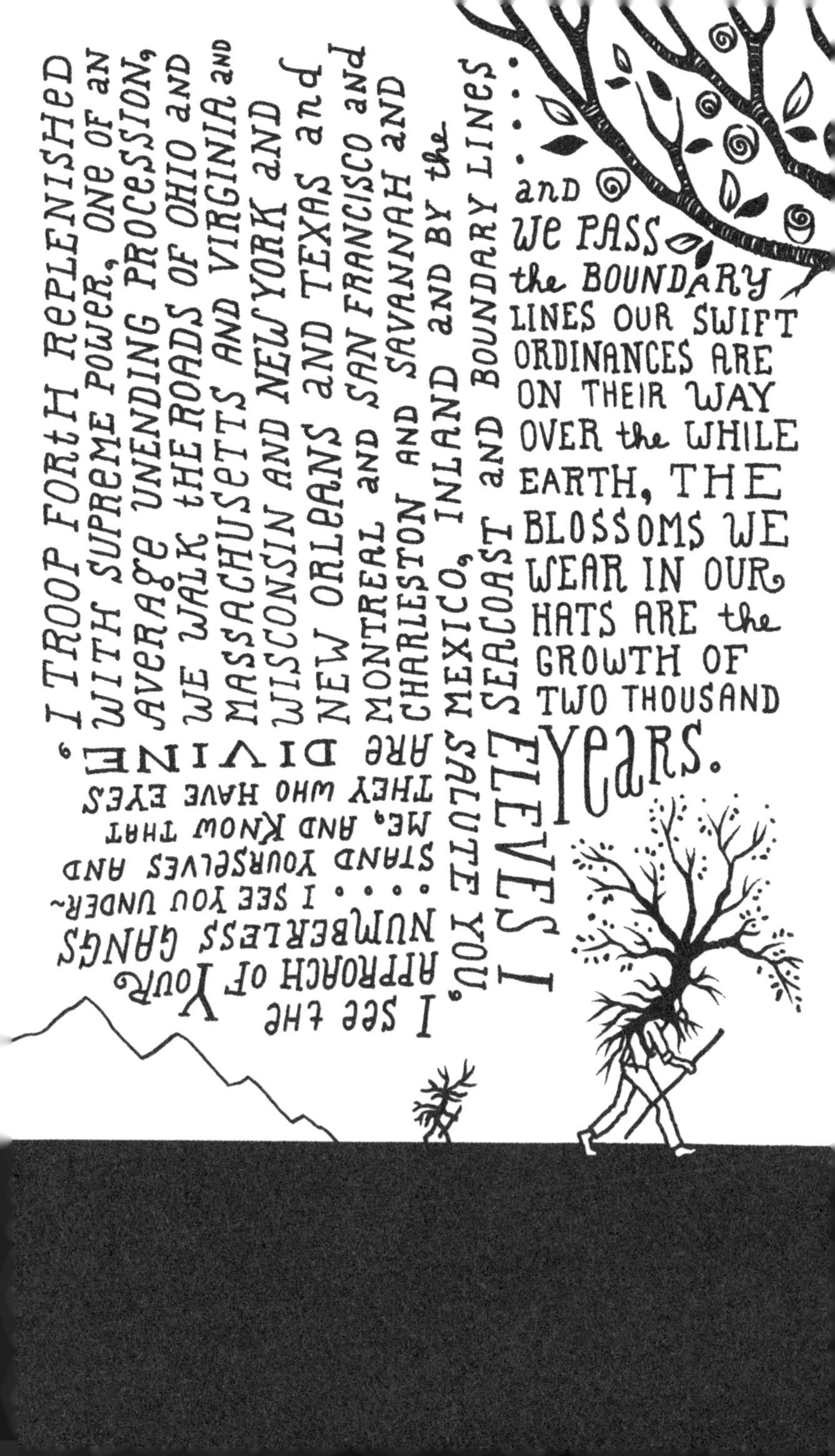
ELEVES I SALUTE YOU,
I SEE THE APPROACH OF YOUR NUMBERLESS GANGS... I SEE YOU UNDER-STAND YOURSELVES AND ME, AND KNOW THAT THEY WHO HAVE EYES ARE DIVINE
"I TROOP FORTH REPLENISHED WITH SUPREME POWER, ONE OF AN AVERAGE UNENDING PROCESSION, WE WALK THE ROADS OF OHIO AND MASSACHUSETTS AND VIRGINIA AND WISCONSIN AND NEW YORK AND NEW ORLEANS AND TEXAS AND MONTREAL AND SAN FRANCISCO AND CHARLESTON AND SAVANNAH AND MEXICO, INLAND AND BY THE SEACOAST AND BOUNDARY LINES...
AND WE PASS THE BOUNDARY LINES OUR SWIFT ORDINANCES ARE ON THEIR WAY OVER THE WHILE EARTH, THE BLOSSOMS WE WEAR IN OUR HATS ARE THE GROWTH OF TWO THOUSAND YEARS.

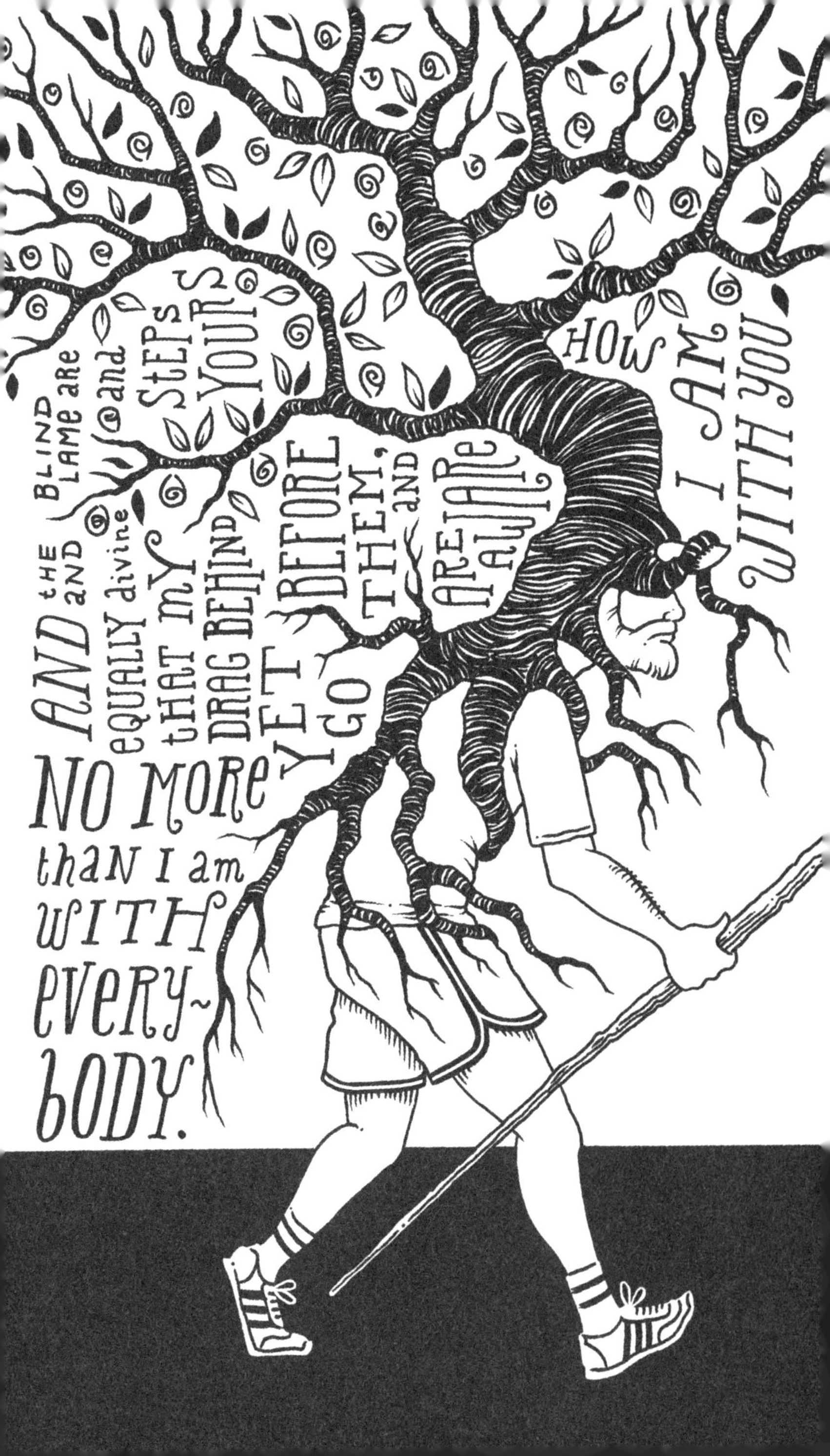
AND the BLIND and LAME are
equally divine and
that my steps
drag behind yours
yet go before them, and are aware
HOW I AM WITH YOU
NO MORE
than I am
WITH
every-
body.

the FRiENDLY
AND FLOWING
SAVAGE .... WHO
is HE?
IS HE
WAITING
FOR
CIVILIZATION
OR PAST IT
AND MASTERING
IT? is he
SOME SOUTHWESTERNER
RAISED OUTDOORS?
is HE CANADIAN?
IS HE FROM the
MiSSiSSiPPi
COUNTRY?
OR FROM
IOWA,
OREGON
OR CALI~
FOR~
NIA?
OR FROM the MOUNtaiN?
OR PRAIRIE LIFE
BUSH~LIFE?
OR.. OR FROM
the SEA?
WHEREVER
He GOES MEN
AND WOMEN
ACCEPT AND
DESIRE HIM,
theY desire he
should like them
and touch tHEM
and speak to
them and staY
WiTH
THEM

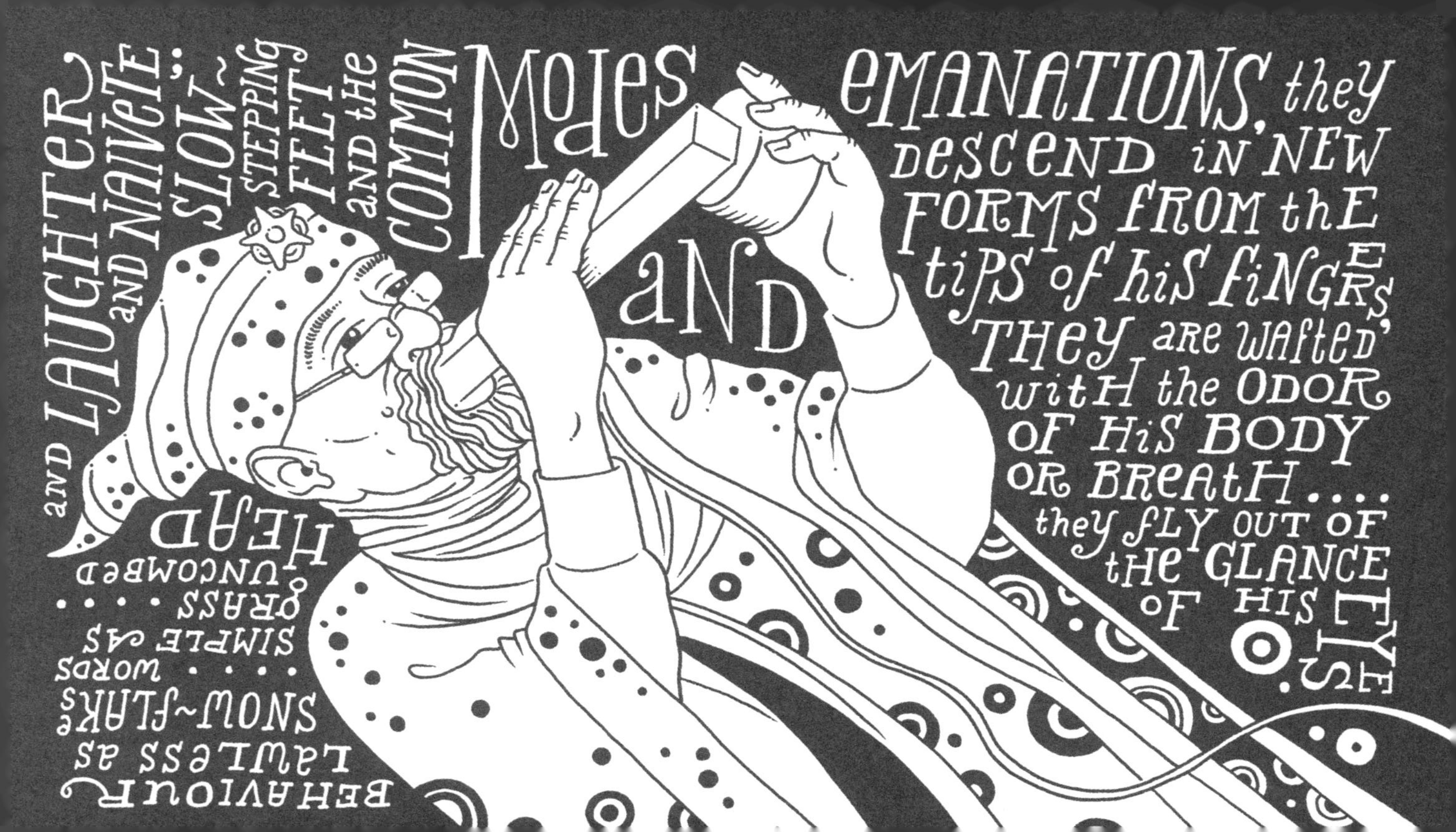
BEHAVIOUR LAWLESS AS SNOW~FLAKES
... WORDS SIMPLE AS GRASS ...
UNCOMBED HEAD
AND LAUGHTER AND NAIVETE;
SLOW~STEPPING FEET
AND THE COMMON
MODES AND EMANATIONS, THEY
DESCEND IN NEW
FORMS FROM THE
TIPS OF HIS FINGERS,
THEY ARE WAFTED
WITH THE ODOR
OF HIS BODY
OR BREATH....
THEY FLY OUT OF
THE GLANCE
OF HIS EYES.

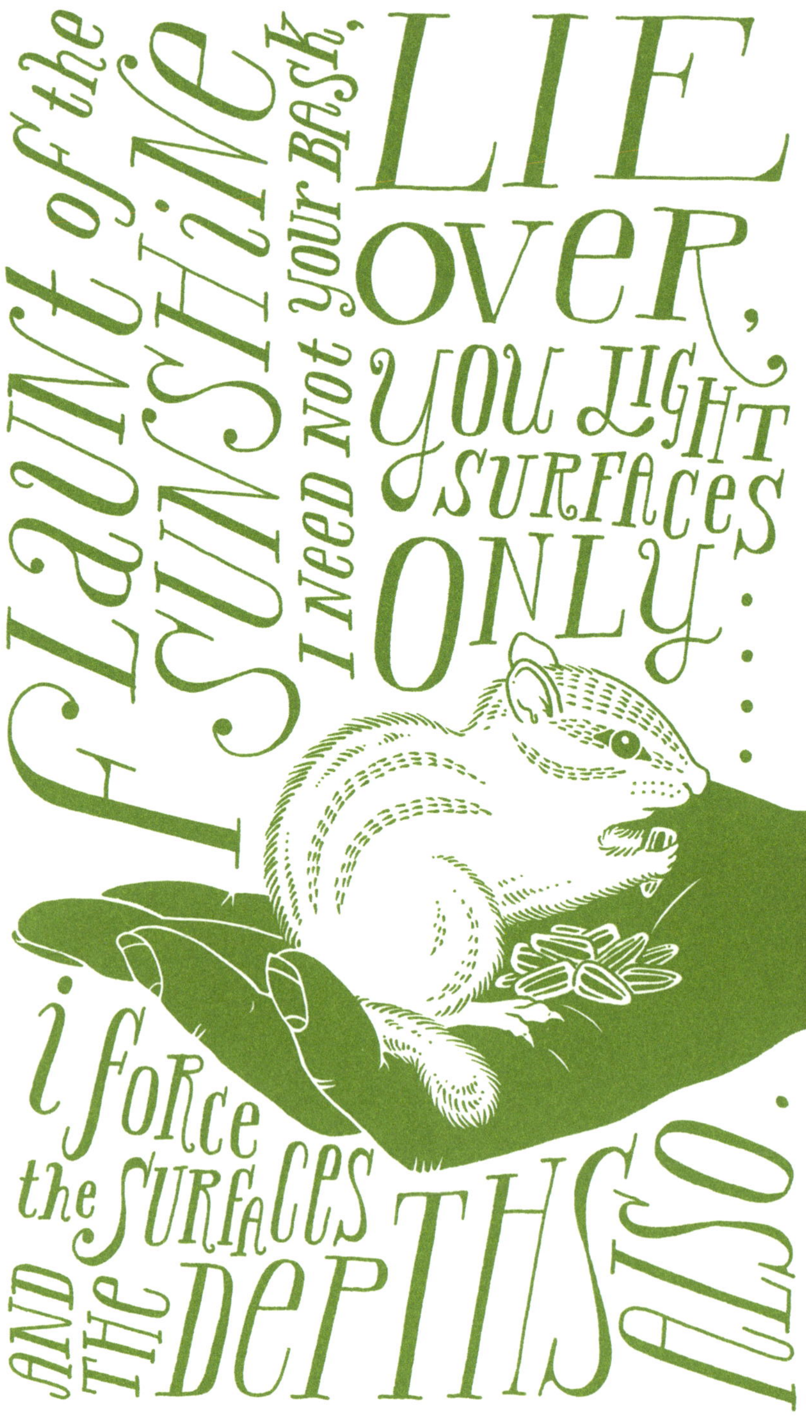
I FLAUNT of the
SUNSHINE
I NEED NOT YOUR BASK,
LIE OVER,
YOU LIGHT SURFACES ONLY…
i FORCE the SURFACES
AND THE DEPTHS ALSO.

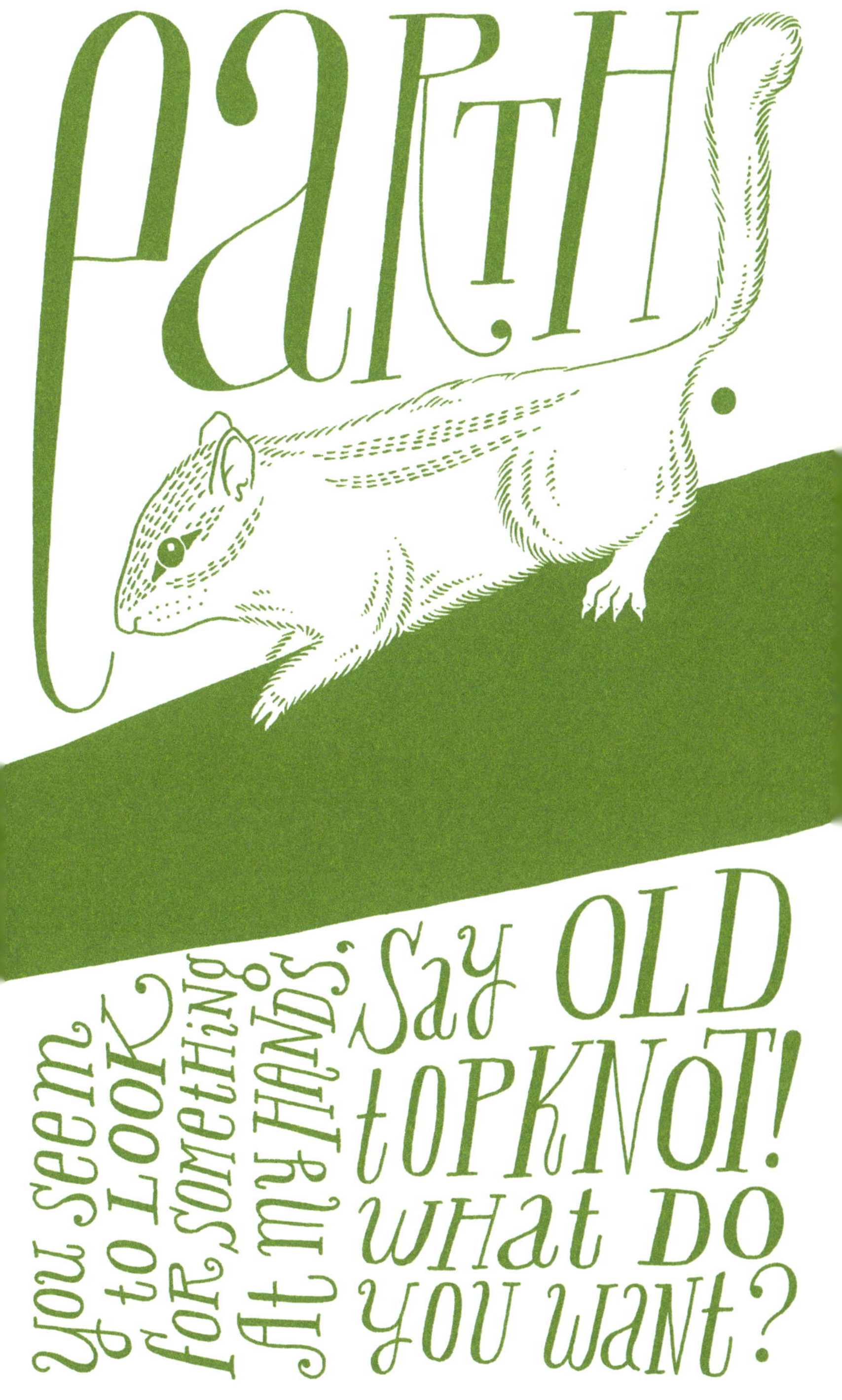
Earth!
"You seem to look for something at my hands," say Old Topknot! What do you want?

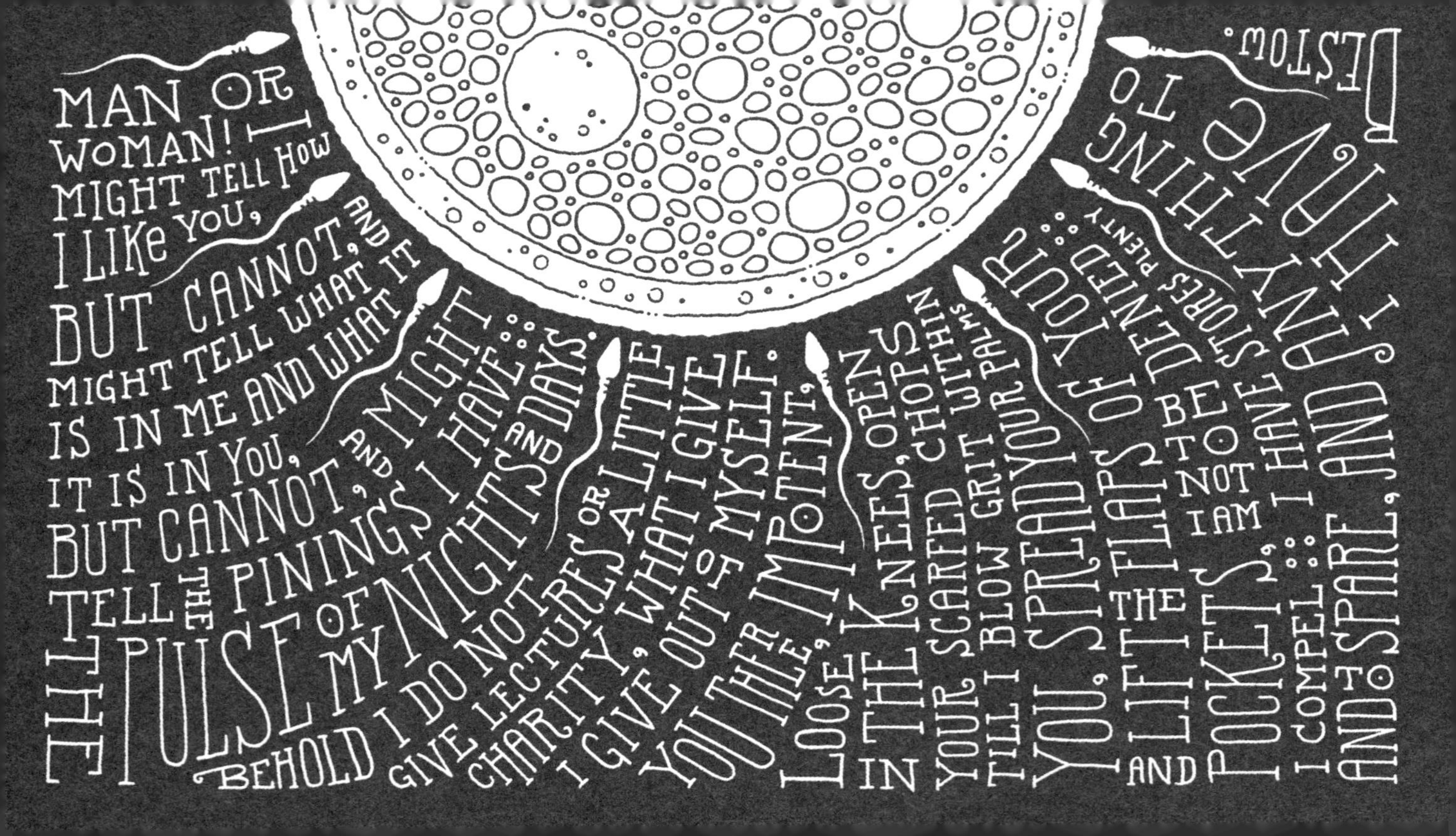
MAN OR WOMAN! I MIGHT TELL HOW I LIKE YOU, BUT CANNOT, AND MIGHT TELL WHAT IT IS IN ME AND WHAT IT IS IN YOU, BUT CANNOT, AND MIGHT TELL THE PININGS I HAVE... THE PULSE OF MY NIGHTS AND DAYS.
BEHOLD I DO NOT GIVE LECTURES OR A LITTLE CHARITY, WHAT I GIVE I GIVE OUT OF MYSELF.
YOU THERE, IMPOTENT, LOOSE IN THE KNEES, OPEN YOUR SCARFED CHOPS TILL I BLOW GRIT WITHIN YOU, SPREAD YOUR PALMS AND LIFT THE FLAPS OF YOUR POCKETS, I AM NOT TO BE DENIED... I COMPEL... I HAVE STORES PLENTY AND TO SPARE, AND ANYTHING I HAVE I BESTOW.

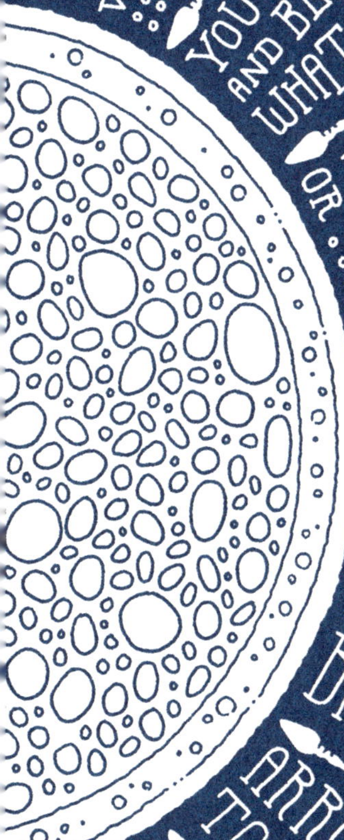

I do not ask who you are: that's not important to me, you can do nothing and be nothing but what I will infold you. To a drudge of the cotton-fields or emptier of privies I lean: on his right cheek I put the family kiss, and in my soul I swear I never will deny him. On women fit for conception I start bigger and nimbler babes, this day I am jetting the stuff of far more arrogant republics. To any one dying: thither I speed and twist the knob of the door. Turn the bedclothes toward the foot of the bed, let the physician and the priest go home.

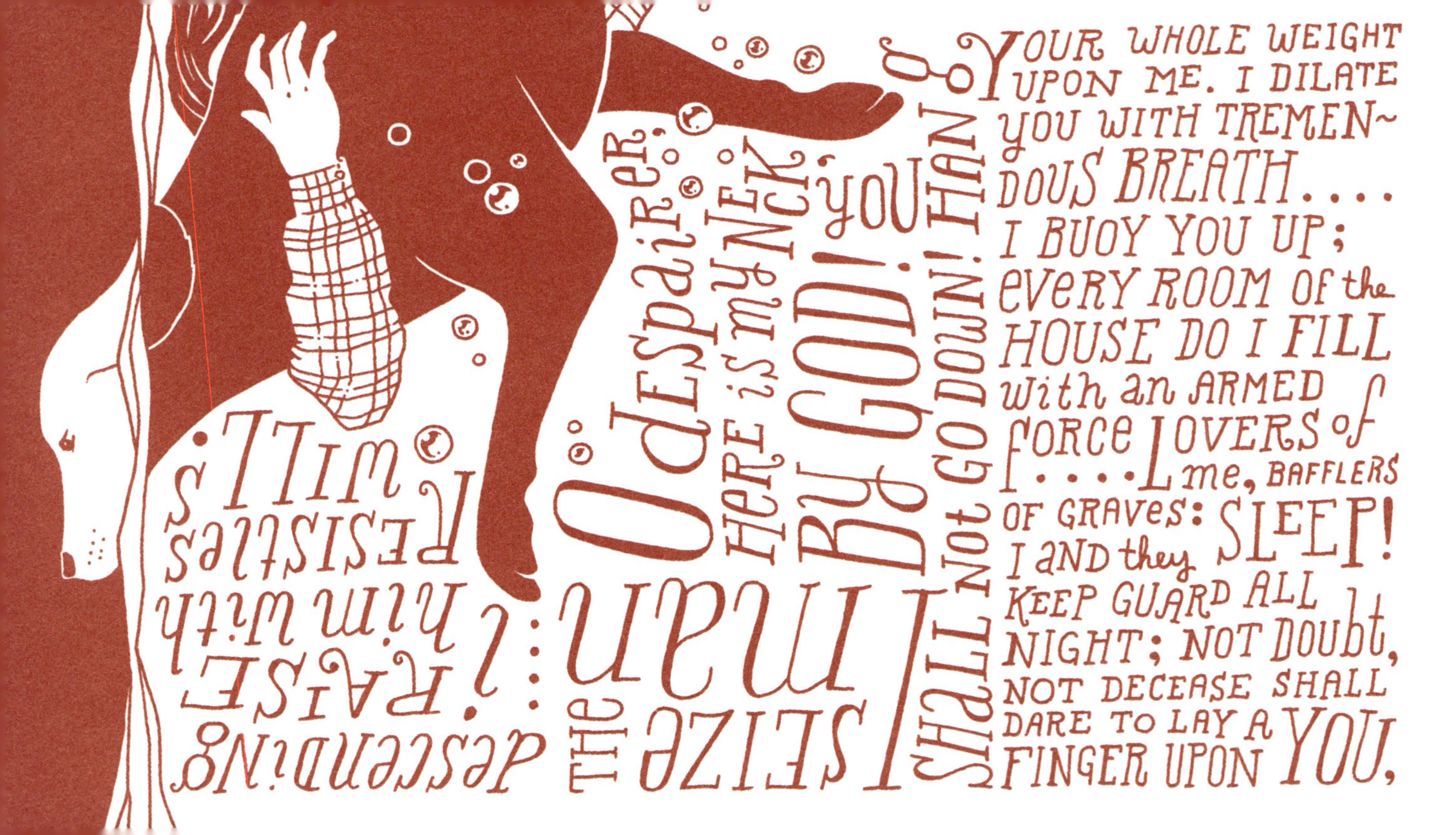

I SEIZE THE descending man... i RAISE him with resistless will...
O despairer, HERE is my NECK,
BY GOD! you SHALL Not GO DOWN! HANg
YOUR WHOLE WEIGHT
UPON ME. I DILATE
YOU WITH TREMEN~
DOUS BREATH....
I BUOY YOU UP;
every ROOM of the
HOUSE DO I FILL
with an ARMED
FORCE LOVERS of
...me, BAFFLERS
OF GRAVES: SLEEP!
I AND they
KEEP GUARD ALL
NIGHT; NOT Doubt,
NOT DECEASE SHALL
DARE TO LAY A
FINGER UPON YOU,

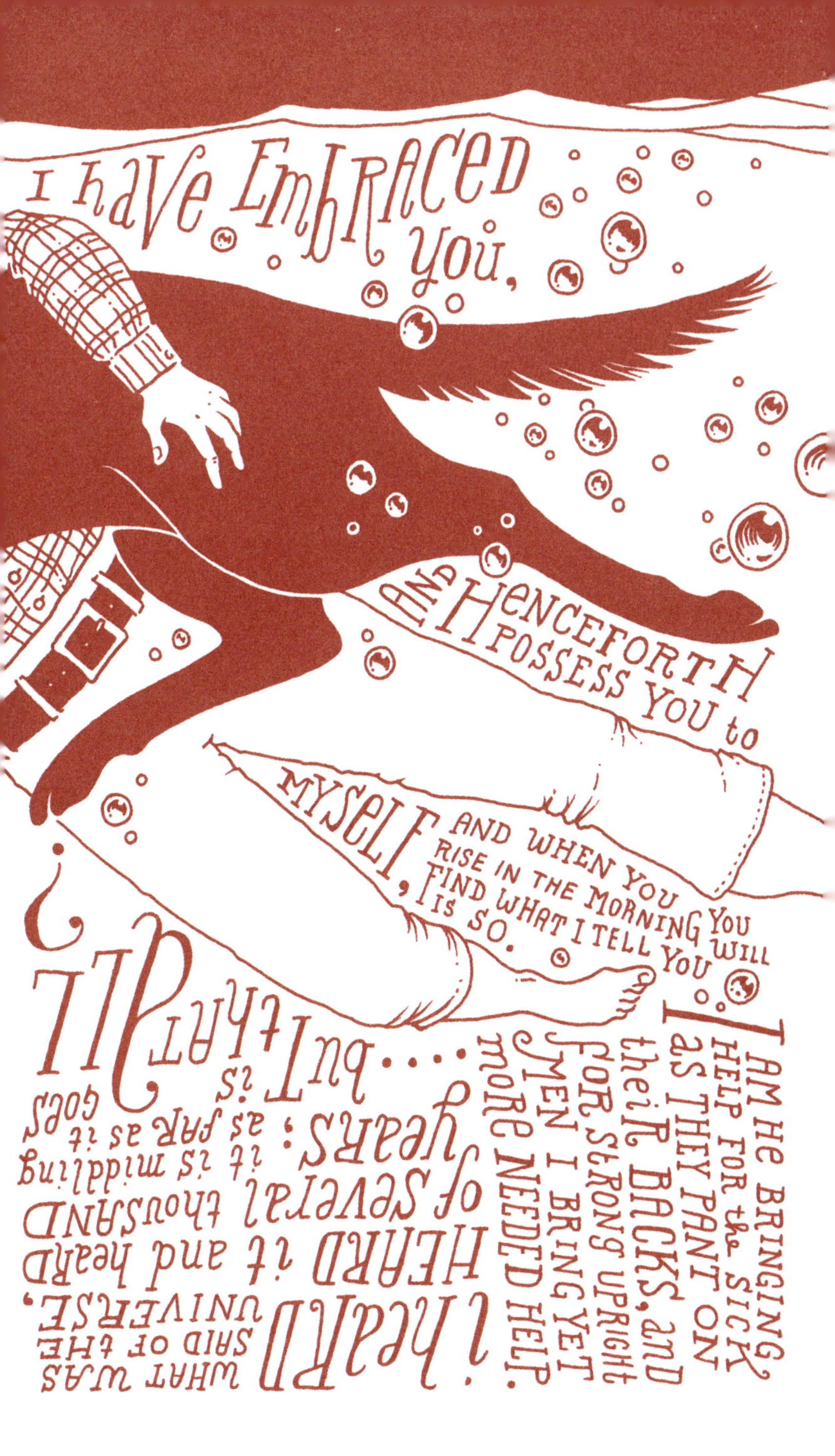
I have Embraced you,
and Henceforth I possess you to
myself,
and when you rise in the morning you will find what I tell you is so.
I am he bringing help for the sick as they pant on their backs, and for strong upright men I bring yet more needed help.
I heard what was said of the universe,
Heard it and heard it of several thousand years;
it is middling as far as it goes
...but is that all?

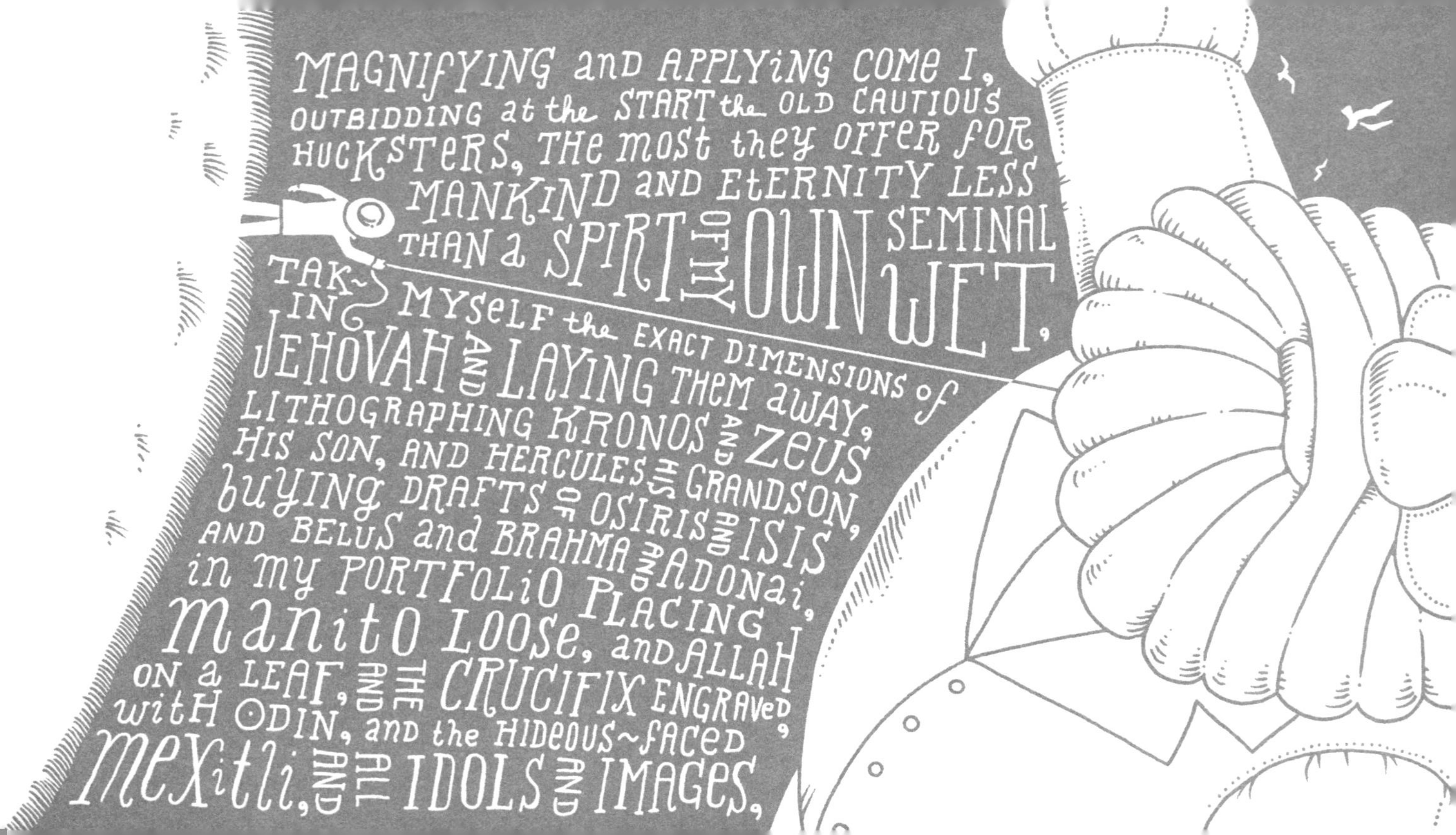
MAGNIFYING and APPLYING COME I,
OUTBIDDING at the START the OLD CAUTIOUS
HUCKSTERS, THE most they OFFER FOR
MANKIND AND ETERNITY LESS
THAN a SPIRT OF MY OWN SEMINAL WET,
TAK-IN MYSELF the EXACT DIMENSIONS of
JEHOVAH AND LAYING THEM AWAY,
LITHOGRAPHING KRONOS AND ZEUS
HIS SON, AND HERCULES HIS GRANDSON,
buying DRAFTS OF OSIRIS AND ISIS
AND BELUS and BRAHMA AND ADONAI,
in my PORTFOLIO PLACING
MANITO LOOSE, and ALLAH
ON a LEAF, AND THE CRUCIFIX ENGRAVED,
witH ODIN, and the HIDEOUS-FACED
MEXITLI, AND ALL IDOLS AND IMAGES,

honestly taking them all
for what ther are worth,
and not a cent more,
admitting they were alive
and did the work of their
day, admitting they bore mites
as for unfledged birds who have
now to rise and fly and sing for
themselves, accepting
the rough deific sketches
to fill out better in myself
. . . . bestowing them freely
on each man and woman I see,

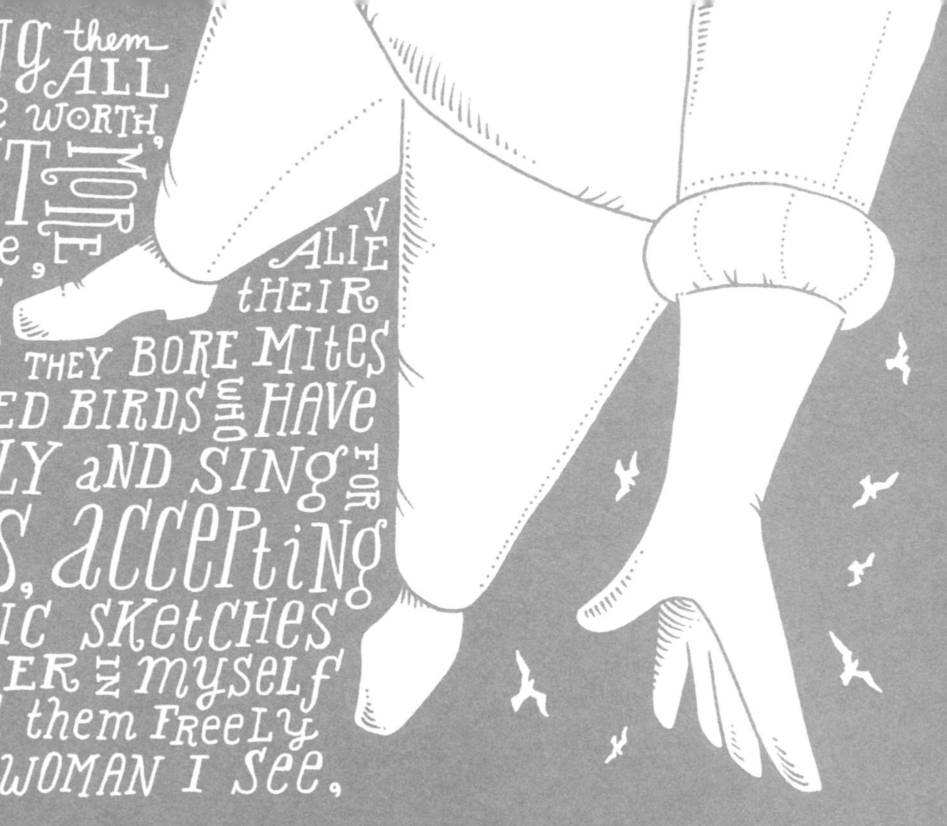

DISCOVERING as much or MORE IN A FRAMER FRAMING A HOUSE, PUTTING HIGHER
CLAIMS FOR HIM THERE WITH HIS ROLLED~UP SLEEVES, DRIVING the MALLET AND CHISEL;
NOT OBJECTING to SPECIAL REVELATIONS • • • CONSIDERING A CURL OF SMOKE OR A
HAIR ON THE BACK OF MY HAND as CURIOUS AS ANY REVELATION; THOSE AHOLD of FIRE~
ENGINES AND HOOK~AND~LADDER ROPES more to me than THE GODS OF the ANTIQUE
WARS, MINDING their VOICES PEAL THROUGH the CRASH of DESTRUCTION, their
BRAWNY LIMBS PASSING SAFE OVER CHARRED LATHS • • • THEIR WHITE FOREHEADS
WHOLE AND UNHURT OUT OF the FLAMES; BY the MECHANIC'S WIFE WITH HER
BABE AT HER NIPPLE INTERCEDING FOR EVERY PERSON BORN;
THREE SCYTHES at HARVEST WHIZZING IN A ROW FROM three
LUSTY ANGELS with SHIRTS BAGGED OUT at their WAISTS;
the SNAG~TOOTHED HOSTLER WITH RED
HAIR REDEEMING SINS PAST AND
TO COME, SELLING ALL HE
POSSESSES, AND
TRAVELING

on foot to fee lawyers for his brother and sit by him while he is tried for forgery:
What was strewn in the amplest strewing the square rod about me, and not filling the square rod then;
The bull and the bug never worshipped half enough,
Dung and dirt more admirable than was dreamed,
The supernatural of no account.... myself waiting my time to be one of the supremes,
The day getting ready for me when I shall do as much good as the best, and be as prodigious,
Guessing when I am it will not tickle me much to recieve puffs out of pulpit or print;
By my life~lumps! becoming already a creator!
Putting myself here and now to the ambushed womb of the shadows!

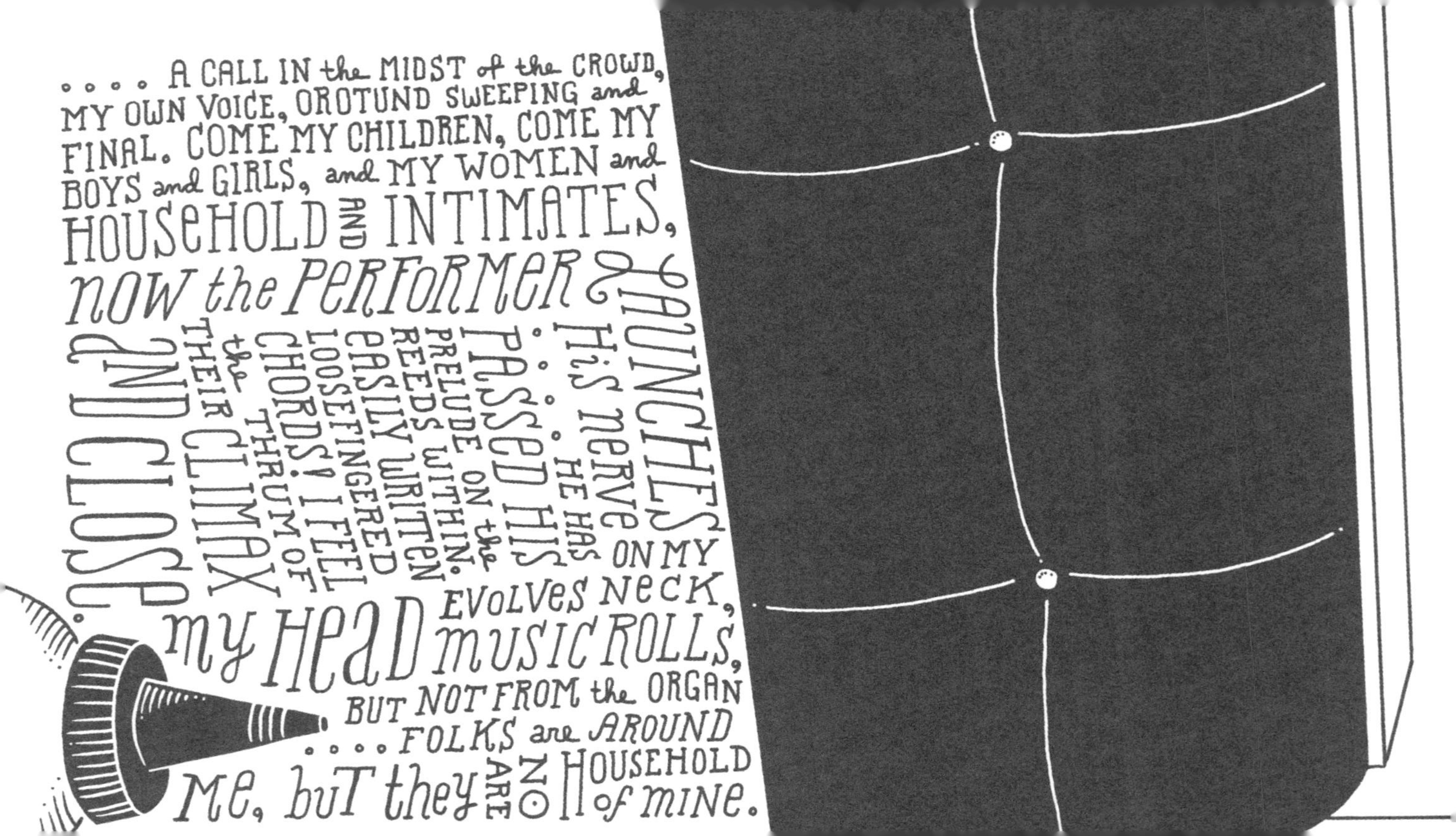
. . . . A CALL IN the MIDST of the CROWD,
MY OWN VOICE, OROTUND SWEEPING and
FINAL. COME MY CHILDREN, COME MY
BOYS and GIRLS, and MY WOMEN and
HOUSEHOLD AND INTIMATES,
NOW the PERFORMER LAUNCHES
His nerve . . . HE HAS
PASSED HIS
PRELUDE ON the
REEDS WITHIN.
EASILY WRITTEN
LOOSEFINGERED
CHORDS! I FEEL
the THRUM OF
THEIR CLIMAX
AND CLOSE.
MY HEAD EVOLVES ON MY NECK,
MUSIC ROLLS,
BUT NOT FROM the ORGAN
. . . . FOLKS are AROUND
ME, BUT they ARE NO HOUSEHOLD of MINE.

EVER the HARD and UNSUNK GROUND,
EVER THE EATERS AND DRINKERS
. . . . EVER the UPWARD AND
DOWNWARD SUN. . . . EVER tHE
AIR and the CEASELESS TIDES,
EVER MYSELF and MY NEIGH~
BORS, Re~FRESHING and WICK~
ED and REAL, EVER the OLD
INEXPLICABLE QUERY. . . .
EVER THAT THORNED
THUMB ~ that BREATH OF
ITCHES and THIRSTS,
EVER the VEXER'S HOOT!
HOOT! till WE FIND where
the SLY ONE HIDES and
BRING HIM FORTH; EVER
LOVE. . . . EVER the
SOBBING LIQUID of
LIFE, EVER the BANDAGE
UNDER the CHIN. . . .
EVER THE TRESTLES
OF DEATH.

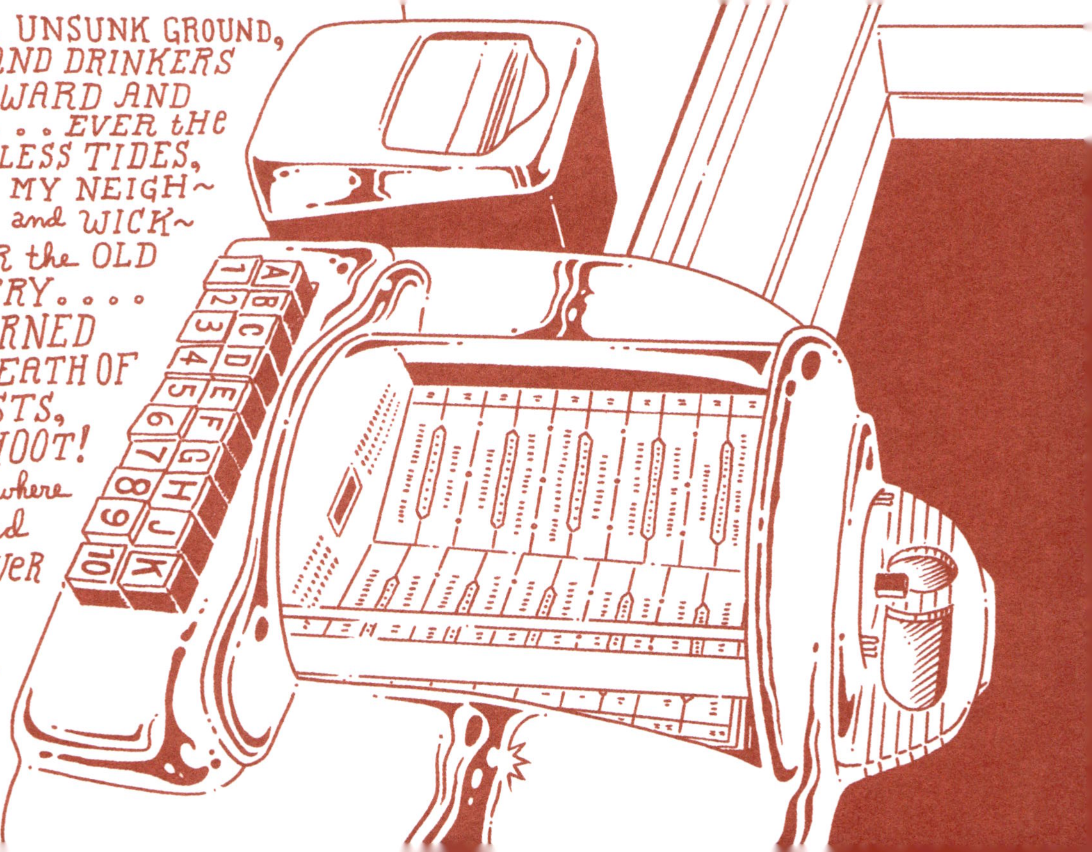

HERE AND THERE WITH DIMES ON THE EYES WALKING,

TO FEED THE GREED OF THE BELLY THE BRAINS LIBERALLY SPOONING, TICKETS BUYING OR TALKING OR SELLING, BUT IN TO THE FEAST NEVER ONCE GOING;

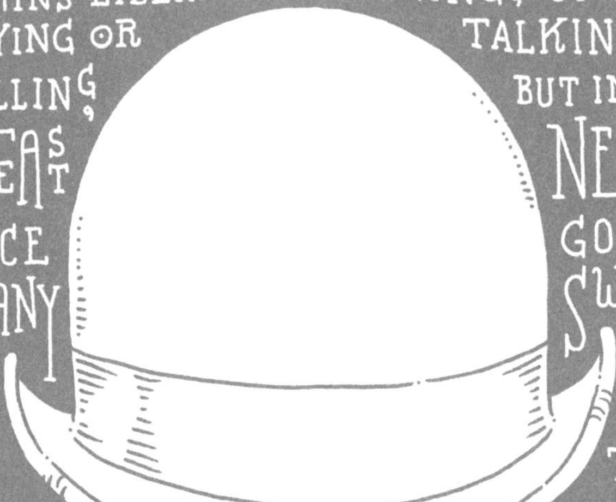

MANY SWEATING AND PLOUGHING AND THRASHING, AND THEN THE CHAFF FOR PAYMENT RECEIVING,

A FEW IDLY OWNING, AND THEY THE WHEAT CONTINUALLY CLAIMING.

THIS IS THE CITY . . . AND I AM ONE OF THE CITIZENS. . . .

WHATEVER INTERESTS THE REST INTERESTS ME: POLITICS, NEWSPAPERS, BENEVOLENT IMPROVEMENTS, TARIFFS, FACTORIES, STOCKS, SCHOOLS, SOCIETIES, BANKS, STEAMSHIPS, MARKETS, AND STORES AND REAL ESTATE AND PERSONAL ESTATE.

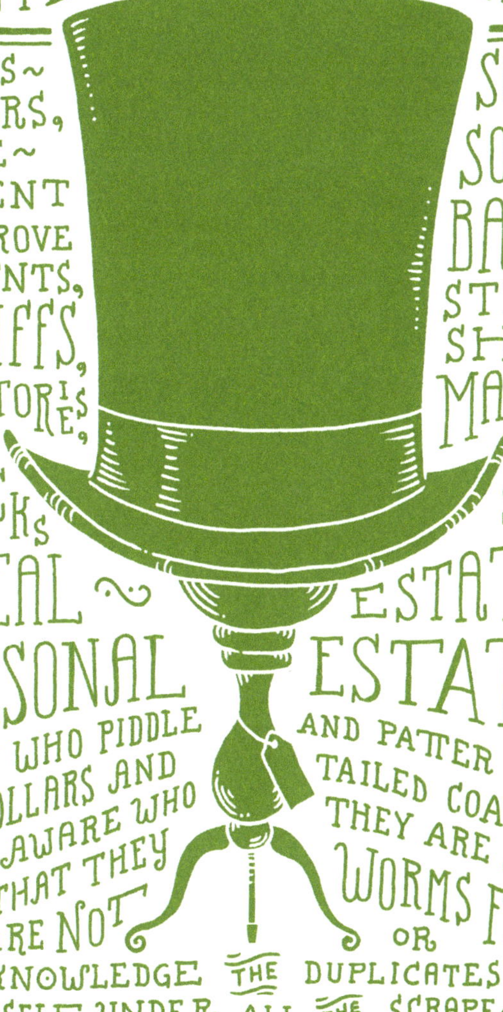

THEY WHO PIDDLE AND PATTER HERE IN COLLARS AND TAILED COATS.... I AM AWARE WHO THEY ARE.... AND THAT THEY ARE NOT WORMS OR FLEAS,

I ACKNOWLEDGE THE DUPLICATES OF MYSELF UNDER ALL THE SCRAPE~LIPPED AND PIPE~LEGGED CONCEALMENTS.

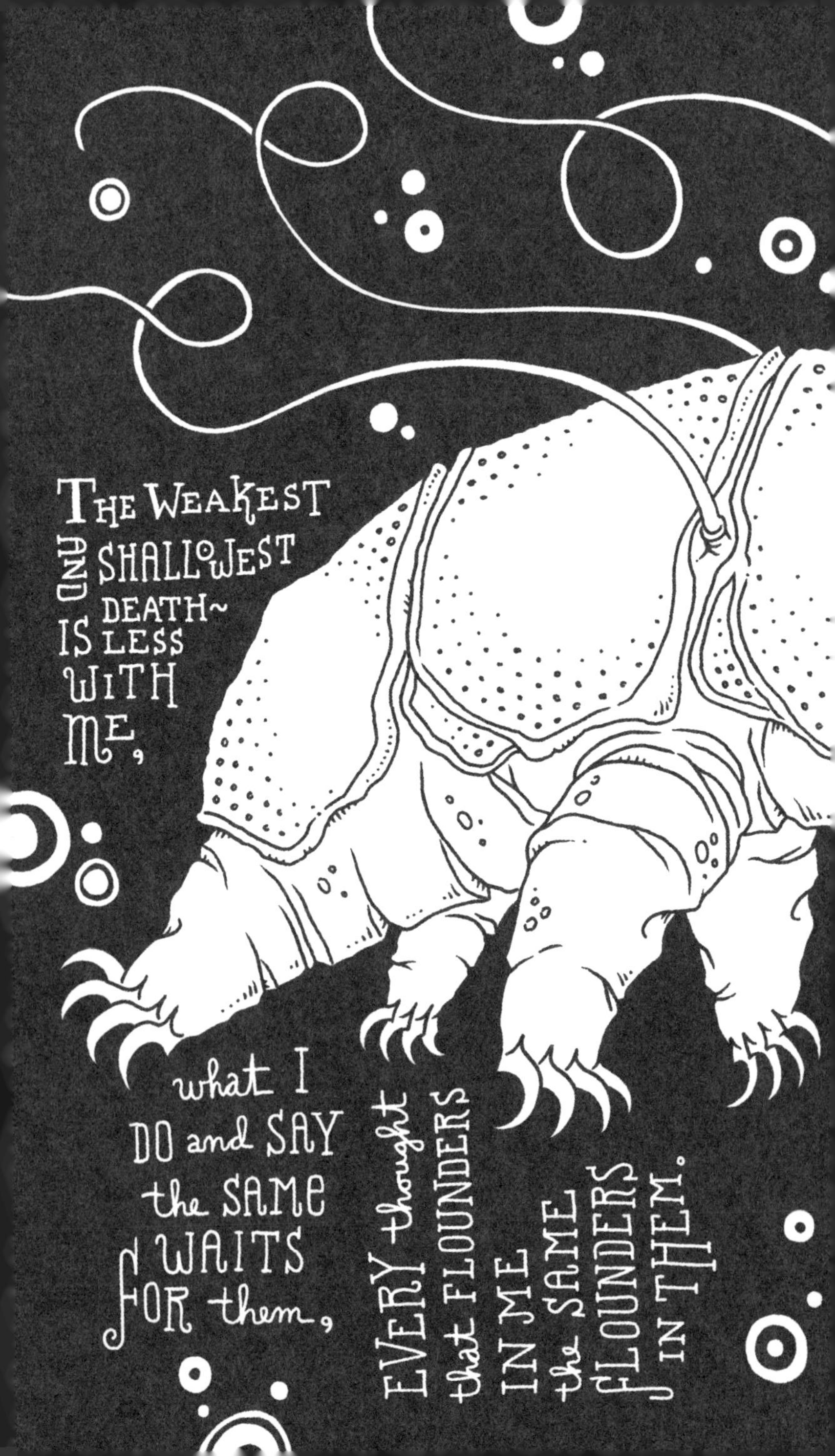
The Weakest and Shallowest is death~less with me,
what I do and say the same waits for them,
Every thought that flounders in me the same flounders in them.

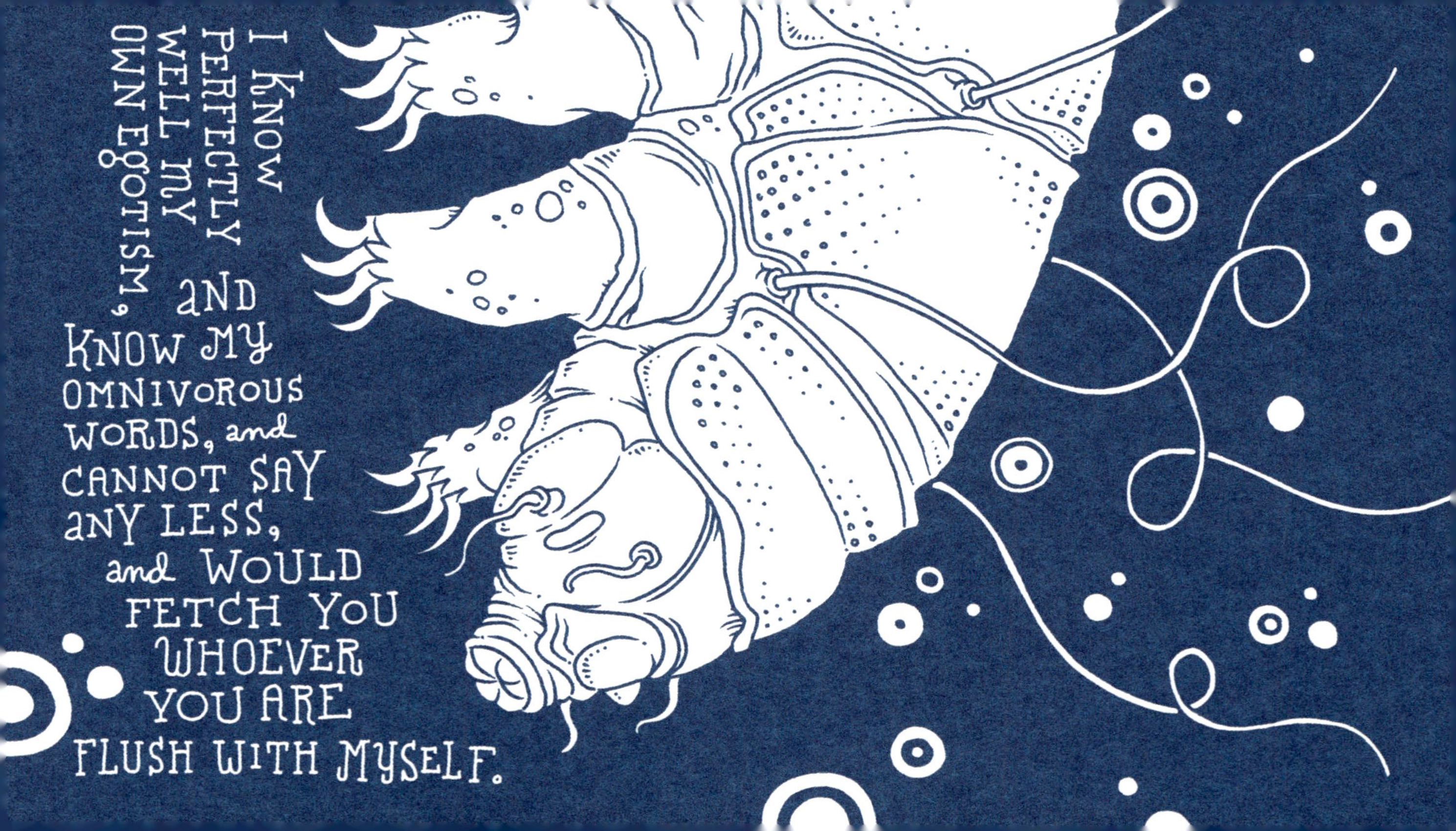
I KNOW
PERFECTLY
WELL MY
OWN EGOTISM,
AND
KNOW MY
OMNIVOROUS
WORDS, and
CANNOT SAY
ANY LESS,
and WOULD
FETCH YOU
WHOEVER
YOU ARE
FLUSH WITH MYSELF.

My words are words of a questioning, and to incite reality; this printed and bound book.... but the printer and the printing office boy? The marriage estate and settlement.... but the body and mind of the bridegroom? also those of the bride? The panorama of the sea.... but the sea itself? The well-taken photographs.... but your wife or friend close and solid in your arms?

the FLEET
of SHIPS of the
LINE
AND all the MODERN
IMPROVEMENTS . . . . BUT
the CRAFT AND PLUCK OF the
ADMIRAL? THE DISHES
AND FARE AND
FURNITURE
. . . . BUT the HOST AND
HOSTESS, and the LOOK OUT
OF THEIR EYES? the SKY
UP THERE . . . . YET HERE
OR NEXT DOOR OR ACROSS
the WAY? THE SAINTS
AND SAGES IN
HISTORY: BUT
YOU
YOURSELF
SERMONS AND CREEDS?
and THEOLOGY. . . . BUT
THE HUMAN BRAIN, and WHAT
IS CALLED REASON, and
WHAT IS CALLED LOVE,
and WHAT
IS CALLED LIFE?

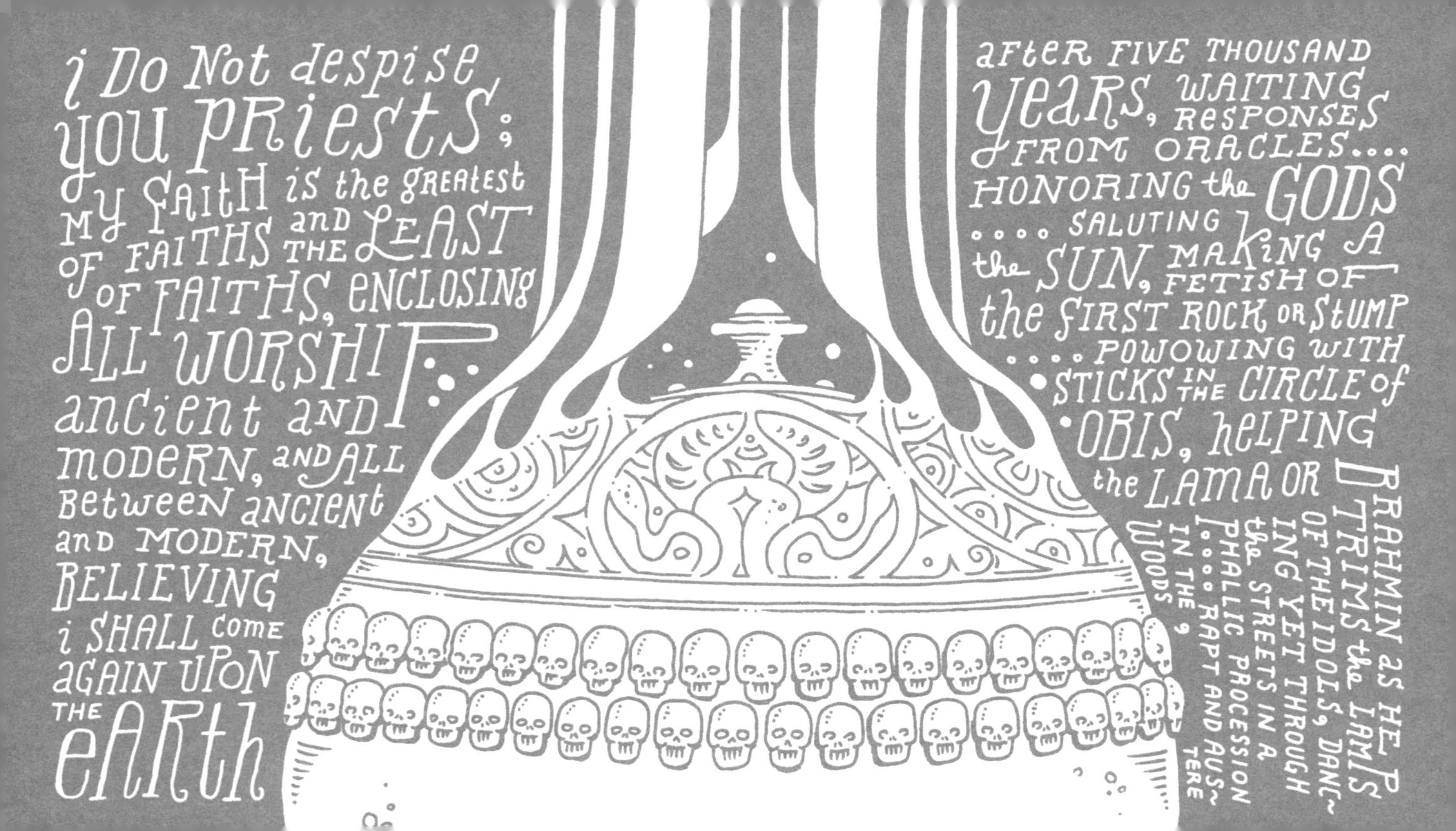

i Do Not despise you PRiests;
my faith is the greatest of faiths and the least of faiths,
enclosing all worship ancient and modern, and all between ancient and modern,
believing i shall come again upon the earth
after five thousand years, waiting responses from oracles.... honoring the gods.... saluting the sun,
making a fetish of the first rock or stump.... powowing with sticks in the circle of obis,
helping the lama or brahmin as he trims the lamps of the idols,
dancing yet through the streets in a phallic procession.... rapt and austere in the woods

a GYMNOSOPHIST, DRINKING MEAD FROM THE SKULL~CUP.... to SHASTA~ and VEDAS ADMIRANT .... MINDING the KORAN, WALKING THE TEOKALLIS, SPOTTED WITH GORE FROM the STONE AND KNIFE~BEATING the SERPENT~SKIN DRUM; ACCEPTING the GOSPELS, ACCEPTING HIM that WAS CRUCIFIED, KNOWING ASSUREDLY THAT HE IS DIVINE, TO the MASS KNEELING~ TO THE PURITAN'S PRAYER RISING ~SITTING PATIENTLY IN A PEW,

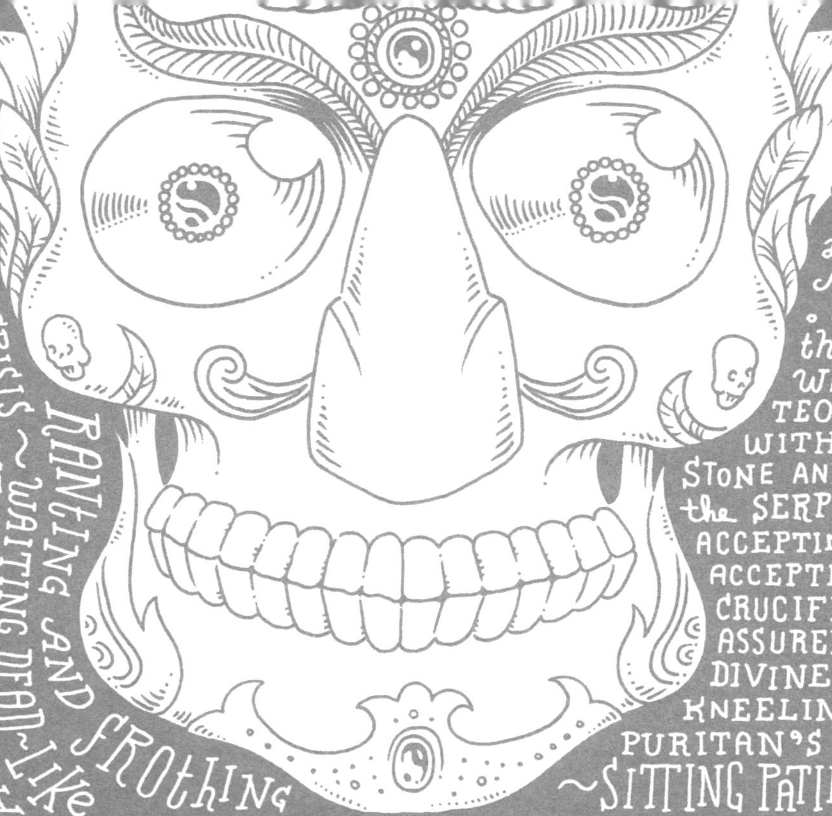

RANTING AND FROTHING IN MY INSANE CRISIS~WAITING DEAD~LIKE TILL MY SPIRIT AROUSES ME; LOOKING FORTH ON PAVEMENT AND LAND, AND OUTSIDE OF PAVEMENT AND LAND, BELONGING TO the WINDERS OF THE CIRCUIT of CIRCUITS.

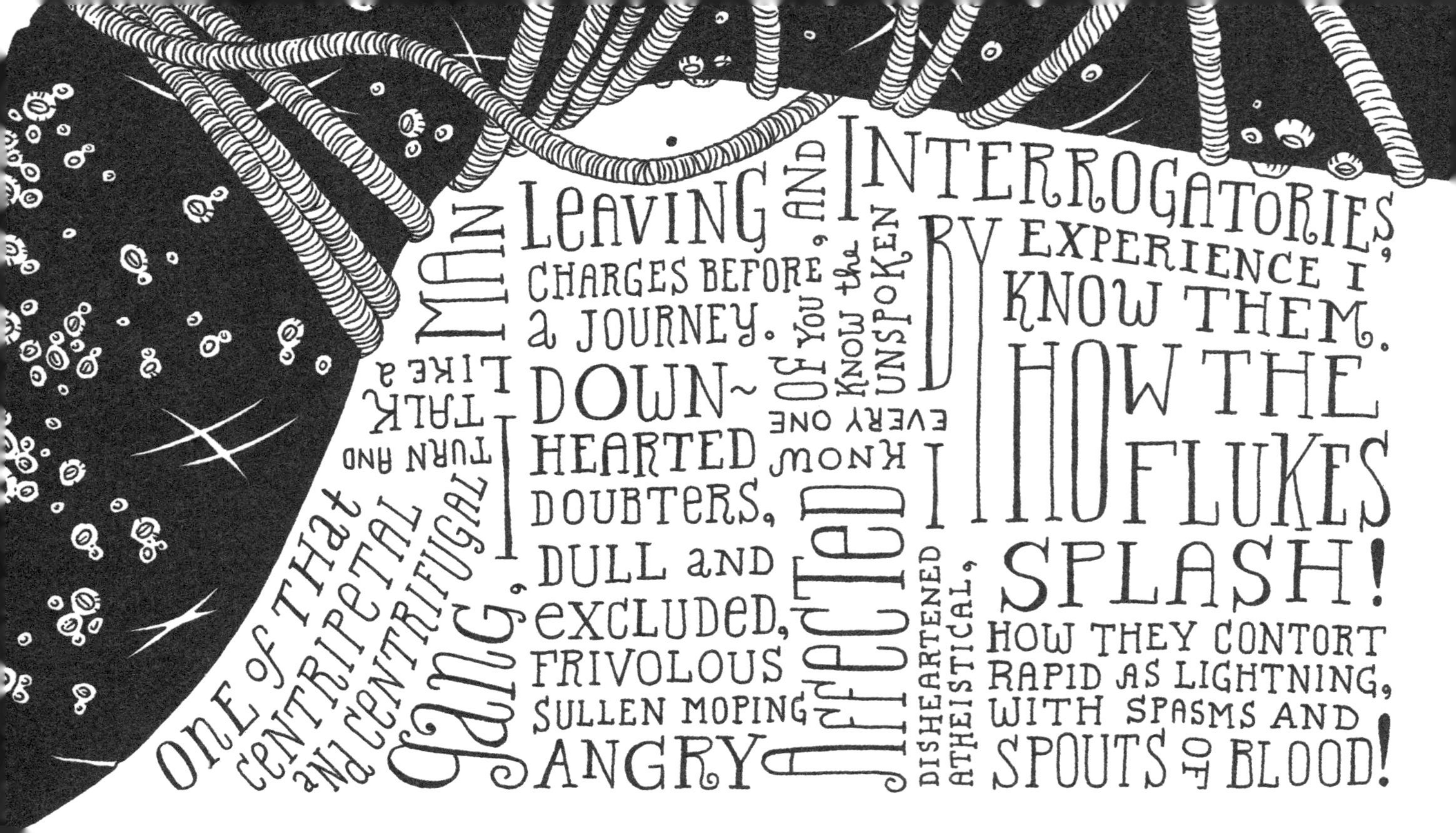

One of that centripetal and centrifugal gang, I turn and talk like a man leaving charges before a journey.
Down~hearted doubters, dull and excluded, frivolous sullen moping angry affected disheartened atheistical, I know every one of you, and know the unspoken interrogatories,
By experience I know them.
How the flukes splash!
How they contort rapid as lightning, with spasms and spouts of blood!

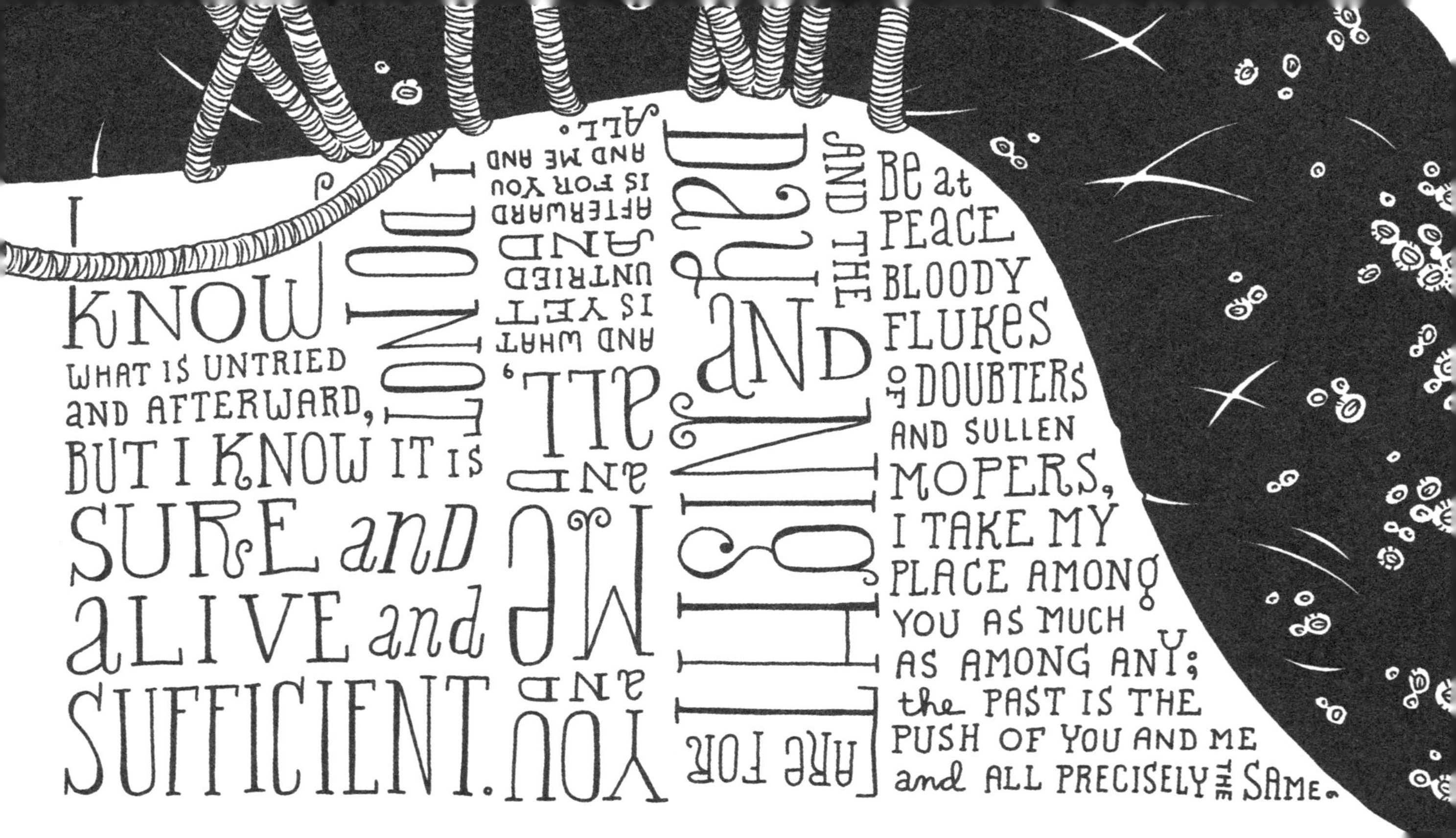
BE at PEACE BLOODY FLUKES OF DOUBTERS AND SULLEN MOPERS,
I TAKE MY PLACE AMONG YOU AS MUCH AS AMONG ANY;
the PAST IS THE PUSH OF YOU AND ME and ALL PRECISELY THE SAME.
AND THE DAY AND NIGHT ARE FOR YOU AND ME AND ALL,
AND WHAT IS YET UNTRIED AND AFTERWARD IS FOR YOU AND ME AND ALL.
I DO NOT KNOW WHAT IS UNTRIED AND AFTERWARD,
BUT I KNOW IT IS SURE AND ALIVE AND SUFFICIENT.

EACH who PASSES IS CONSIDERED, and EACH who STOPS IS CONSIDERED, and NOT A SINGLE ONE CAN IT FAIL.

IT CANNOT FAIL the YOUNG MAN WHO DIED and WAS BURIED, NOR the YOUNG WOMAN WHO DIED AND WAS PUT BY HIS SIDE,

NOR the LITTLE CHILD THAT PEEPED IN AT THE DOOR, and THEN DREW BACK AND WAS NEVER SEEN AGAIN,

NOR THE OLD MAN WHO HAS LIVED WITHOUT PURPOSE, and FEELS IT WITH BITTERNESS WORSE THAN GALL,

NOR HIM IN THE POORHOUSE TUBERCULED BY RUM and THE BAD DISORDER,

NOR the NUMBERLESS SLAUGHTERED and WRECKED . . . NOR the BRUTISH KOBOO, CALLED the ORDURE OF HUMANITY, NOR the SACS MERELY FLOATING WITH OPEN MOUTHS FOR FOOD TO SLIP IN,

NOR ANY THING IN THE EARTH, OR DOWN IN THE OLDEST GRAVES OF THE EARTH,

NOR ANY THING IN THE MYRIADS OF SPHERES, NOR ONE OF THE MYRIADS OF MYRIADS THAT INHABIT THEM,

NOR the PRESENT, NOR the LEAST WISP THAT IS KNOWN.

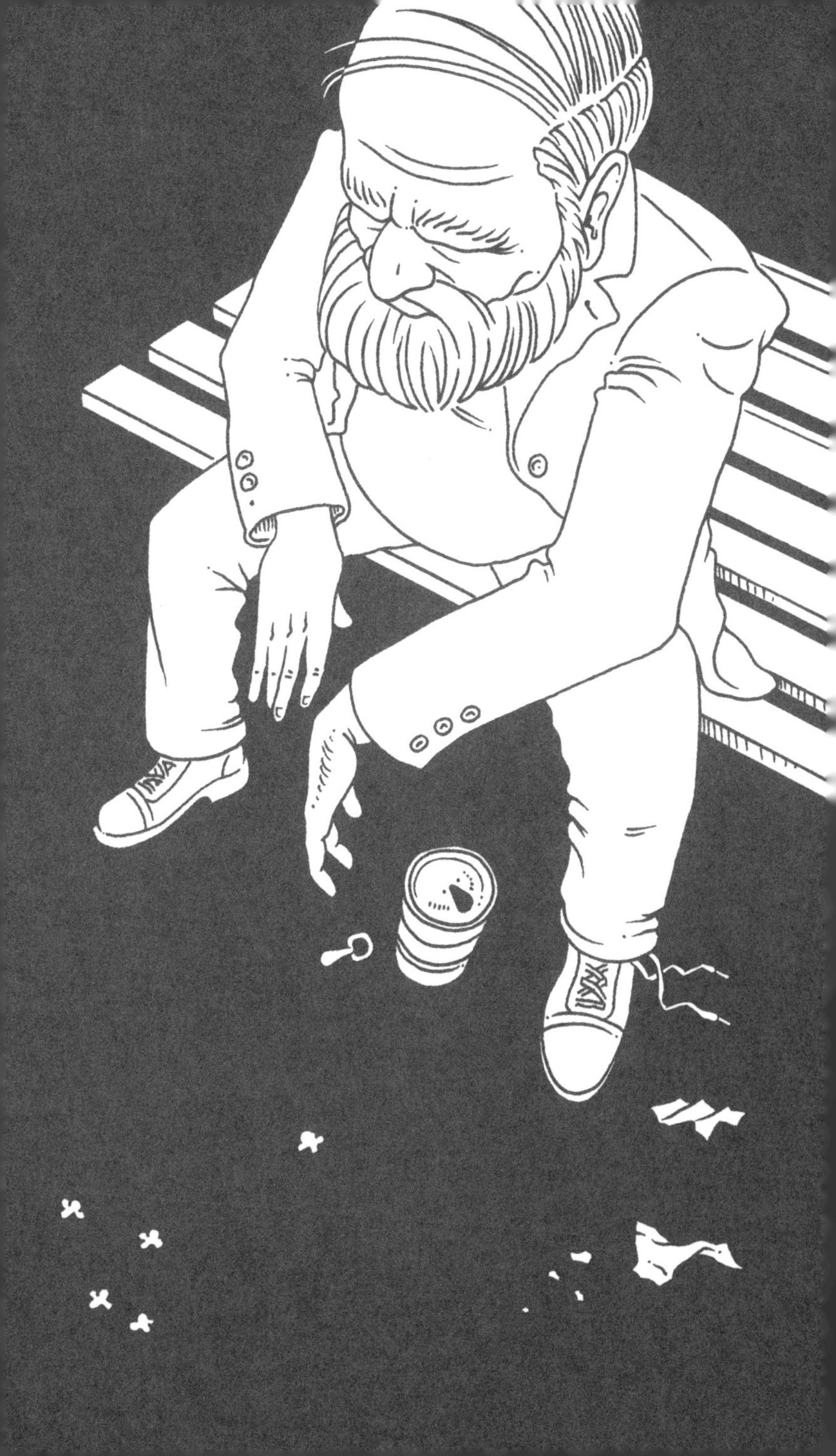

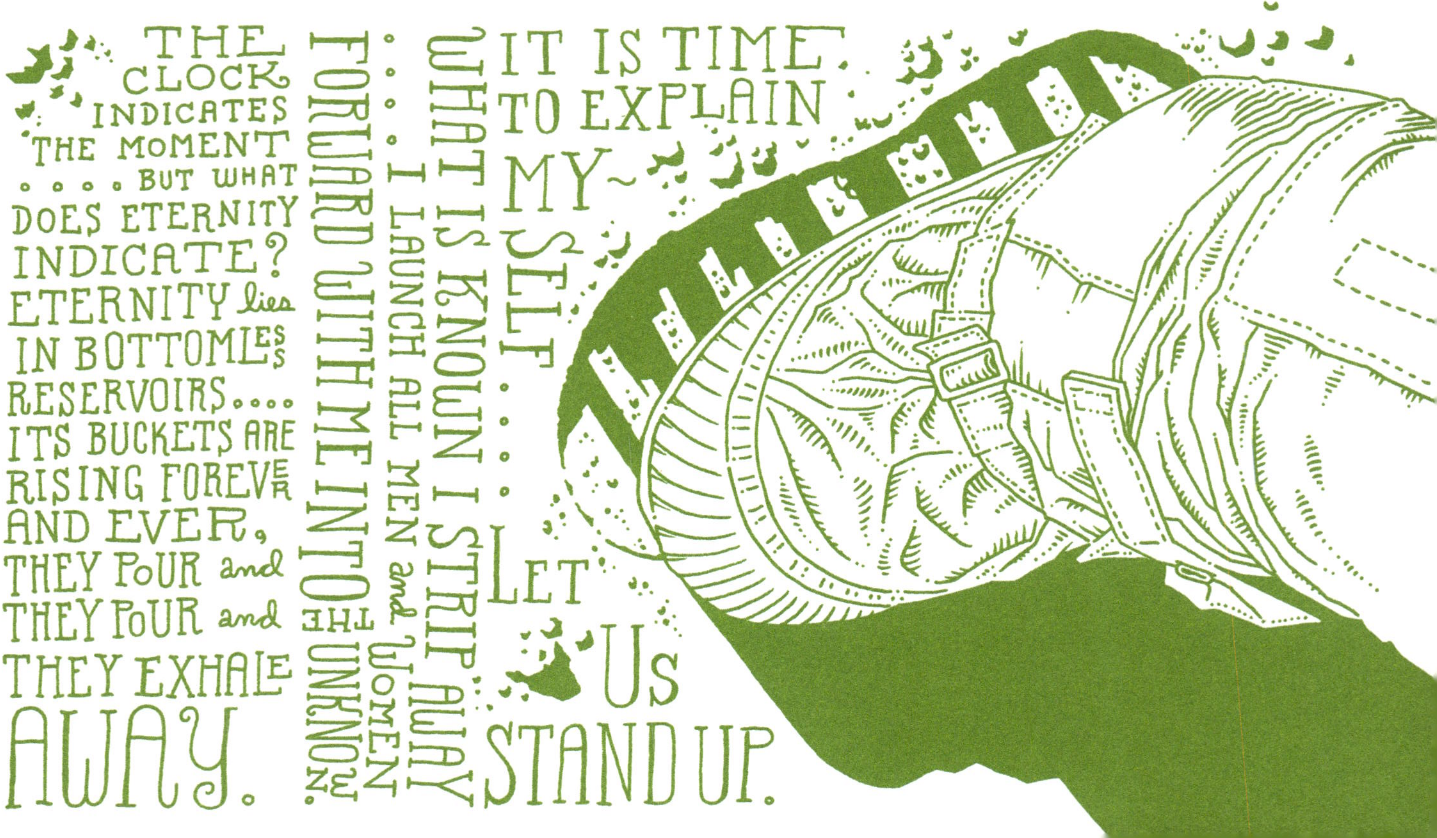
IT IS TIME
TO EXPLAIN
MY~
SELF....
LET
US
STAND UP.
WHAT IS KNOWN I STRIP AWAY
....I LAUNCH ALL MEN and WOMEN
FORWARD WITH ME INTO THE UNKNOWN.
THE
CLOCK
INDICATES
THE MOMENT
....BUT WHAT
DOES ETERNITY
INDICATE?
ETERNITY lies
IN BOTTOMLESS
RESERVOIRS....
ITS BUCKETS ARE
RISING FOREVER
AND EVER,
THEY POUR and
THEY POUR and
THEY EXHALE
AWAY.

WE HAVE thus FAR EXHAUSTED TRILLIONS OF WINTERS and SUMMERS; THERE ARE TRILLIONS AHEAD, and TRILLIONS AHEAD OF THEM. BIRTHS HAVE BROUGHT US RICH~NESS and VARIETY, AND OTHER BIRTHS WILL BRING US RICH~NESS and VARIETY. I DO CALL ONE NOT GREATER AND ONE SMALLER,

THAT WHICH FILLS ITS PERIOD AND IS EQUAL TO ANY.

WERE MANKIND MURDER~OUS OR JEALOUS UPON YOU MY BROTHER OR MY SISTER? I AM SORRY FOR YOU . . . . THEY are NOT MURDEROUS or JEALOUS UPON ME; ALL HAS BEEN GENTLE WITH ME . . . . I KEEP NO ACCOUNT WITH LAMENTATION;

WHAT HAVE I TO DO WITH LAMENTATION?

I AM AN ACME OF THINGS ACCOMPLISHED, and I AN ENCLOSER OF THINGS TO BE. MY FEET STRIKE AN APEX OF THE APICES OF THE STAIRS,

ON EVERY STEP BUNCHES OF AGES, and LARGER BUNCHES BETWEEN THE STEPS, ALL BELOW DULY TRAVELED ~ and STILL I MOUNT AND MOUNT.

RISE AFTER RISE BOW
the PHANTOMS BEHIND
ME, AFAR DOWN I SEE
the HUGE FIRST
NOTHING,
the VAPOR FROM THE
NOSTRILS OF DEATH,
I KNOW I WAS EVEN THERE
. . . . I WAITED UNSEEN
AND ALWAYS, and SLEPT
while GOD CARRIED ME
THROUGH the LETH~
ARGIC MIST, and
TOOK MY TIME
. . . . AND TOOK
NO HURT FROM
the FOETID
CARBON.

LONG I was HUGGED
CLOSE. . . . LONG AND LONG.

IMMENSE HAVE BEEN
the PREPARATIONS for
ME, FAITHFUL and
FRIENDLY the ARMS
that HAVE HELPED ME.
CYCLES FERRIED MY CRADLE,
ROWING AND ROWING LIKE
CHEERFUL BOATMEN;

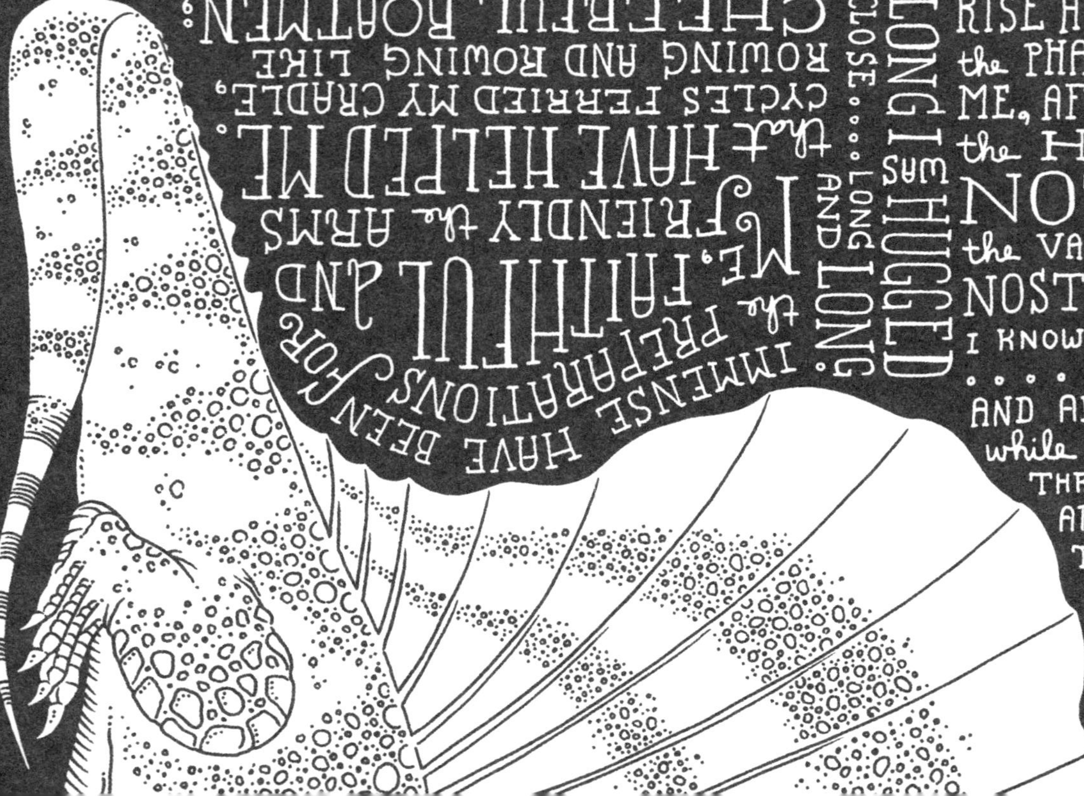

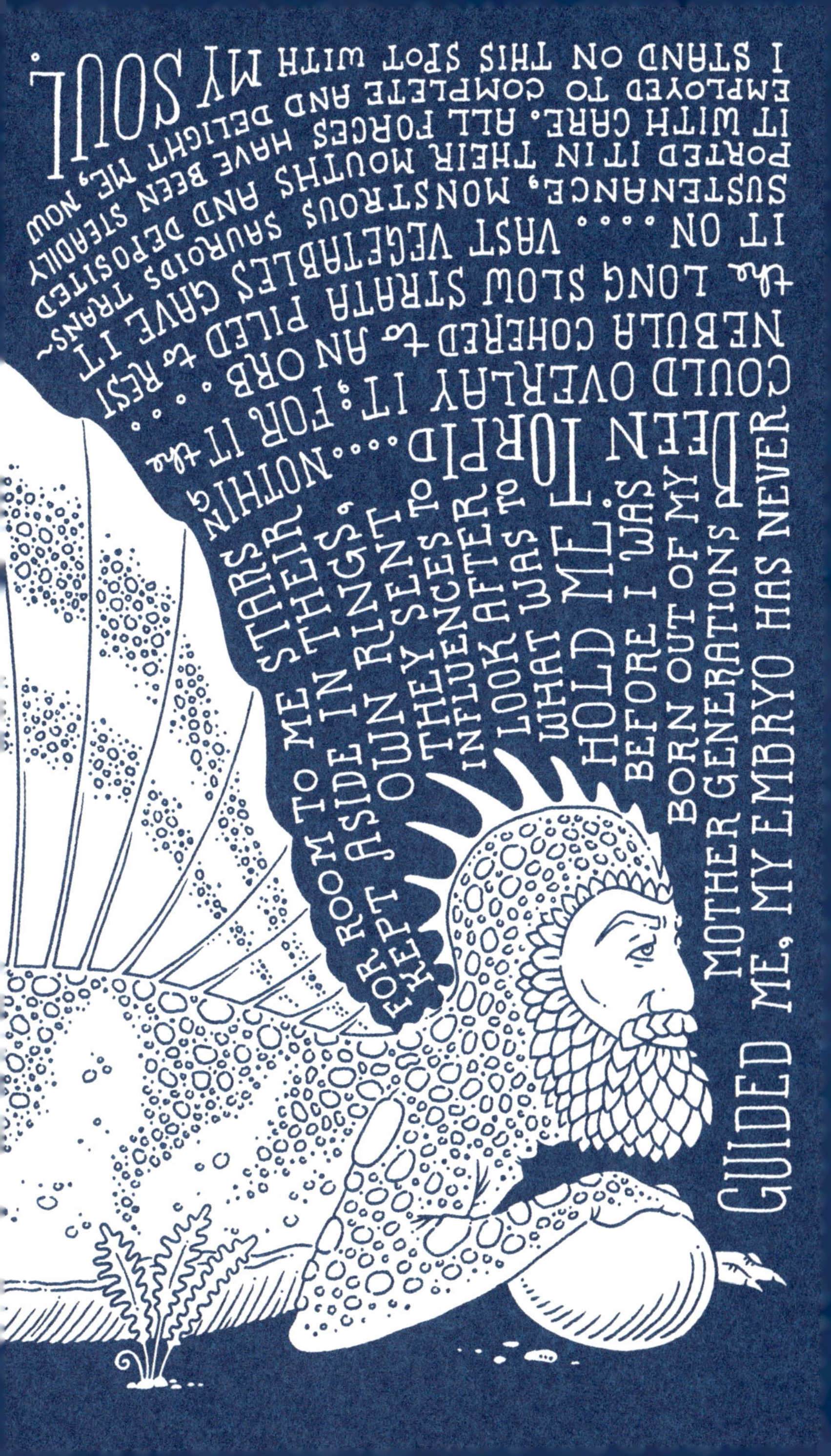
FOR ROOM TO ME STARS
KEPT ASIDE IN THEIR
OWN RINGS,
THEY SENT
INFLUENCES TO
LOOK AFTER
WHAT WAS TO
HOLD ME.
BEFORE I WAS
BORN OUT OF MY
MOTHER GENERATIONS
GUIDED ME, MY EMBRYO HAS NEVER
BEEN TORPID
NOTHING.... COULD OVERLAY IT: FOR IT the
NEBULA COHERED to AN ORB....
the LONG SLOW STRATA PILED to REST
IT ON.... VAST VEGETABLES GAVE IT
SUSTENANCE, MONSTROUS SAUROIDS TRANS-
PORTED IT IN THEIR MOUTHS AND DEPOSITED
IT WITH CARE. ALL FORCES HAVE BEEN STEADILY
EMPLOYED TO COMPLETE AND DELIGHT ME, NOW
I STAND ON THIS SPOT WITH MY SOUL.

SPAN OF YOUTH! EVER~PUSHED ELASTICITY! MANHOOD BALANCED AND FLORID AND FULL! MY LOVERS SUFFOCATE ME! CROWDING MY LIPS, and THICK in the PORES of MY SKIN, JOSTLING ME THROUGH STREETS and PUBLIC HALLS.... COMING NAKED to ME at NIGHT, CRYING BY DAY AHOY FROM the ROCKS of the RIVER.... SWI~NGING and CHIRPING OVER my HEAD, CALLING MY NAME FROM FLOWERBEDS OR VINES or TANGLED UNDERBRUSH, OR WHILE I SWIM IN the BATH

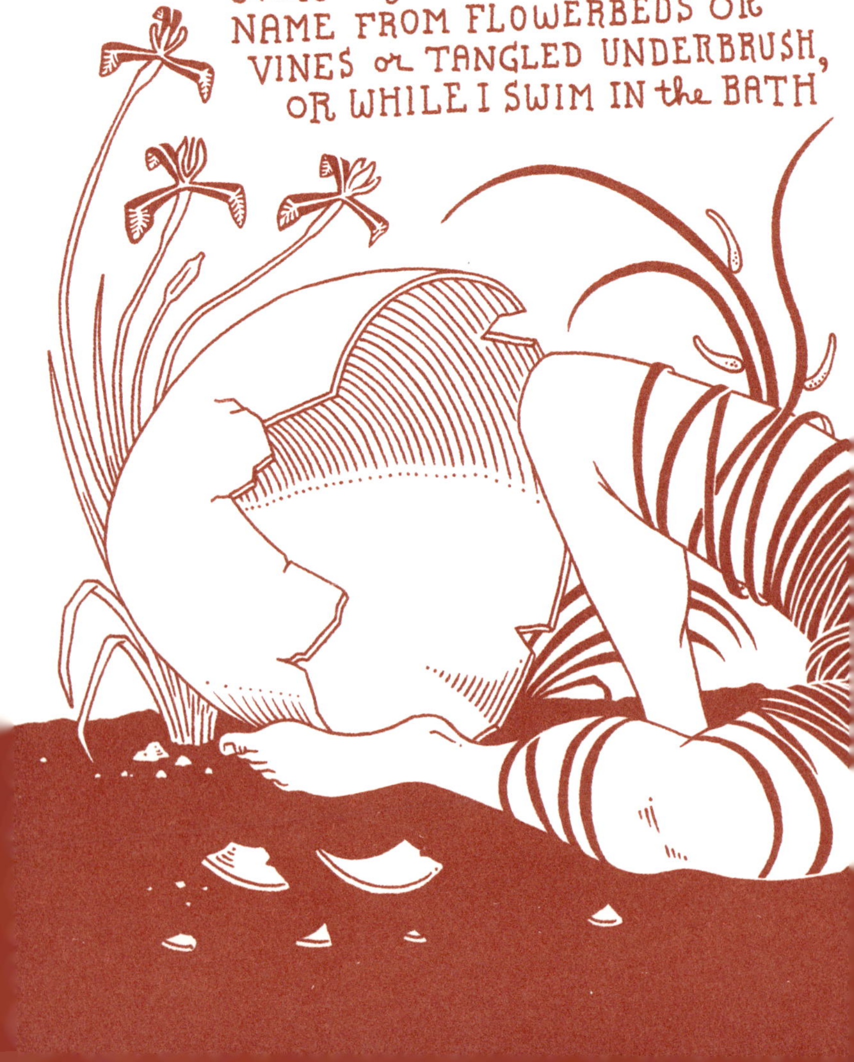

. . . . OR DRINK FROM the PUMP at THE CORNER . . . . OR the CURTAIN IS DOWN at the OPERA . . . . OR I GLIMPSE at A WOMAN'S FACE IN the RAILROAD CAR; LIGHTING ON EVERY MOMENT OF MY LIFE, BUSSING MY BODY WITH SOFT and BALSAMIC BUSSES, NOISELESSLY PASSING HANDFULS OUT of THEIR HEARTS and GIVING THEM to BE MINE.

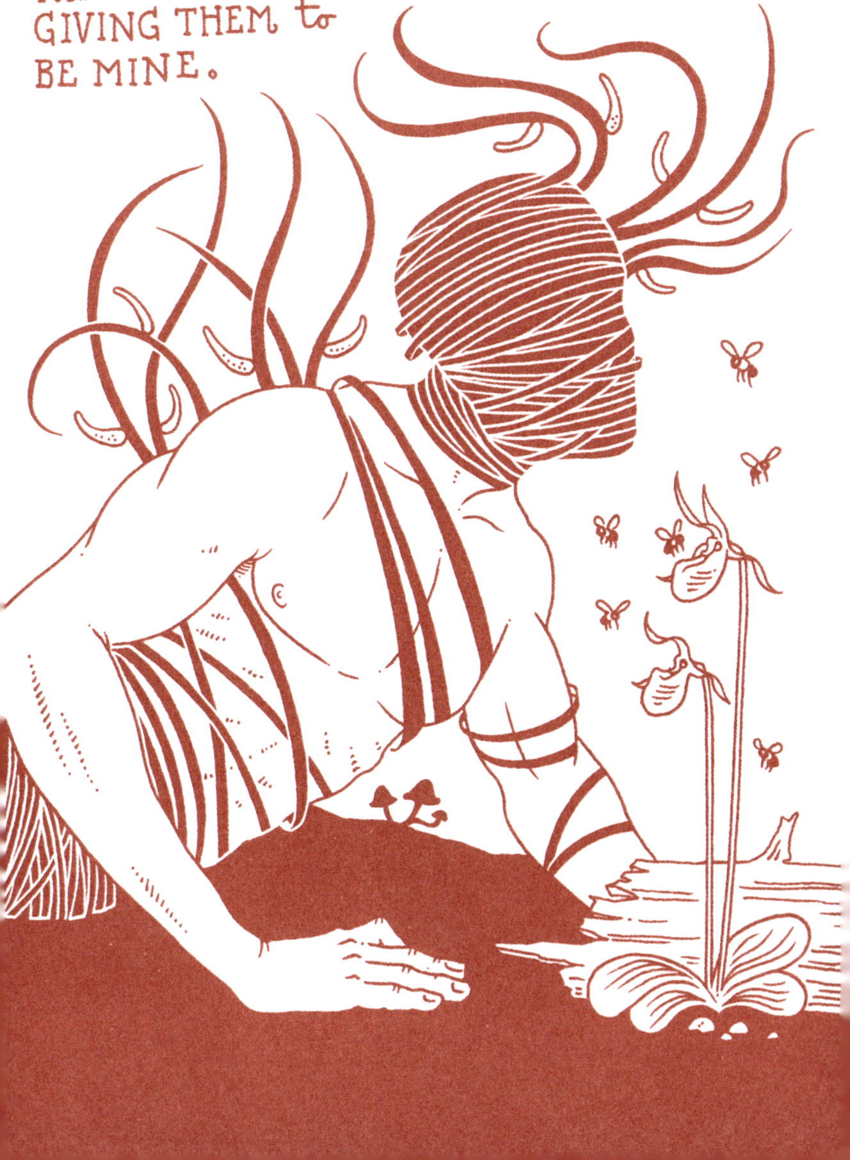

OLD AGE SUPERBLY RISING! INEFFABLE GRACE of DYING DAYS!

EVERY CONDITION PROMULGES NOT ONLY ITSELF.... IT PROMULGES WHAT GROWS AFTER AND OUT OF ITSELF, AND THE DARK HUSH PROMULGES AS MUCH AS ANY.

I OPEN MY SCUTTLE AT NIGHT AND SEE the FAR-SPRINKLED SYSTEMS,

AND ALL I SEE, MULTIPLIED AS HIGH AS I CAN CIPHER, EDGE BUT THE RIM OF THE FARTHER SYSTEMS.

WIDER AND WIDER THEY SPREAD, EXPANDING AND ALWAYS EXPANDING,

OUTWARD AND OUTWARD AND FOREVER OUTWARD.

MY SUN HAS HIS SUN, AND ROUND HIM OBEDIENTLY WHEELS,

HE JOINS WITH HIS PARTNERS A GROUP OF SUPERIOR CIRCUIT,

AND GREATER SETS FOLLOW, MAKING SPECKS OF THE GREATEST INSIDE THEM.

THERE IS NO STOPPAGE, AND NEVER CAN BE STOPPAGE; IF I AND YOU AND THE WORLDS AND ALL BENEATH OR UPON THEIR SURFACES, AND ALL THE PALPABLE LIFE, WERE THIS MOMENT REDUCED BACK TO A PALLID FLOAT, IT WOULD NOT AVAIL IN THE LONG RUN,

WE SHOULD SURELY BRING UP AGAIN WHERE WE NOW STAND, AND AS SURELY GO AS MUCH FARTHER, AND THEN FARTHER AND FARTHER.

A FEW QUADRILLIONS OF ERAS, A FEW OCTILLIONS OF CUBIC LEAGUES, DO NOT HAZARD THE SPAN, OR MAKE IT IMPATIENT, THEY ARE BUT PARTS.... ANY THING IS BUT A PART.

SEE EVER SO FAR... THERE IS LIMITLESS SPACE OUTSIDE OF THAT, COUNT EVER SO MUCH... THERE IS LIMITLESS TIME AROUND THAT.

OUR RENDEZVOUS IS FITLY APPOINTED.... GOD WILL BE THERE AND WAIT TILL WE COME.

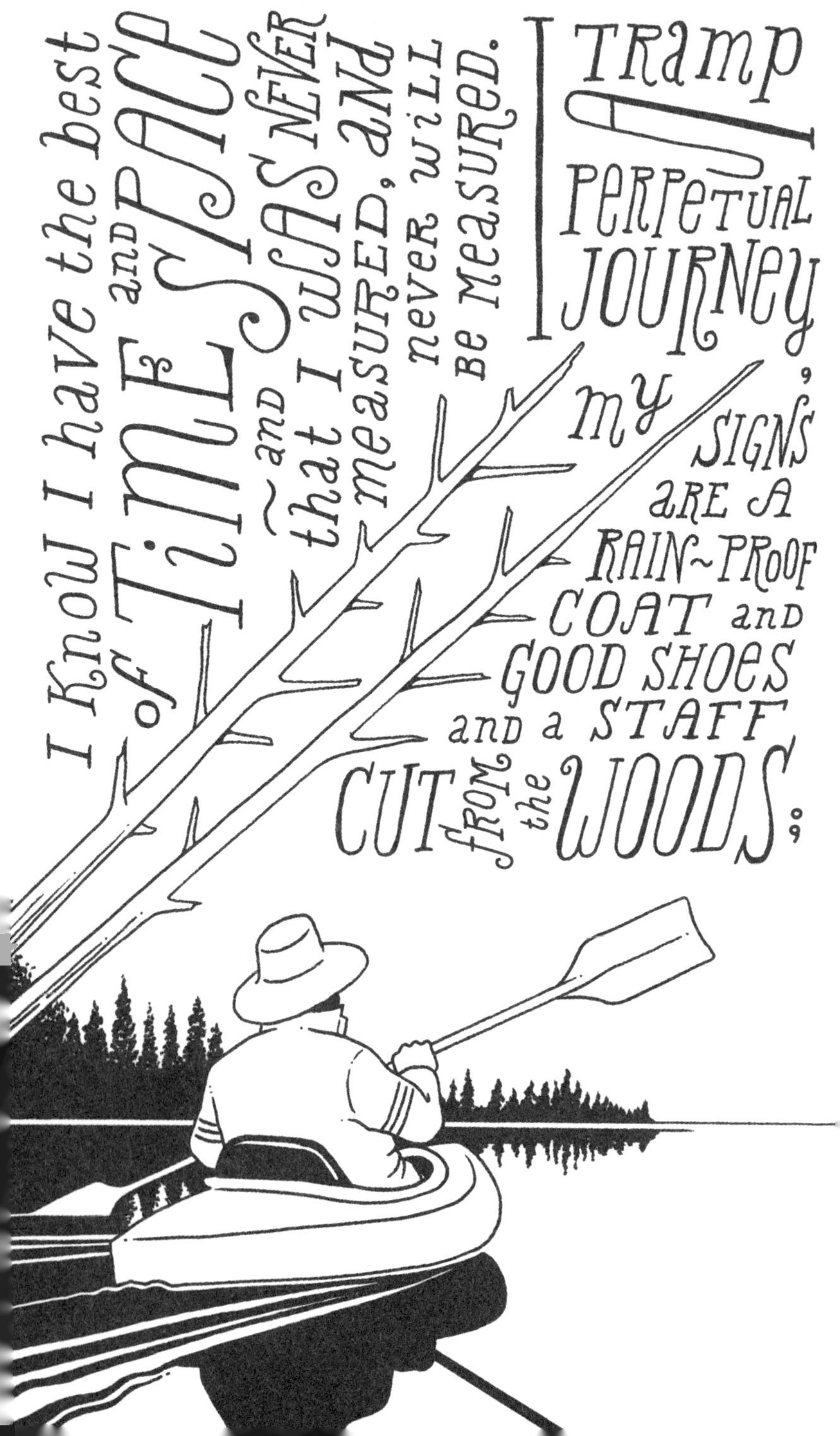
I know I have the best of Time and Space and that I was never measured, and never will be measured.
I tramp a perpetual journey, my signs are a rain-proof coat and good shoes and a staff cut from the woods;

No friend of mine takes his ease in my chair, I have no chair, nor church, nor philosophy;

I lead no man to a dinner-table or library or exchange, but each man and each woman of you I lead upon a knoll, my left hand hooks you round the waist, my right hand points to landscapes of continents, and a plain public road.

Not I, not any one else can travel that road for you, you must travel it for yourself.

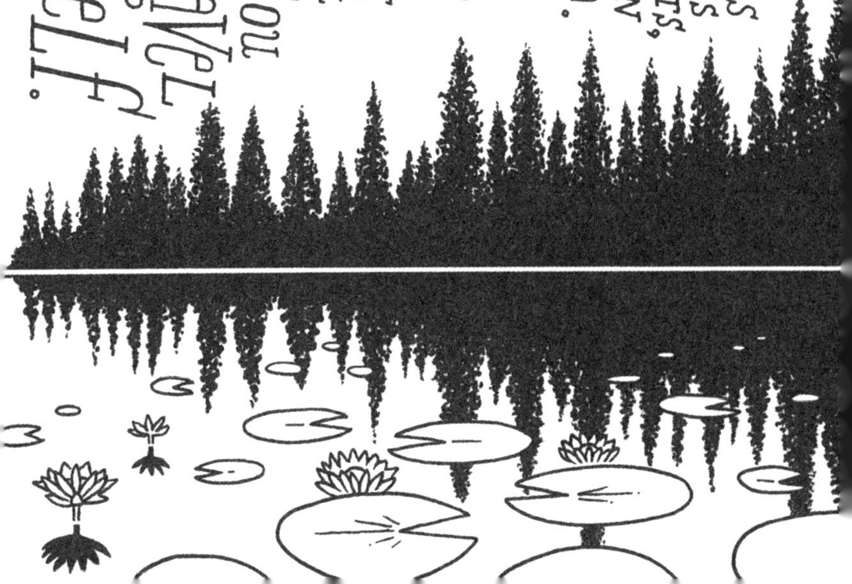

it is not far.... it is within reach,

Perhaps you have been on it since you were born, and did not know,

Perhaps it is every where on water and on land.

Shoulder your duds, and I will mine, and let us hasten forth; wonderful cities and free nations we shall fetch as we go.

If you tire, give me both burdens, and rest the chuff of your hand on my hip, and in DUE TIME you SHALL Repay the SAME Service TO Me; for after we start we never lie by again.

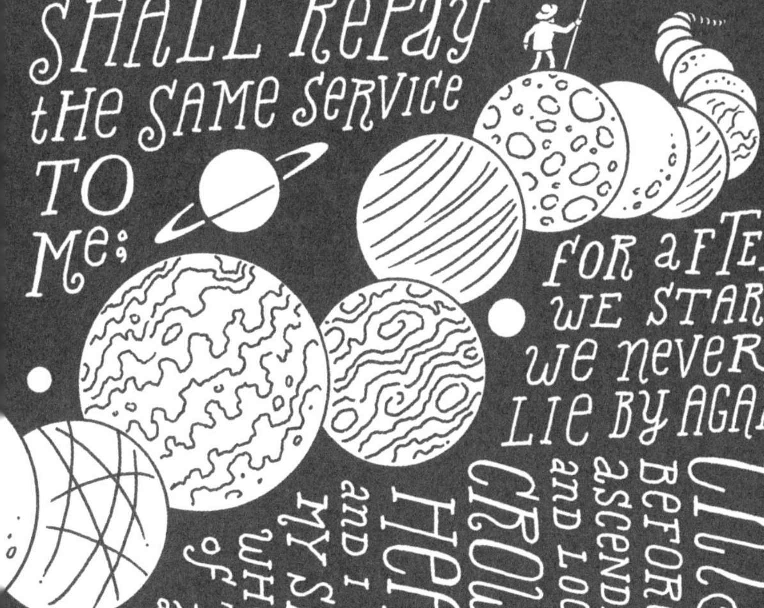

this Day before dawn I ascended a hill and looked at the crowded heaven, and I said to my spirit, when we become the enfolders of those orbs and the pleasure and knowledge of every thing in them, shall we be filled and satisfied then!

and my spirit said NO, we level that lift to pass and continue beyond.

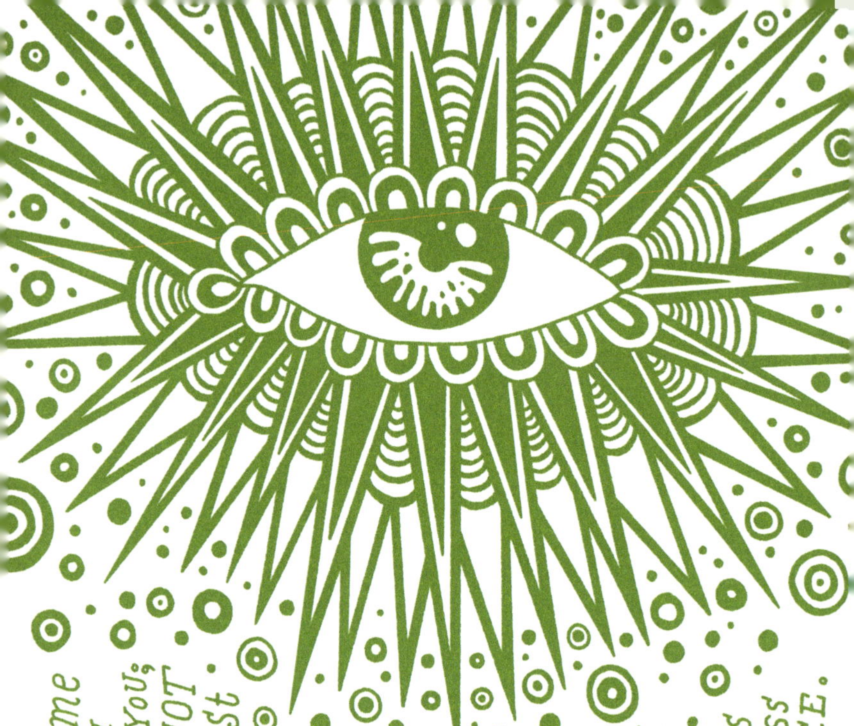

You are also asking me questions, and I hear you; I answer that I cannot answer... you must find out for yourself. Sit awhile wayfarer, here are biscuits to eat and here is milk to drink, but as soon as you sleep and renew yourself in sweet clothes I will certainly kiss you with my goodbye kiss and open the gate for your egress hence.

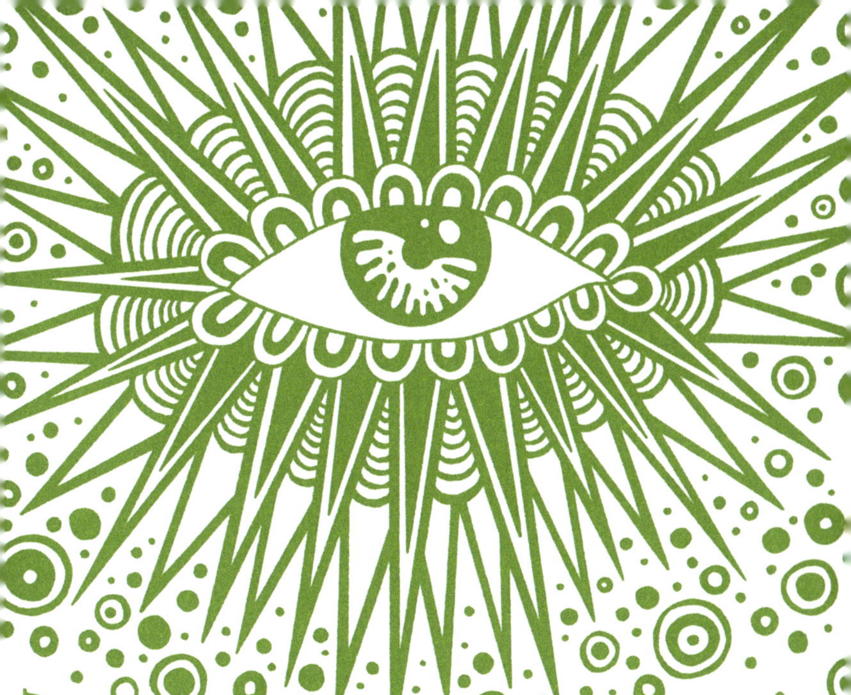

LONG ENOUGH HAVE YOU DREAMED CONTEMPTIBLE DREAMS, NOW I WASH the GUM FROM YOUR EYES, YOU MUST HABIT YOURSELF TO THE DAZZLE OF THE LIGHT and OF EVERY MOMENT OF YOUR LIFE.

LONG HAVE YOU TIMIDLY WADED, HOLD~ING A PLANK BY the SHORE, NOW I WILL YOU TO BE A BOLD SWIMMER, TO JUMP OFF IN THE MIDST OF THE SEA, AND RISE AGAIN AND NOD TO ME and SHOUT, AND LAUGHINGLY DASH WITH YOUR HAIR.

I am the teacher of Athletes, He that By mE SPREADS a WIDER BREAST than my OWN PROVES the WIDTH of MY OWN,

He MOST HONORS MY STYLE WHO LEARNS UNDER IT TO DESTROY THE TEACHER.

the BOY I LOVE, THE SAME BECOMES A MAN NOT THROUGH DER~IVED POWER BUT IN HIS OWN RIGHT, WICKED, RATHER THAN VIRTUOUS OUT OF CONFORMITY OR FEAR, FOND OF HIS SWEETHEART, RELISHING WELL HIS STEAK, UNREQUITED LOVE OR a SLIGHT CUTTING WORSE than A WOUND CUTS, FIRST RATE to RIDE, to FIGHT, to HIT the BULL'S EYE, to SAIL A SKIFF, to SING a SONG OR PLAY ON the BANJO,

PREFERRING SCARS and FACES PITTED WITH SMALLPOX OVER ALL LATHERERS and THOSE THAT KEEP OUT of the SUN.

I DO NOT SAY THESE THINGS FOR A DOLLAR, OR TO FILL UP THE TIME WHILE I WAIT FOR A BOAT; IT IS YOU TALKING JUST AS MUCH AS MYSELF. . . . I ACT AS THE TONGUE OF YOU, IT WAS TIED IN YOUR MOUTH. . . . IN MINE IT BEGINS TO BE LOOSENED.

I TEACH STRAYING FROM ME, YET WHO CAN STRAY FROM ME? I FOLLOW YOU WHOEVER YOU ARE FROM THE PRESENT HOUR; MY WORDS ITCH AT YOUR EARS TILL YOU UNDERSTAND THEM.

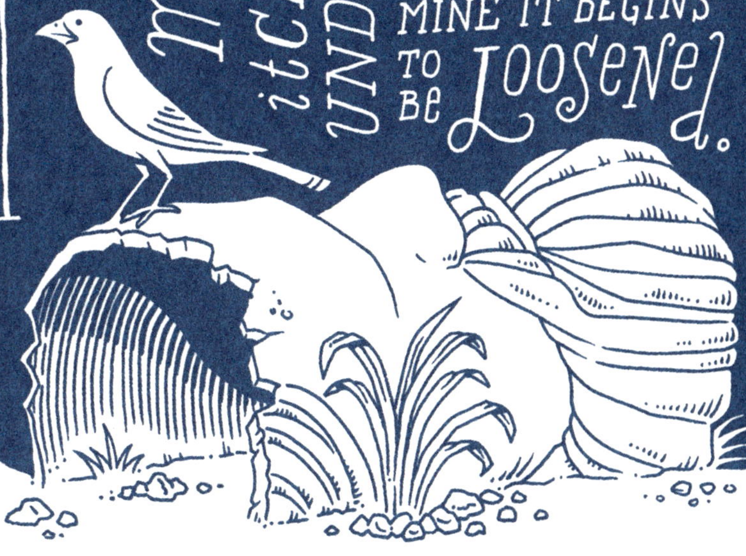

I SWear I WILL
neveR mention
LOVE OR DeATH
INSIDE A HOUSE, and
I SWEAR I NEVER WILL
TRANSLATE MYSELF AT
ALL, ONLY TO HIM OR
HER WHO PRIVATELY
STAYS WITH ME IN
the OPEN AIR. IF
YOU WOULD UNDER~
STAND ME GO TO the
HEIGHTS or WATER~
SHORE, THE NEAREST
GNAT IS AN EXPLANATION
and A DROP OR the MOTION
OF WAVES a KEY, the
MAUL the OAR and the
HANDSAW SECOND MY
WORDS. NO SHUTTERED
ROOM OR SCHOOL CAN COMMUNE WITH ME,

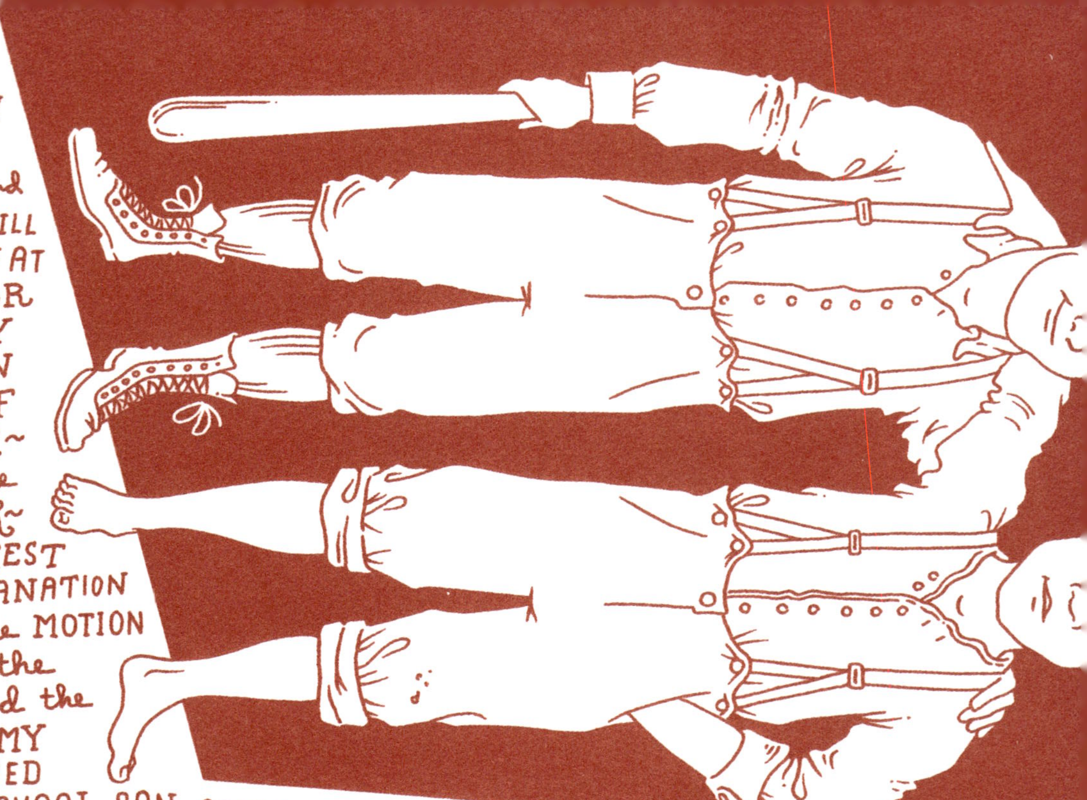

BUT ROUGHS and LITTLE CHILDREN BETTER THAN THEY. the YOUNG MECHANIC IS CLOSEST TO ME .... HE KNOWS ME PRETTY WELL, the WOODMAN that TAKES HIS AXE and JUG WITH HIM SHALL TAKE ME WITH HIM ALL DAY, tHE FARMBOY PLOUGHING IN THE FIELD FEELS GOOD at the SOUND OF MY VOICE, IN VESSELS THAT SAIL MY WORDS MUST SAIL .... I GO WITH FISHERMEN AND SEAMEN, AND LOVE THEM, MY FACE RUBS to the HUNTER'S FACE WHEN HE LIES DOWN ALONE IN HIS BLANKET, tHe DRIVeR THINKING OF ME DOES NOT MIND the JOLT OF HIS WAGON.

tHe YOUNG MotHeR and OLD MOTHER SHALL COMPREHEND me, the GIRL and the WIFE Rest the NeeDLe a moment AND forget where they ARE, they AND ALL would Resume WHAT I have told them.

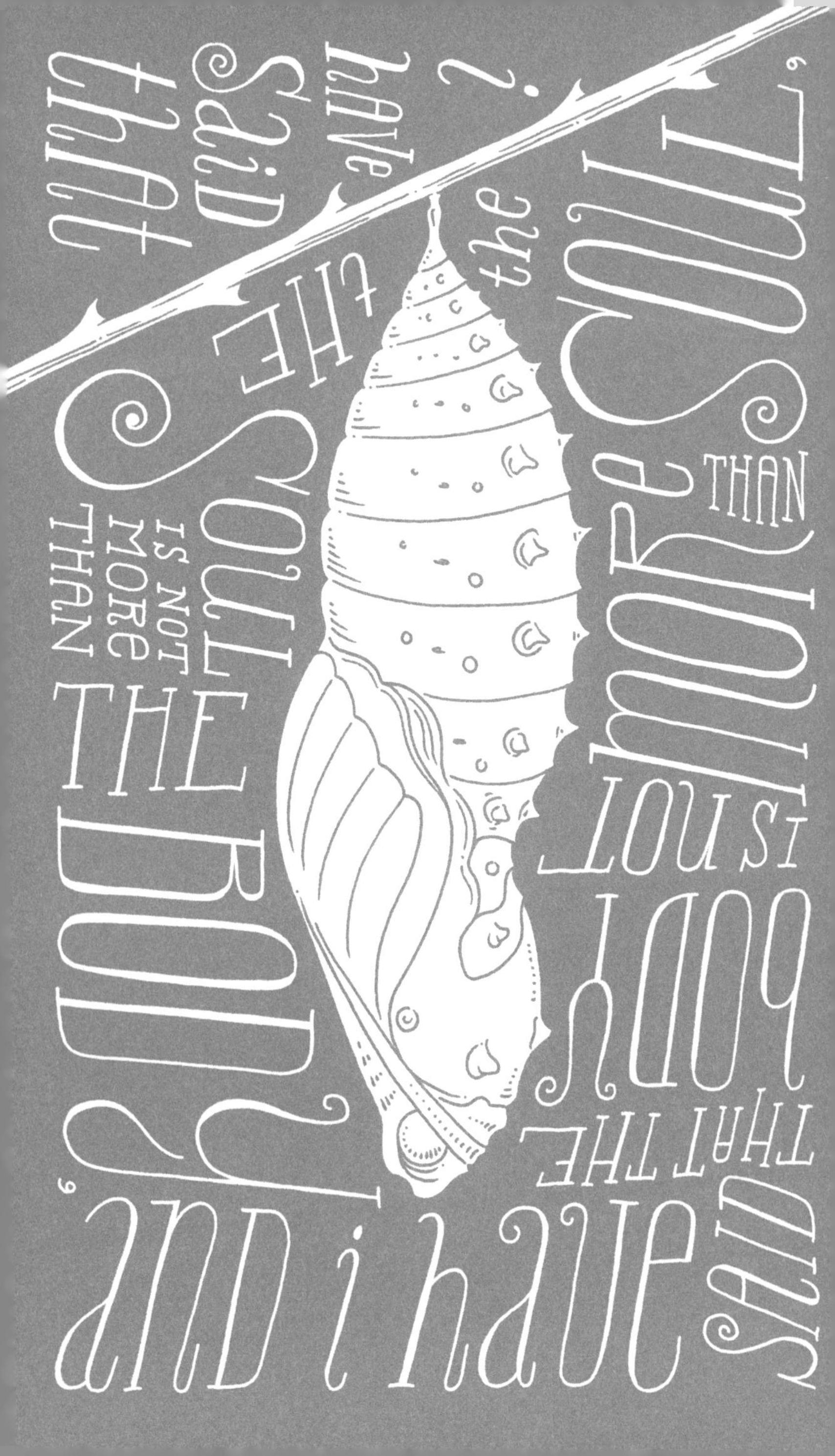
"I have said that the soul is not more than the body,
and I have said that the body is not more than the soul"

AND NOTHING, NOT GOD
is greater to ONE
than ONE'S SELF IS, AND
WHOEVER WALKS A FURLONG
WITHOUT SYMPATHY WALKS to his
OWN FUNERAL, DRESSED IN HIS SHROUD,
AND I OR YOU POCKETLESS OF A DIME
MAY PURCHASE the PICK OF
the EARTH, AND to
GLANCE WITH AN EYE OR SHOW
A BEAN IN ITS POD CONFOUNDS
the LEARNING OF ALL TIMES,
AND THERE is no TRADE
OR EMPLOYMENT BUT
the YOUNG
MAN
following
IT MAY BECOME
a HERO,
AND there is no
OBJECT
SO SOFT BUT
IT MAKES A HUB
FOR THE WHEELED
UNIVERSE, AND ANY MAN
OR WOMAN SHALL STAND COOL AND SUPER~
CILIOUS BEFORE A MILLION UNIVERSES.

And I Call to Mankind, Be not curious about God, for I who am curious about each am not curious about God, no array of terms can say how much I am at peace about God and about death.

I hear and behold God in every object, yet I understand God not in the least, nor do I understand who there can be more wonderful than myself.

Why should I wish to see God better than this day?

I see something of God each hour of the twenty-four, and each moment then, in the faces of men and women I see God, and in my own face in the glass;

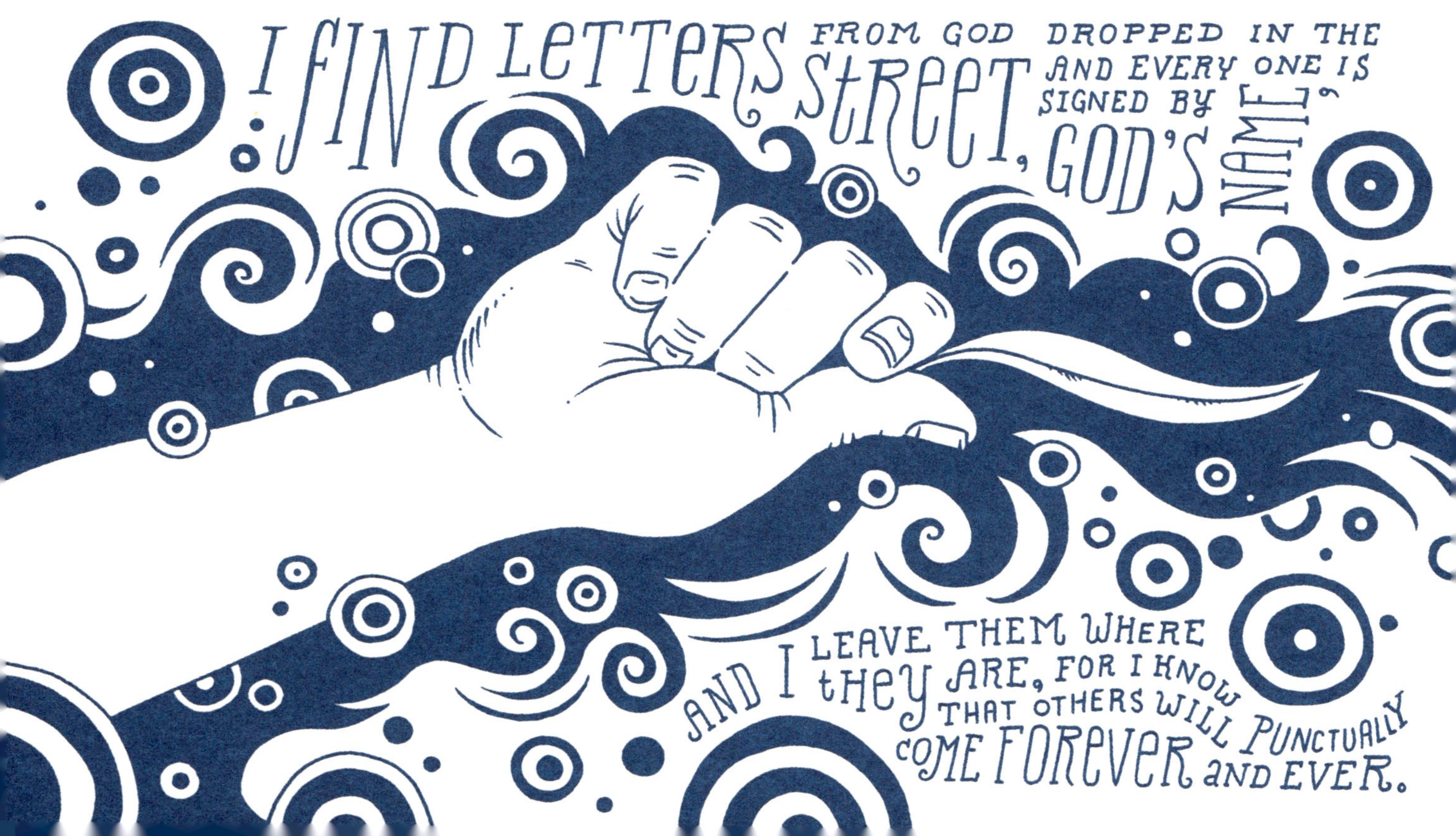
I FIND LETTERS FROM GOD DROPPED IN THE STREET, AND EVERY ONE IS SIGNED BY GOD'S NAME,
AND I LEAVE THEM WHERE THEY ARE, FOR I KNOW THAT OTHERS WILL PUNCTUALLY COME FOREVER AND EVER.

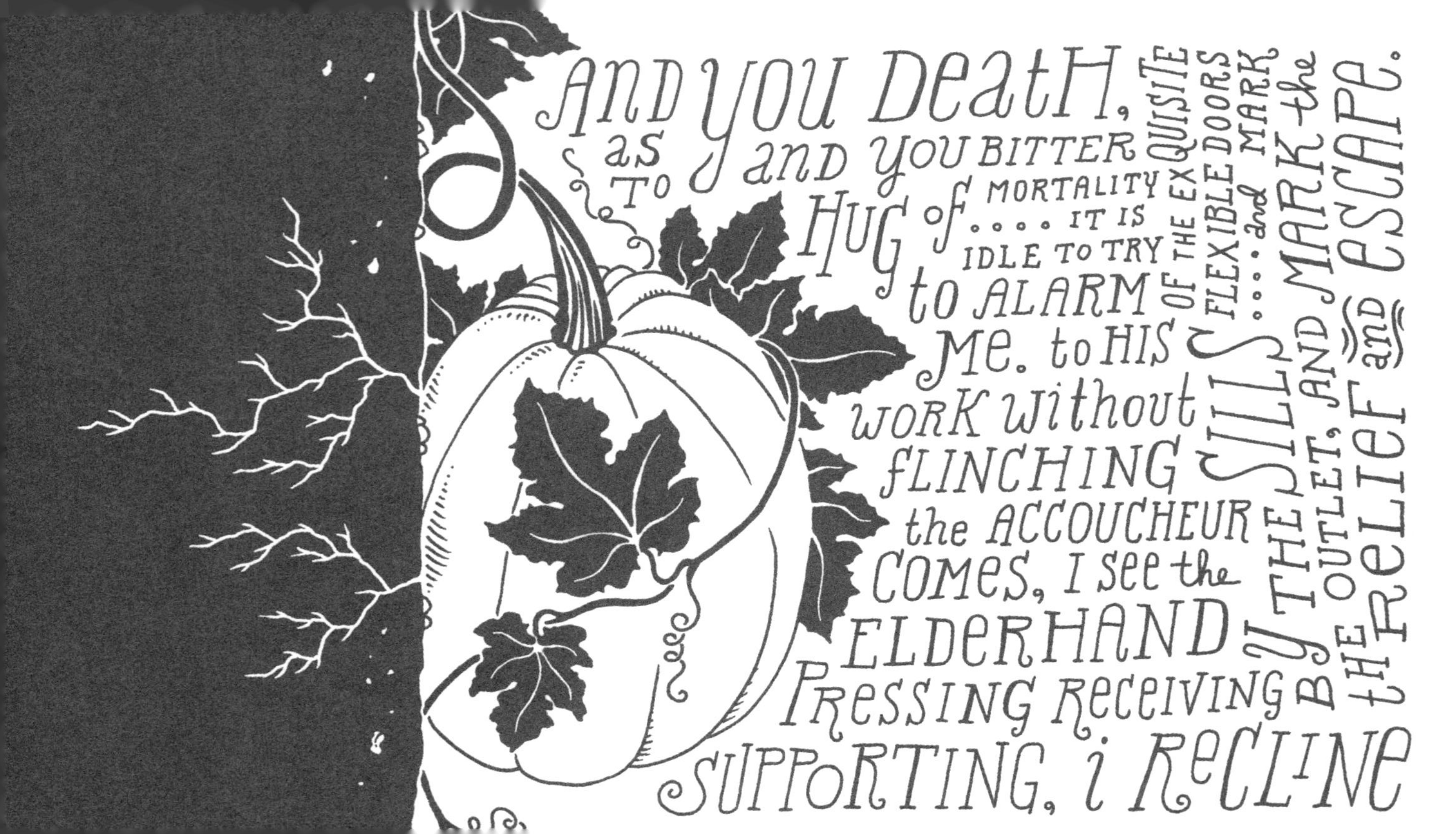
And you Death, and you bitter hug of mortality.... it is idle to try to alarm me.
To his work without flinching the accoucheur comes, I see the elderhand pressing receiving supporting,
I recline by the sills of the exquisite flexible doors.... and mark the outlet, and mark the relief and escape.

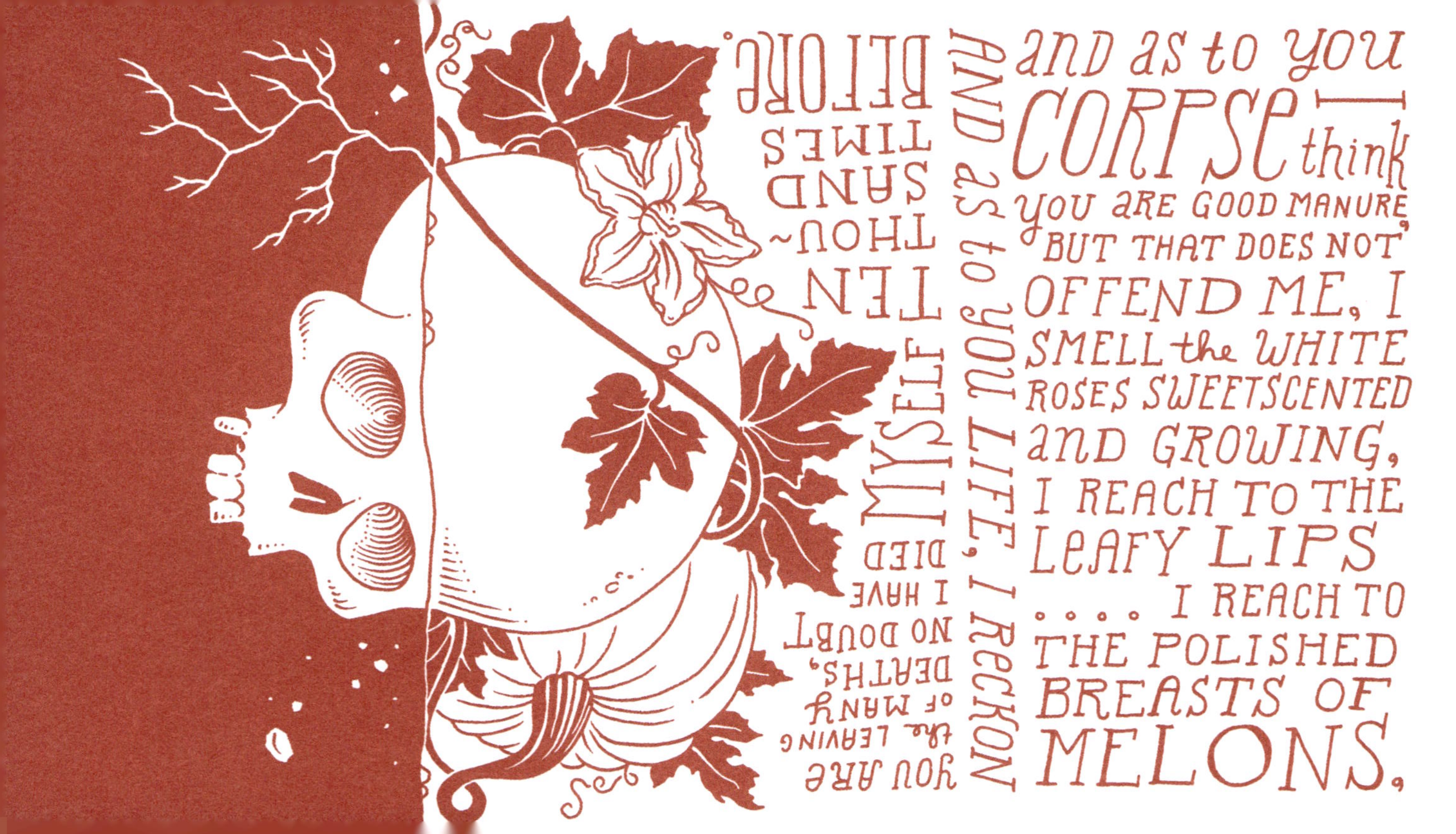

and as to you
CORPSE I think
you are good manure,
but that does not
offend me, I
smell the white
roses sweetscented
and growing,
I reach to the
leafy lips
.... I reach to
the polished
breasts of
melons,
AND as to you LIFE, I reckon
you are
the leaving
of many
deaths,
no doubt
I have
died
myself
ten
thou~
sand
times
before.

I HEAR YOU WHISPERING THERE O STARS OF HEAVEN, O SUNS.... O GRASS OF GRAVES.... O PERPETUAL TRANSFERS AND PROMOTIONS .....IF YOU DO NOT SAY ANYTHING HOW CAN I SAY ANYTHING?

OF THE TURBID POOL THAT LIES IN THE AUTUMN FOREST, OF THE MOON THAT DESCENDS THE STEEPS OF THE SOUGHING TWILIGHT, TOSS, SPARKLES OF DAY AND DUSK.... TOSS ON THE BLACK STEMS THAT DECAY IN THE MUCK, TOSS TO THE MOANING GIBBERISH OF DRY LIMBS.

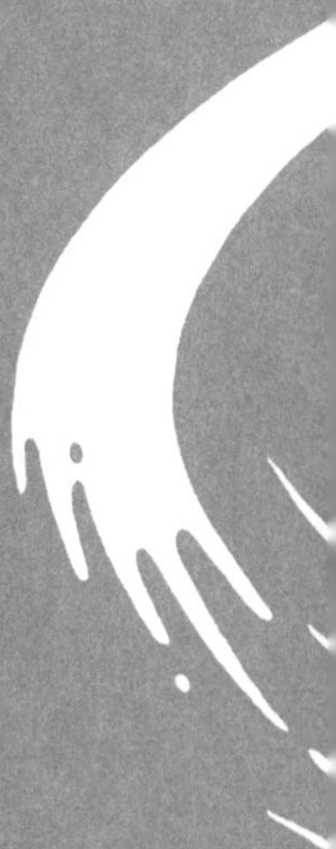

I ASCEND FROM THE MOON.... I ASCEND FROM THE NIGHT, AND PERCEIVE OF THE GHASTLY GLITTER THE SUNBEAMS REFLECTED, AND DEBOUCH TO THE STEADY AND CENTRAL FROM THE OFFSPRING GREAT OR SMALL.

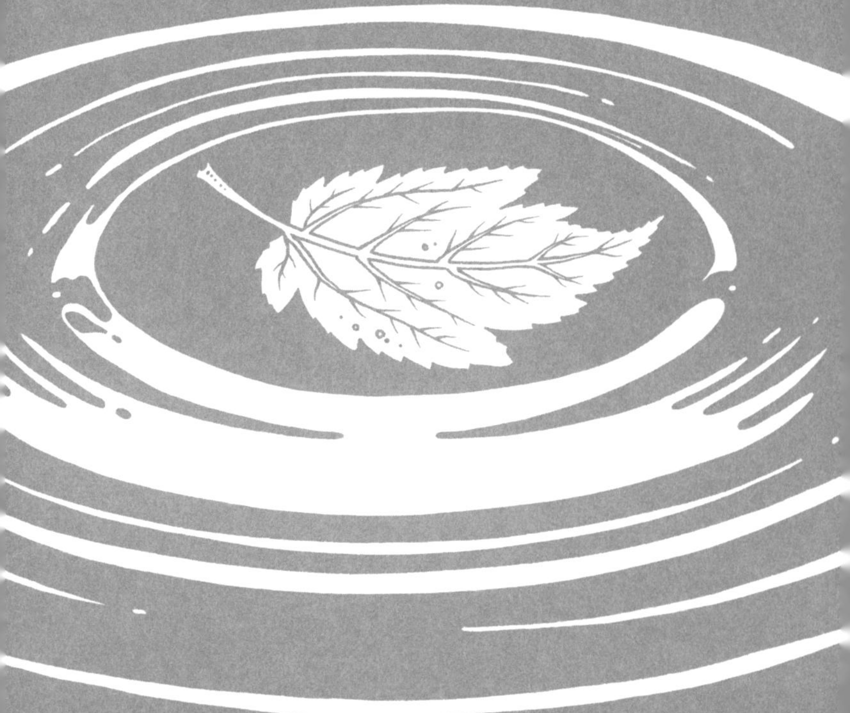

there is that
in me
.... I DO
NOT KNOW
WHAT IT IS
.... BUT
I KNOW IT IS
IN
ME.

WRENCHED AND SWEATY....
CALM AND COOL THEN
MY BODY BECOMES
.... I SLEEP
.... I SLEEP LONG.

i DO NOT
KNOW IT.... it
IS WITHOUT
NAME....
IT IS A WORD
UNSAID, IT IS NOT
IN ANY DICTIONARY
OR UTTERANCE OR
SYMBOL. SOMETHING
IT SWINGS ON MORE
THAN the EARTH
I SWING ON,
TO IT THE CREATION
IS the FRIEND
WHOSE EMBRACING
AWAKES ME.

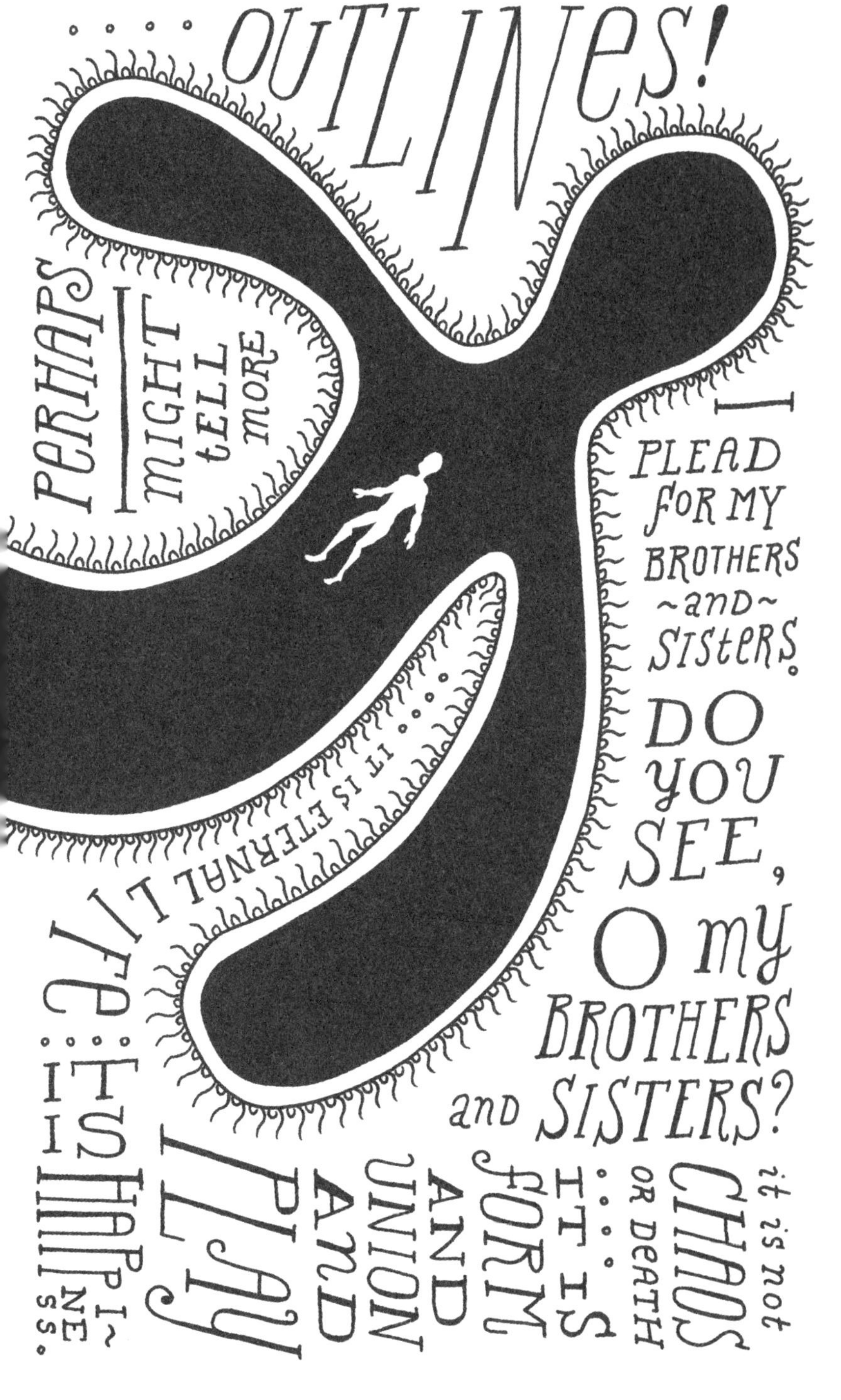

....OUTLINES!
PERHAPS I MIGHT tELL MORE
I PLEAD FOR MY BROTHERS ~and~ SISters.
DO YOU SEE, O my BROTHERS and SISTERS?
it is not CHAOS OR DEATH
...IT IS FORM, AND UNION AND PLAY
...IT IS ETERNAL
LIFE: IT IS HAPPI~NESS.

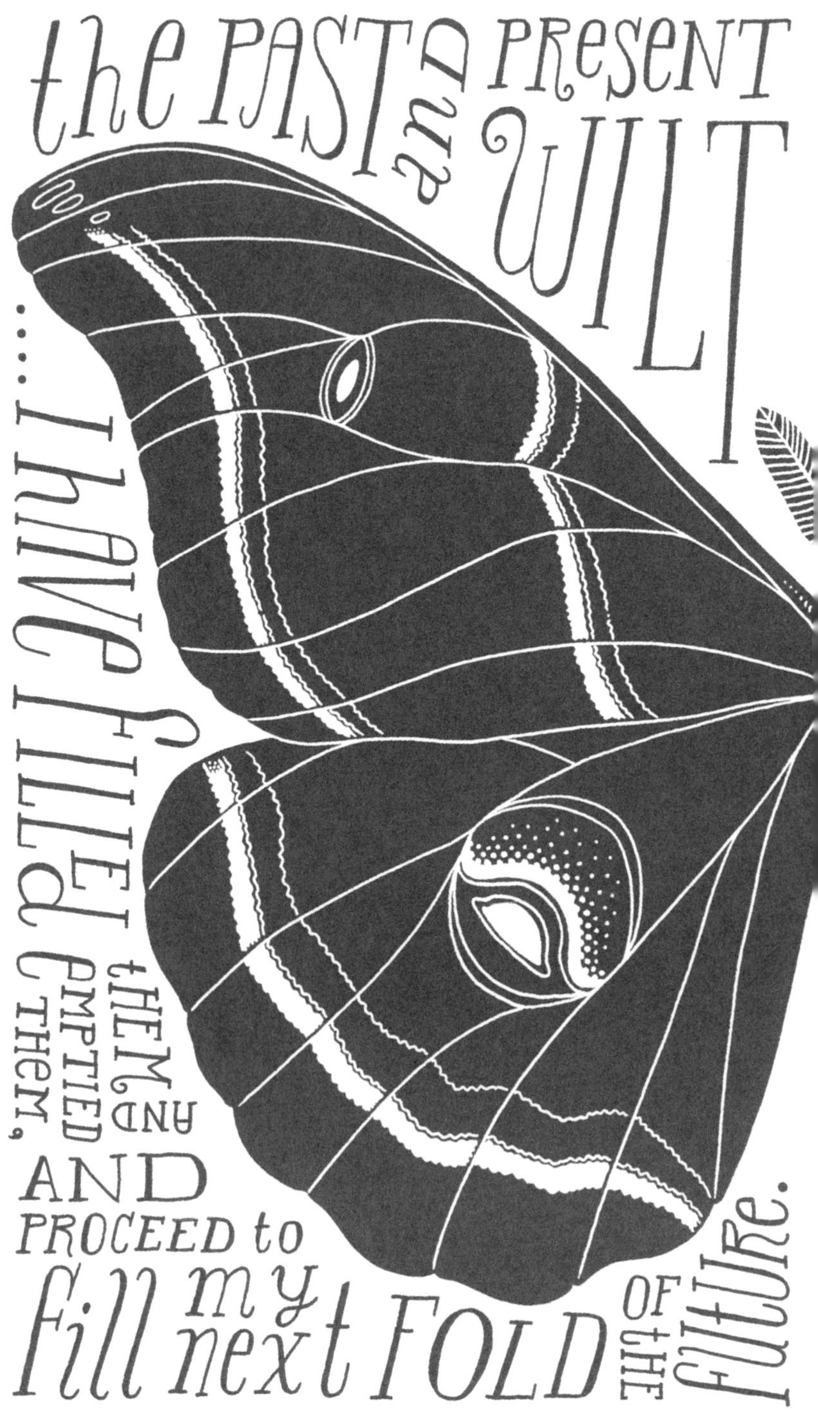
the PAST and PRESENT WILT
...I have filled them and emptied them,
AND PROCEED to fill my next FOLD of the FUTURE.

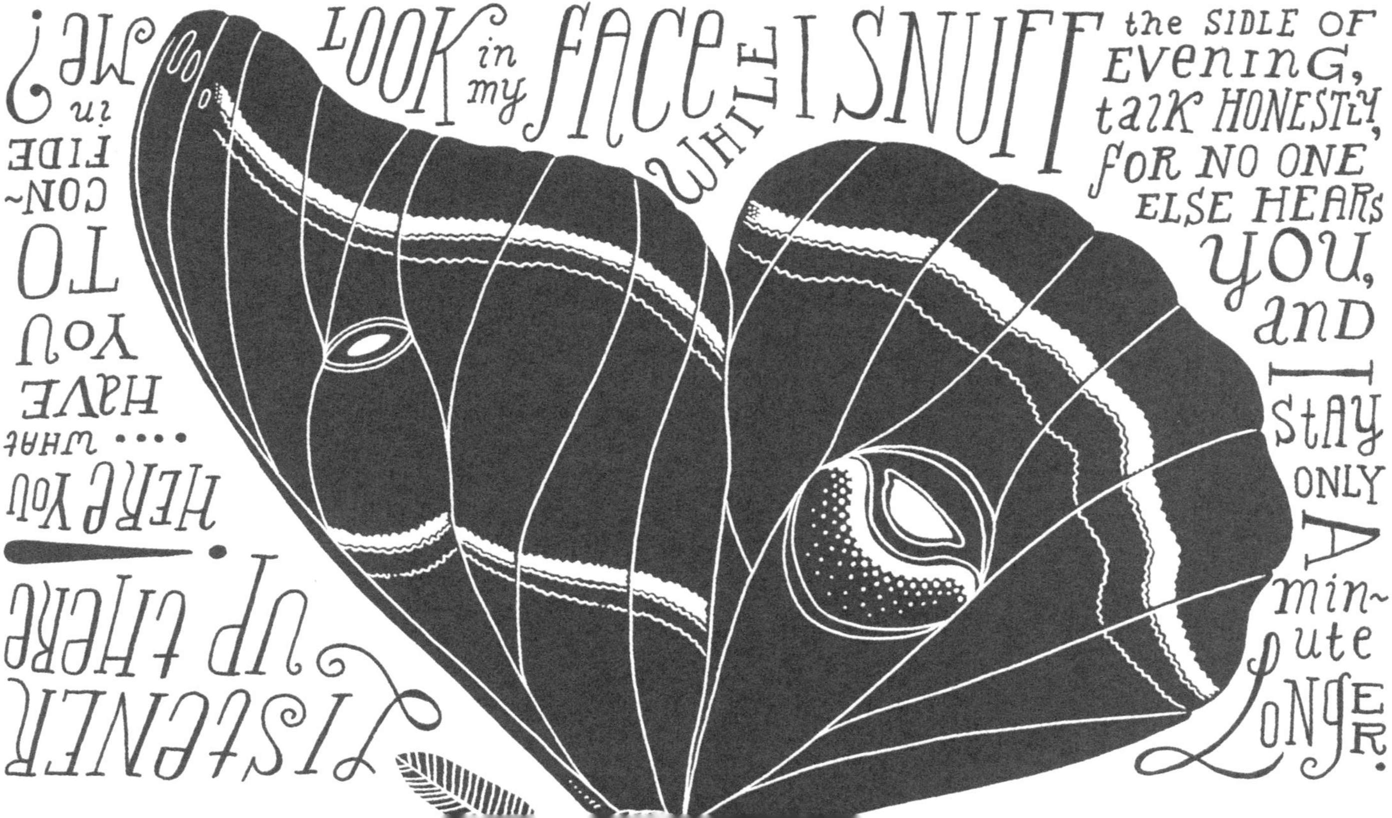

Listener up there!
Here you .... what have you to con-fide in me?
Look in my face while I snuff the sidle of evening,
talk honestly, for no one else hears you,
and I stay only a minute longer.

do i contra-dict myself?

VERY Well then....
i contradict myself.

I AM LARGE....

i contain MULTI-TUDES.

i concentrate
toward them
that are nigh....
I Wait on the
DOOR~SLAB.

WHO has DONE
his day's work
and WILL SOONEST
BE THROUGH with
HIS SUPPER?

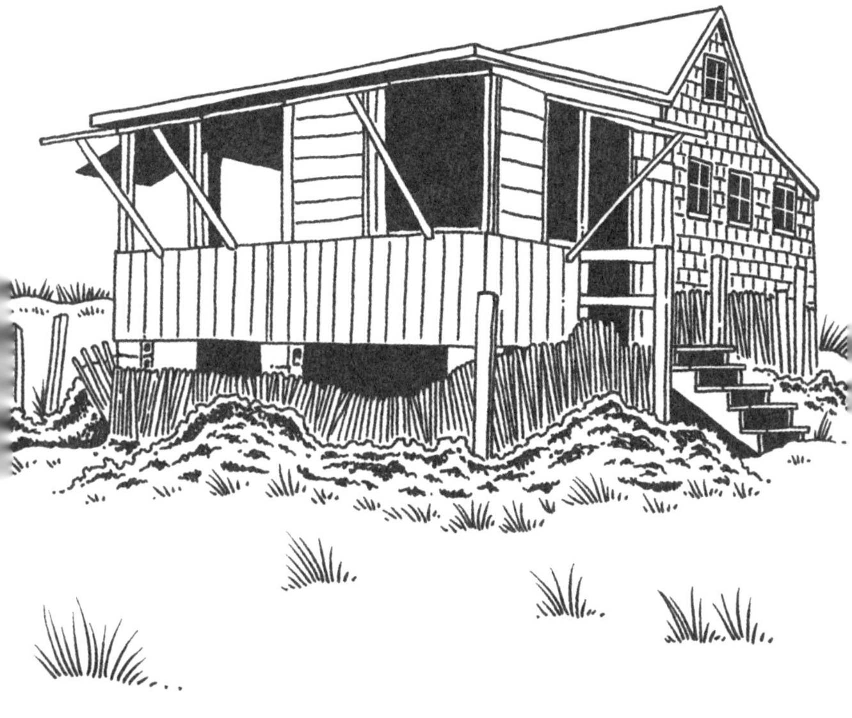

WHO WISHES to WALK WITH me?

WILL YOU SPEAK BEFORE I am GONE?

WILL YOU PROVE ALREADY too LATE?

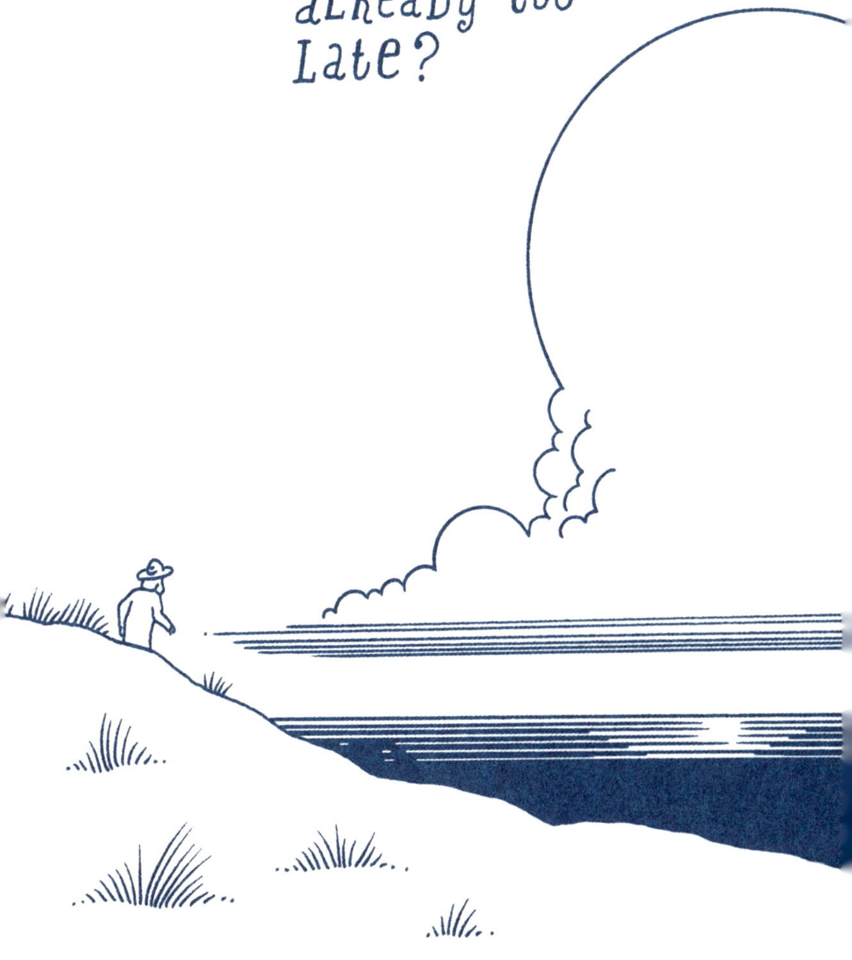

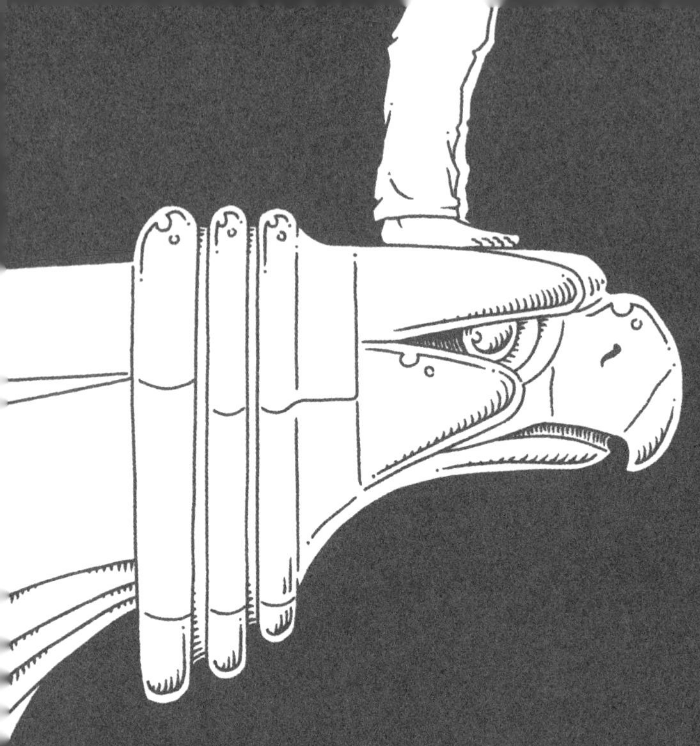

THE SPOTTED HAWK SWOOPS BY AND ACCUSES ME....

HE COMPLAINS OF MY GAB AND MY LOITERING.

I TOO AM NOT
A BIT TAMED
. . . . I TOO AM
UNTRANSLATABLE.

I SOUND MY
BARBARIC YAWP
OVER the ROOFS
OF THE WORLD.

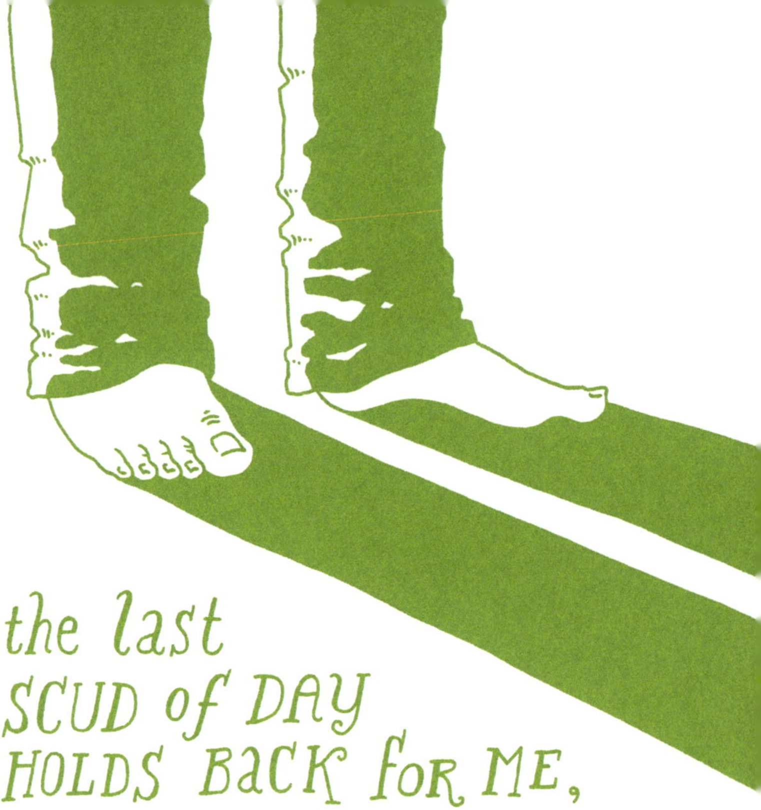

the last
SCUD of DAY
HOLDS BACK for ME,

it FLINGS my
Likeness after
the Rest and
true as any on
the SHADOWED
WILDS,

it coaxes me
to the vapor
and the dusk.

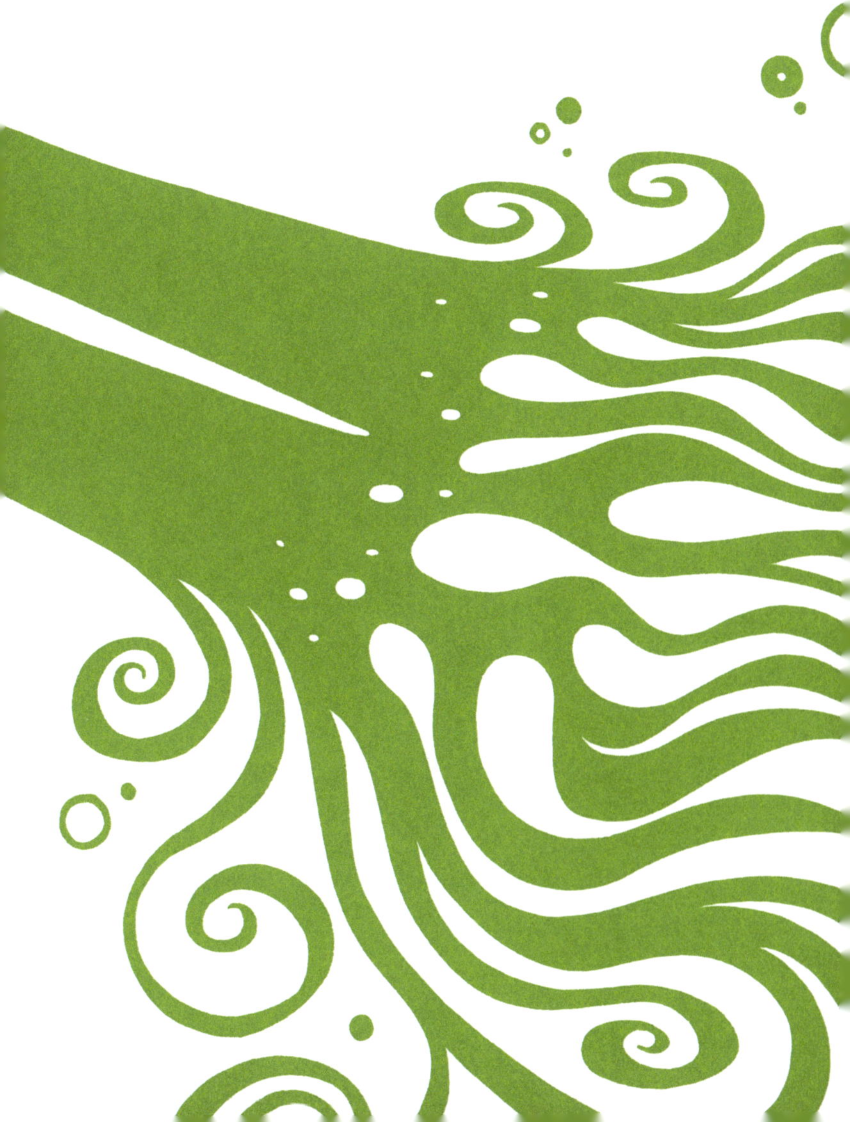

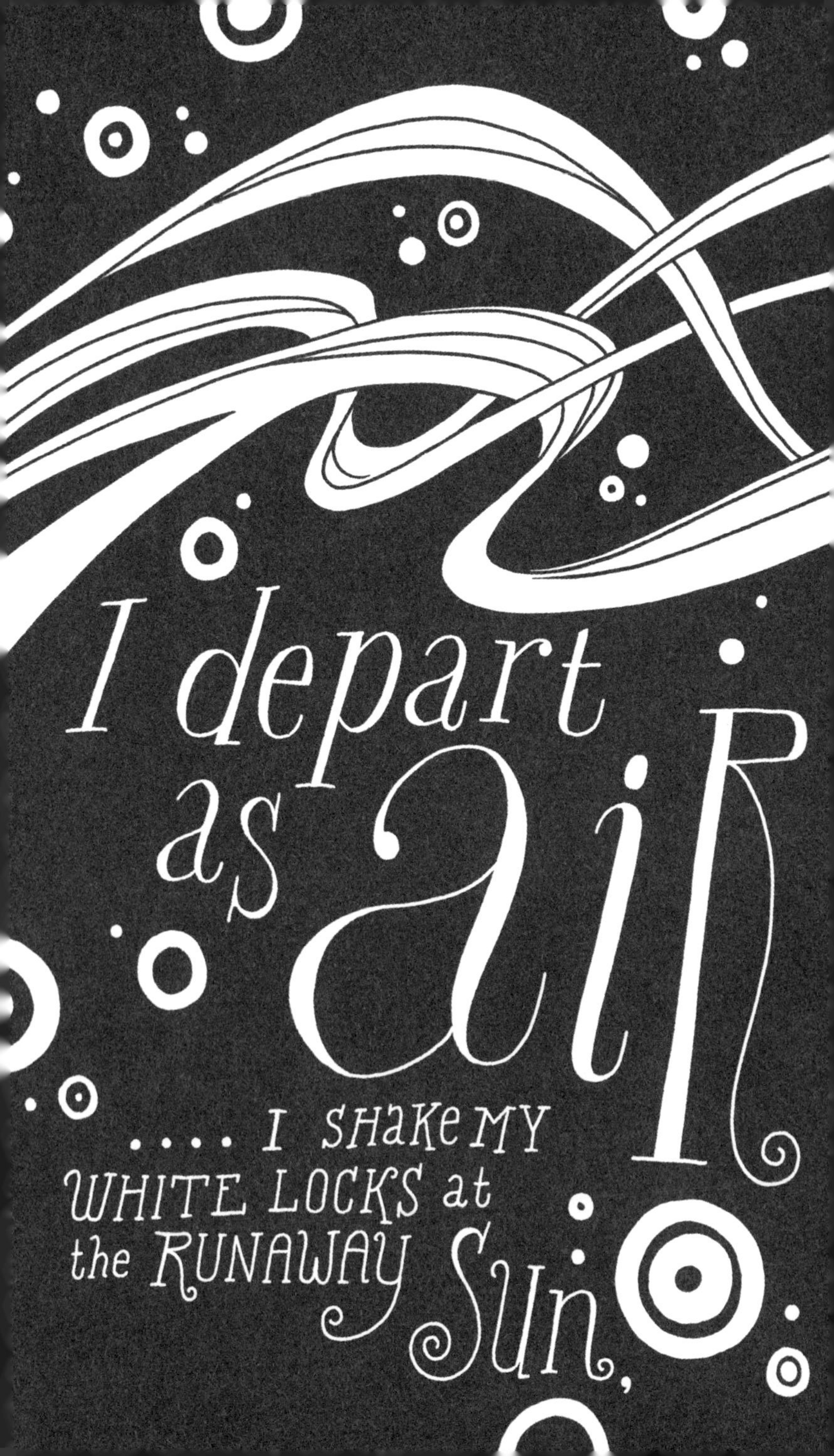
I depart as air
.... I shake my
white locks at
the runaway sun,

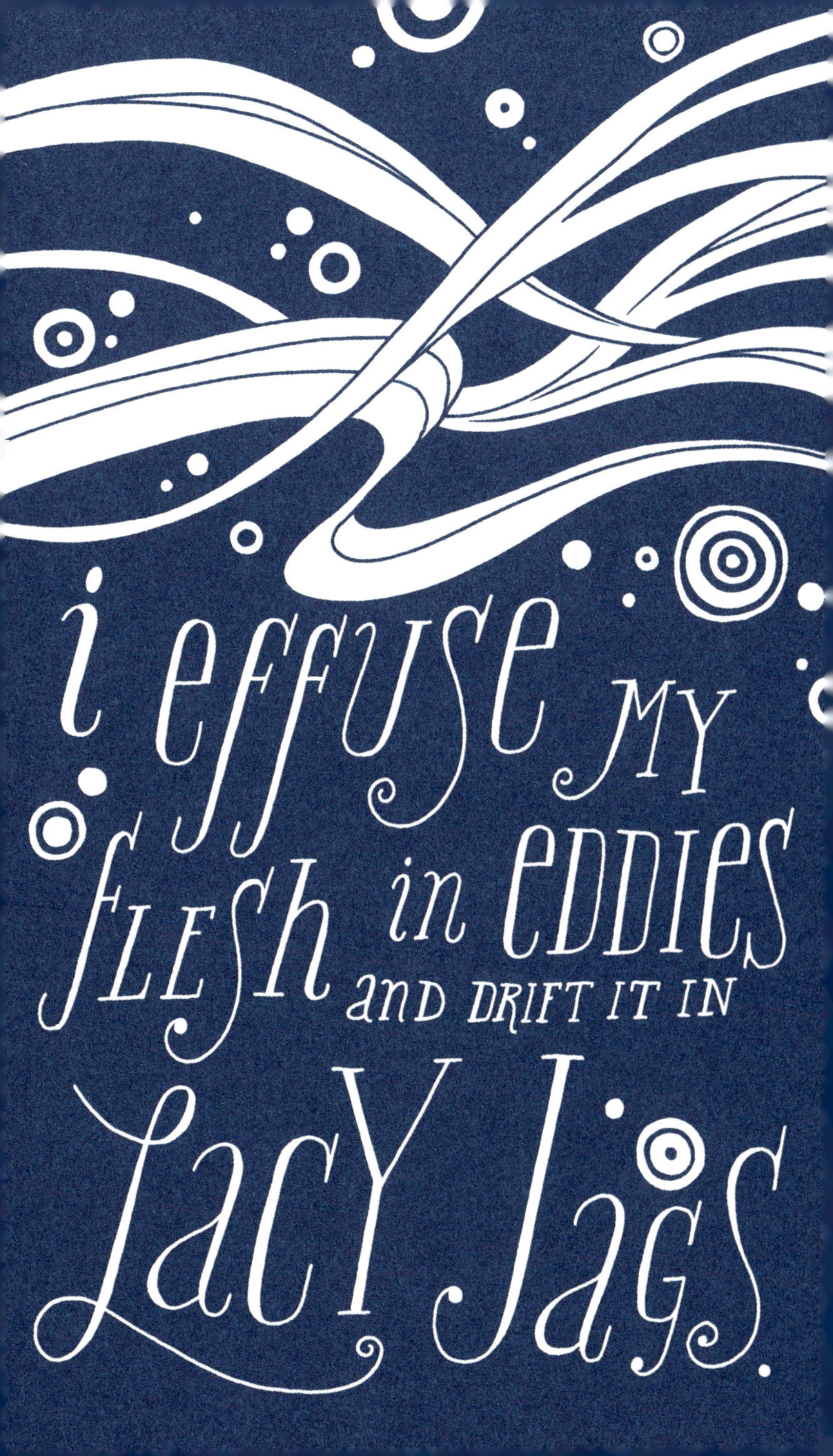

i effuse my
flesh in eddies
and drift it in
lacy jags.

I bequeath myself
to the dirt to
grow from
the grass
I love,

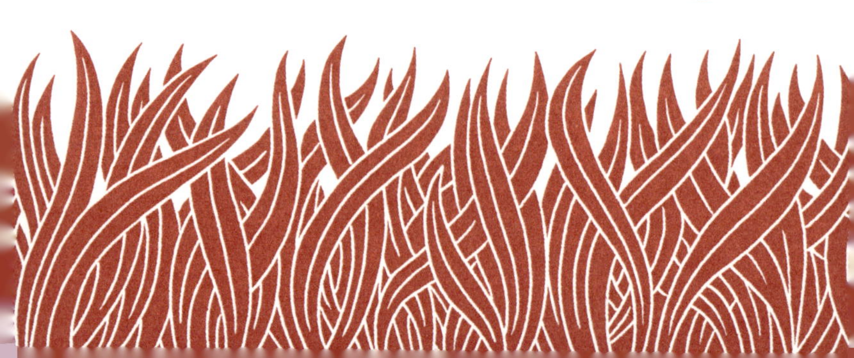

if you want me again look for me under your bootsoles.

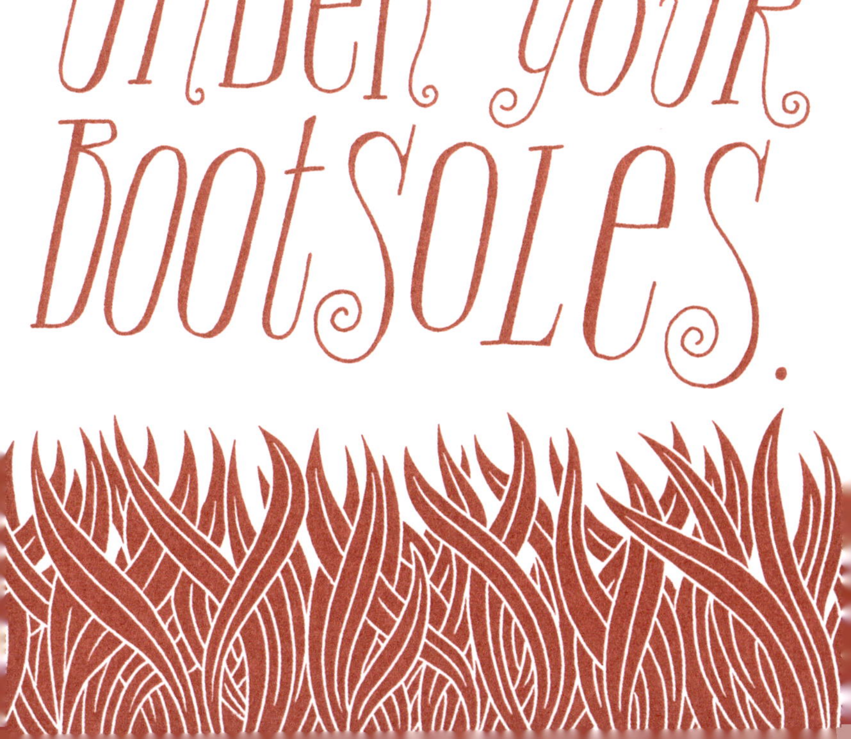

YOU WILL HARDLY KNOW WHO I AM OR WHAT I MEAN,

but i shall be good health to you nevertheless, and filter and fibre your blood.

Failing to fetch me at first keep encouraged,
Missing me one place search another,

i STOP
SOMEWHERE
WAITING
FOR YOU

ACKNOWLEDGEMENTS

This book owes its existence to: My agent Peter Steinberg, who champions my ridiculous schemes and makes them possible. My editor Tony Perez, whose patience and astute perspective were invaluable. Tin House's art director Diane Chonette, whose keen eye made this book shine. Tin House's director of publicity Nanci McCloskey, who put this book before your eyes and into your hands. Emilie Parker and Farrar Fitzgerald of the Rosenbach Museum and Library, who allowed me to attend their Whitman reading group for free. Arielle Middleman of The Library Company of Philadelphia, who allowed me to leaf through their copy of Whitman's 1855 edition of *Leaves of Grass*. Paul Schopp, who provided me with a rich historical context. Bill Bolger, who embodies Whitman's sensibilities. David Kessler and Ben Warfield, who created a beautiful video about this book. My friends and family, whose fine qualities are the stuff of Whitman's songs. And finally, my wife, partner, and friend, Susan Crawford, whose insight and devotion have never failed me over the past twenty-five years. A truer comerado, there never was.

WALT WHITMAN

Walt Whitman (May 31, 1819~March 26, 1892) was an American poet, essayist, and journalist. Whitman's great work, *Leaves of Grass*, was very controversial in its time but now holds an exalted place in the American canon. "Song of Myself" is considered by many to be the foundation of Whitman's poetic vision, as well as the heart of the original 1855 edition of *Leaves of Grass*.

ALLEN CRAWFORD

Allen Crawford is an illustrator, designer, and writer. He and his wife Susan are proprietors of the design/illustration studio Plankton Art Co. (planktonart.com) Their most notable project to date is the collection of 400 species-identification illustrations that are on permanent display at the American Museum of Natural History's Milstein Hall of Ocean Life. Under the pseudonym Lord Breaulove Swells Whimsy (lordwhimsy.com), he wrote, designed, and illustrated *The Affected Provincial's Companion, Volume One* (Bloomsbury, 2006), which was optioned by Infinitum Nihil, Johnny Depp's production company.